CAMBRIDGE LIBRARY COLLECTION

Books of enduring scholarly value

Archaeology

The discovery of material remains from the recent or the ancient past has always been a source of fascination, but the development of archaeology as an academic discipline which interpreted such finds is relatively recent. It was the work of Winckelmann at Pompeii in the 1760s which first revealed the potential of systematic excavation to scholars and the wider public. Pioneering figures of the nineteenth century such as Schliemann, Layard and Petrie transformed archaeology from a search for ancient artifacts, by means as crude as using gunpowder to break into a tomb, to a science which drew from a wide range of disciplines - ancient languages and literature, geology, chemistry, social history - to increase our understanding of human life and society in the remote past.

A History of Sinai

The feminist, medievalist and political theorist Lina Eckenstein (1857–1931) spent the excavations seasons from 1903 to 1906 working with Flinders Petrie (of whose wife Hilda she was a close friend) at Saqqara, Abydos and elsewhere. This 1921 publication was inspired by her experiences at the site of Serabit in the Sinai peninsula (Petrie's account of the excavation is also reissued in this series). Eckenstein describes it as a 'little history which will, I trust, appeal to those who take an interest in the reconstruction of the past and in the successive stages of religious development'. The narrative begins in the prehistoric period, suggesting that the inhospitable landscape (caused by ancient deforestation) and climate dissuaded large-scale permanent settlement until the first hermit and monastic communities of the Christian era (although the Egyptians had been drawn there by resources of turquoise and copper), and continues down to the nineteenth century.

T0381717

Cambridge University Press has long been a pioneer in the reissuing of out-of-print titles from its own backlist, producing digital reprints of books that are still sought after by scholars and students but could not be reprinted economically using traditional technology. The Cambridge Library Collection extends this activity to a wider range of books which are still of importance to researchers and professionals, either for the source material they contain, or as landmarks in the history of their academic discipline.

Drawing from the world-renowned collections in the Cambridge University Library and other partner libraries, and guided by the advice of experts in each subject area, Cambridge University Press is using state-of-the-art scanning machines in its own Printing House to capture the content of each book selected for inclusion. The files are processed to give a consistently clear, crisp image, and the books finished to the high quality standard for which the Press is recognised around the world. The latest print-on-demand technology ensures that the books will remain available indefinitely, and that orders for single or multiple copies can quickly be supplied.

The Cambridge Library Collection brings back to life books of enduring scholarly value (including out-of-copyright works originally issued by other publishers) across a wide range of disciplines in the humanities and social sciences and in science and technology.

A History of Sinai

LINA ECKENSTEIN

CAMBRIDGE
UNIVERSITY PRESS

CAMBRIDGE
UNIVERSITY PRESS

University Printing House, Cambridge, CB2 8BS, United Kingdom

Cambridge University Press is part of the University of Cambridge.

It furthers the University's mission by disseminating knowledge in the pursuit of education, learning and research at the highest international levels of excellence.

www.cambridge.org
Information on this title: www.cambridge.org/9781108082334

This edition first published 1921
This digitally printed version 2018

ISBN 978-1-108-08233-4 Paperback

A HISTORY OF SINAI

BY

LINA ECKENSTEIN

AUTHOR OF "WOMAN UNDER MONASTICISM"

WITH MAPS AND ILLUSTRATIONS

LONDON
SOCIETY FOR PROMOTING
CHRISTIAN KNOWLEDGE
NORTHUMBERLAND AVENUE, W.C.
NEW YORK: THE MACMILLAN CO.
1921

PRINTED BY
WILLIAM CLOWES AND SONS, LIMITED,
LONDON AND BECCLES.

FOREWORD

In the winter of 1905–6 Professor Flinders Petrie undertook the examination of the Egyptian remains in Sinai. After working at Wadi Maghara he removed into the Wadi Umm Agraf to copy the inscriptions and excavate the temple ruins at Serabit. His work is described in "Researches in Sinai, 1906," and the inscriptions are in course of publication by the Egypt Exploration Fund. Among the workers at Serabit was myself. I had long been interested in the hermit life of the peninsula and in the growing belief that the Gebel Musa was not the Mountain of the Law. The excavations at Serabit and the non-Egyptian character of the ancient hill sanctuary supplied new material for reflection. In the hours spent in sorting fragments of temple offerings and copying temple inscriptions it occurred to me that we might be on the site which meant so much in the history of religion. Studies made after our return suggested further points of interest. The outcome is this little history which will, I trust, appeal to those who take an interest in the reconstruction of the past and in the successive stages of religious development.

LINA ECKENSTEIN

Easter, 1920.

APPROXIMATE DATING OF EGYPTIAN DYNASTIES

DYNASTY

I.	B.C. 5500.	Monument of Semerkhet in Sinai
IV.	,, 4800.	,, Khufu ,,
VI.	,, 4300.	,, the Pepys ,,
XII.	,, 3600.	Amen-em-hats and Sen-userts
XV.	,, 2500.	Hyksos Conquest
	,, ,,	Time of Abraham and Joseph
XVIII.	,, 1580.	Amen hotep and Tahutmes
	,, 1380.	Akhenaten (Amenhotep IV), (?) time of Moses
XIX.	,, 1328–1202.	Ramessides
	,, 1300–1234.	Ramessu II.

v

RULERS OF PHARAN AND THE CONVENT OF SINAI

LIST TENTATIVELY ENLARGED FROM CHEIKHO

BISHOPS OF PHARAN—
Moses.
Natyr.
Macarius.
Photius.
Theodor.

BISHOPS OF SINAI—
Constantine, 869.
Marcus I, 869.
Jorius, 1033.
John I, 1069.
Zacharias, 1103 or 1114.
George, 1133 or 1143.
Gabriel I, 1146.
John II, 1164.
Simeon (Archbishop),1203–53.
Euthymius, 1223.
Macarius I, 1224.
Germanus I, 1228.
Theodosius, 1239.
Macarius II, 1248.
Simeon (? II), 1258.
John III, 1265.
Arsinius, 1290.
Simeon, 1306.
Dorotheus, 1324–33.
Germanus II, 1333.
Marcus II, 1358.
Job.

BISHOPS OF SINAI—*continued*.
Athanasius.
Sabbas.
Abraham.
Gabriel II.
Michael.
Silvanus.
Cyrillus.
Solomon.
Macarius of Cyprus, 1547.
Eugenius, 1565–83.
Anastasius, 1583–92.
Laurentius, 1572–1617.
Joasaph, 1617–58.
(Nectarius)
Ananias (1667–77), 1658–68.
Joannicus I. (1677–1703), 1668–1703.
Cosmas, 1705.
Athanasius of Bari, 1706–18.
Joannicus II of Mytilene, 1718–29.
Nicephorus Mortales, 1729–49.
Constantius I, 1749–59.
Cyrillus II, 1759–90.
Dorotheus of Byzantium, 1794–96.
Constantius II, 1804–59.
Cyrillus III, 1859–67.
Callistratus, 1877–85
Porphyrius, 1885.

CHIEF AUTHORITIES

*For other works and writers see Alphabetical Index and
page referred to.*

BREASTED, J. H., "Ancient Records of Egypt, 1906."

" Perigraphe of Holy Mount Sinai, 1817." (In Greek.)

PETRIE, W. M. FLINDERS, " Researches in Sinai, 1906."

WEILL, RAYMOND, "La Presqu'île de Sinai, 1908."

WILSON & PALMER, " Ordnance Survey, 1870–71."

CONTENTS

ILLUSTRATIONS

A HISTORY OF SINAI

CHAPTER I

INTRODUCTORY [1]

SINAI is the peninsula, triangular in form, which projects into the Red Sea between Egypt and Arabia. The name used to be applied to the mountainous region of the south, now it is made to comprise the land as far north as the Mediterranean.

Sinai is famous for the part which it has played in the religious history of mankind. It was at one time a centre of moon-cult, before it became the seat of the promulgation of the Law to the Jews at the time of Moses. In Christian times it was one of the chief homes of the hermits, and the possession of the relics of St. Katherine in the great convent of the south, caused Sinai to be included in the Long Pilgrimage throughout the Middle Ages.

A history of Sinai deals with the people who visited the peninsula at different times, rather than with its permanent inhabitants, who, in the course of the centuries, seem to have undergone little change. They still live the life of the huntsman and the herdsman as in the days of Ishmael, sleeping in the open, and adding to their meagre resources by carrying dates and charcoal to the nearest centres of intercourse, in return for which they receive corn.

The country geographically belongs to Egypt, ethnologically to Arabia. It naturally falls into three regions.

In the north, following the coast line of the Mediterranean, lies a zone of drift sand, narrowest near Rafa on the borders of Palestine, widening as it is prolonged in a westerly direction

---

[1] Wilson and Palmer: *Ordnance Survey*, 1870–71; Hull, Ed.: *Mount Seir, Sinai and Western Palestine*, 1885, *with geological map* ; Weill, R.: *La presqu'île de Sinai*, 1908.

1

towards Egypt, where it is conterminous with the present Suez Canal. This desert was known in Biblical days as Shur (the wall) of Egypt. "And Saul smote the Amalekites from Havilah (north Arabia), until thou comest to Shur that is over against Egypt" (1 Sam. xv. 7). The military highway from Egypt to Syria from ancient times followed the coast line of the Mediterranean, the settlements along which were modified on one side by the encroachment of the sea, on the other by the invasion of sand.

Adjoining this zone of drift sand, the land extends south with increased elevation to the centre of the peninsula, where it reaches a height of about 4000 ft., and abruptly breaks off in a series of lofty and inaccessible cliffs, the upper white limestone of which contrasts brilliantly in some places with the lower red sandstone. This region is, for the most part, waterless and bare. It is known in modern parlance as the Badiet Tîh (the plain of wandering). Its notable heights include the Gebel el Ejneh and the Gebel Emreikah. This plain is drained in the direction of the Mediterranean by the great Wadi el Arish and its numerous feeders, which, like most rivers of Sinai, are mountain torrents, dry during the greater part of the year, and on occasion like the *fiumare* of Italy, flowing in a spate. The Wadi el Arish is the River of Egypt of the Bible (Gen. xv. 18; Num. xxxiv. 5), the *Nahal Muzur* of the annals of King Esarhaddon.

The Badiet Tîh is crossed from east to west by the road from Akaba to Suez, along which the Holy Carpet, which is made at Cairo, was annually conveyed to Mecca. Halfway between Suez and Akaba, at Kalaat el Nakhl, the road is crossed by one coming from Gaza, which is prolonged south in several directions down precipitous passes. Kalaat en Nakhl is an important watering place, and was for a time a military station. It was known in the Middle Ages as a *puteus Soldani* (well of the Sultan).

The roads coming from Nakhl lead down the escarpment of Tîh to a belt of sand and gravel, varying in width, which, with the arid stretches adjoining it, covers an area of some thirty square miles. This is the Gebbeter Ramleh (belt of sand). Its western parts including the Wadi Jarf is the wilderness of Sin of the Bible (Exod. xvi. 1).

South of this great belt of sand, red sandstone reappears

in shelving masses leading up to the great mountainous district
which forms Sinai proper, the third region of the peninsula.
These mountains are traversed by many river-beds or wadies.
Some of them, according to the ways of the country, do not bear
the same name throughout their course, but the main stream
frequently takes another name when it is joined by a tributary.
Thus the Wadi Nasb after its junction with the Wadi Beda
becomes the Wadi Baba, and so forth.

This sandstone district is cut into by deep gorges and
canyons, that have sheer falls of several hundred feet in places.
It comprises the mountains which yielded turquoise and copper,
products that brought the neighbouring people into Sinai.
Beads of turquoise were found in the pre-dynastic tombs of
Egypt which probably came from Sinai, while there was an
increasing demand for copper in the surrounding countries
from the close of the Neolithic Age. If the name Milukhkha
of the Babylonian records refers to Sinai, these people also
came there several thousand years before our era.

Turquoise appears in a ferruginous layer in the sandstone
at the height of about 2650 ft. at Serabit, and at the height of
about 1170 ft. at Maghara above sea-level. The copper ore
occurs in the Wadi Nasb, and in the Wadi Khalig, somewhat
extensively in the latter, together with iron and manganese.
Enormous slag heaps lie at the head of the Wadi Nasb and
near the outlet of the Wadi Baba, which bear evidence to
former smelting activity. Again, in the Wadi Sened, a dyke rich
in copper traverses syenite for a distance of nearly two miles.

The district which was worked by the ancient Egyptians
was comprised between the valley system of the Wadi Baba
on the north, and that of the Wadi Sidreh on the south, both
of which have their outlet in the direction of the coastal plain
of El Markha. It was from this side that the ancient Egyptians
approached Sinai. The chief height of the district is the
Tartir ed Dhami (black cap), so called from the dark basalt
that forms its summit, which rises to a height of 3531 ft.
There is also the double-peaked Umm Riglên (mother of
two feet) which rises to the south of the Wadi Umm Agraf
and dominates the height of Serabit.

To the south of the ancient mining district the sandstone
is connected in a manner highly interesting to the geologist
with the plutonic rock which gives its imposing character to

the mountains of the south. Here lies the Wadi Feiran, one of the best watered and fruitful valleys of the peninsula, to the south of which Mount Serbal rises abruptly from a comparatively low elevation to the height of 6734 ft. This mountain has been described as one great lump of diorite, and its majestic appearance led some recent travellers, including Lepsius [1] and Bartlett,[2] to identify it as the Mountain of the Law. Further south lies the great group of mountains which include the Gebel Musa, 7359 ft. high, and the Gebel Katrîn with its three peaks, the highest of which rises to 8527 ft. The Gebel Musa from early Christian times was generally looked upon as the Mountain of the Law. At its foot lies the great convent of Sinai, at one time known as the Bush, which has carried on to the present day the traditions of the early Christian hermits, who settled in the peninsula. The Gebel Katrîn lying further south, was looked upon during the later Middle Ages, as the height on which the angels deposited the body of St. Katherine. Another imposing height of the group is the Ras Safsaf, 6540 ft. high, which has been put forward in recent times as a possible Mountain of the Law.

These mountains of the south contain many natural springs and fruitful valleys, which were formerly the home of Christian ascetics. They are divided from the Gulf of Suez on the west by the desert of El Kaa, which drains a large amphitheatre of hills, and becomes a coastal plain that extends as far as Ras Mohammad, the southernmost point of the peninsula. The desert of El Kaa has a harder subsoil which is so tilled that the accumulated moisture is thrown up at the coast near Tur, the chief harbour of the peninsula, and possibly an ancient Phœnician colony. Near it lay Raithou, a place of many oases and large date-palm plantations which were carefully tended by the monks during the Middle Ages.

The south-eastern parts of the peninsula are rarely visited by Europeans. There are some high mountains, including the Gebel Thebt (7883 ft.), the Gebel Umm Shomer (8449 ft.), and the Gebel Umm Iswed (8236 ft.), in districts that were recently explored by Dr. Hume.[3] The eastern coast-line

[1] Lepsius: *Reise nach Sinai*, 1846, p. 19 ff.
[2] Bartlett, W. H.: *Forty Days in the Desert*, 1849, p. 88.
[3] Hume, W. F.: *Topography and Geology of the South-eastern Portion of Sinai*, 1906.

of the peninsula is relatively inaccessible. There are some creek ports at Sherm, some ten miles north of Ras Mohammad, and some palm trees with a good supply of water at Nakhb. From here it is less than eight miles across the sea to Ras Fartak, the nearest point of Arabia. Further north, opposite the coastland of what is now reckoned the land of Midian, lies Dahab and, beyond it, Ain en Nuêbeh, where the road that leads from the convent to Akaba at the head of the Gulf of Akaba, reaches the coast. From Akaba the mountains are prolonged in the direction of Palestine on both sides of the Wadi el Arabah, the great depression that extends northwards to the Dead Sea. This is " the land of Seir, the country of Edom " of the Bible (Gen. xxxii. 3). Edom signifies red in Hebrew, and the land may have been so called owing to the red sandstone of the district.

Sinai, generally speaking, is a country of stern desolation. Its mountains are bare, its plains are swept by the wind, its river beds are to all appearance waterless. But clusters of bushes that follow the valley floors or rise from the plains, show that moisture percolates the soil beneath the surface, and is procurable by digging down to the harder subsoil, (*i.e.* " striking the rock ") as was done at the time of the passage of the Israelites. Such digging is done by the Bedawyn at the present day, the holes for water being called *hufrah* in Arabic. In some places, however, the water along the valleys is thrown up and forms natural oases as in the Wadi Gharandel, the Wadi Feiran, and at Tur. In others, it is raised by means of the mechanical device of a water-wheel and by a *shaduf*.

Rain falls in the peninsula in sudden downpours, often in connection with a thunderstorm. When we camped in the Wadi Umm Agraf in January of 1906, it rained without ceasing for two days and a night, creating rivulets and a waterfall down the mountain slope. A week later the valley floor was carpeted with verdure and flowers, and the thorny bushes were masses of bloom. Rainstorms may result in a spate, the dreaded *seil* of the Bedawyn, which often appears several miles below where the rain has actually fallen. In the winter of 1914–15 the Wadi el Arish was twice in spate, and left extensive pools of water behind. The effect of a spate, seen on Dec. 3, 1867, in the Wadi Feiran by the Rev. F. W. Holland, was described by him. In little more than an hour, the Wadi Feiran, at this point about 300 yards wide, was filled with a raging torrent from eight to ten feet deep. Men, animals, and trees were swept past upon the flood, and huge boulders ground along the wady bed with a noise of a hundred mills at work. In this spate perished thirty persons, scores of sheep and goats, camels, and donkeys, and it swept away an entire encampment that had been pitched at the mouth of a small valley on the north side of Mount Serbal.[1]

Disasters of this kind are in part attributable to the reckless deforestation of the country which has gone on unchecked for thousands of years, and continues at the present day. To this is attributable also the calamitous invasion of sand along the shores of the Mediterranean recorded by Arabic writers. In ancient times wood was extensively used for smelting purposes in different parts of the peninsula, as is shown by enormous slag-heaps in the Wadi Baba and in the Wadi Nasb. A great bed of wood ashes beneath the temple-floor at Serabit showed that wood was freely used in offering the holocaust in a district that is now entirely denuded of trees. According to the Mosaic Law, charcoal was used in early times at the Temple service as we gather from "a censer full of burning coals" (Lev. xv. 12).[2] For domestic use it was exported during the Middle Ages, and was regularly delivered by the Bedawyn as tribute to the Pasha in the nineteenth century. Its export continues to this day.

The heathen past tried to stem the ravages of deforestation by marking off certain valley floors, the use of which was reserved to the sanctuaries. Inside this holy ground, the *hima*, no animal might be hunted and no tree might be cut down. Many valleys of Sinai to this day contain one tree of great age and often of prodigious size, which is accounted holy and is therefore left untouched.[3] But the mass of the trees and with them the hope of a copious undergrowth, has gone. At the time of the passage of the Israelites, there must have been extensive tamarisk groves, since it is the tamarisk which yields manna, a product well-known in ancient Egypt.

[1] *Ordnance Survey*, i. 226.
[2] In this and other passages of the Bible, the word that stands as coal should be understood as charcoal.
[3] Palmer, H. S. : *Sinai from the Fourth Dynasty*, revised by Prof. Sayce, 1892, p. 47.

Its abundance must have made an appreciable difference in their food-supply. Only a few tamarisk groves remain in the more southern mountains at the present day, chief among them the groves of Tarfat el Gidaran. Again neglect has destroyed the palm groves of which enormous plantations existed in the Middle Ages. We read of a plantation of over 10,000 date-palms at Tur, and the date since the earliest times was a staple article of diet. According to Arab tradition the land along the shores of the Mediterranean was of great fruitfulness before it was invaded by sand drifts. It was the same with the numerous fruit and vegetable gardens which were once cultivated by the monks and the hermits. With the exception of the garden belonging to the convent, they have passed away. Journeying across the wide stretches of the country which were formerly a wilderness and are now a desert, one wonders if a wise government could not impose restrictions which would stop the destruction of the under-growth and regulate the water-supply. This would extend the cultivation of the date-palm, the tamarisk and of other food products, for the Bedawyn, the present inhabitants of the penin-sula, live in a state of semi-starvation. Their various means of subsistence have steadily grown less with the centuries. Deforestation has influenced the fauna to the detriment of the huntsmen. The herds of gazelles which were numerous as late as the Middle Ages, are few and far between. Pasture lands which formerly fed sheep and goats were encroached upon by the introduction of the camel. The transport of goods and of pilgrims which gave occupation to the owners of camels during the Middle Ages has practically ceased. The convent formerly helped to tide over difficult times by means of its resources, but the advent in the east of the Turk reduced these resources to a minimum, and the convent is nowadays hardly able to satisfy its own needs. In the face of this state of things, it seems worth recalling the different periods in the past when Sinai held the attention of the outside world and helped in the making of history. For the recognition of her solitary ruins, and of her literary wealth still enshrined in the convent, taken with the needs of her people, may stimulate effort to inaugurate a new era to the profit of Christian and of Moslim alike.

CHAPTER II

SINAI A CENTRE OF MOON-CULT

THE name Sinai is first mentioned in the Song of Deborah. (Judges v. 5), which is dated to about B.C. 1000, and in the story of Exodus. It perpetuates the early form of belief of the inhabitants of the peninsula. For the word Sinai together with Sin (Exod. xvi. 1) and Zin (Num. xiii. 21), all date back to Sin, a name of the moon-god in ancient Babylonia.

The word Sin appears as part of the name of Naram-Sin, king of Accad in Babylonia (c. B.C. 3700), whose great stele of victory, now in the Louvre, represents his conquest of Elam (Persia). The acts of Naram-Sin were considered in the light of lunar influence, for his Annals state that "the moon was favourable for Naram-Sin who at this season marched into Maganna." [1] Maganna, otherwise Magan, was frequently named in early annals and inscriptions, notably on the great statues of King Gudea (B.C. 2500). It was the place where the diorite came from out of which the statues were made. The same inscriptions mention Milukhkha. [2] An ancient fragment of Assyrian geography which was engraved about the year B.C. 680, but the original of which is considered much older, names side by side : " The country of Milukhkha as the country of blue stone, and the country of Maganna as the country of copper." [3] Of these names Maganna may refer to Sinai while the word Milukhkha recalls the Amalekites who dwelt in the peninsula. In any case the name Sin goes back to Babylonian influence, probably to the Semites who were powerful in the land of Arabia in the days of Khamurabbi.

---

[1] Birch, S. : *Records of the Past.* New Series. Edit. Sayce, I. 41.
[2] *Ibid.*, II, 75, 83.
[3] Birch, S. : *Records of the Past*, XI. 148.

8

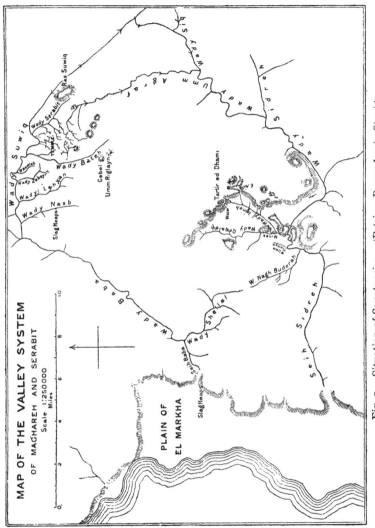

Fig. I.—Situation of Sanctuaries.   (Petrie: *Researches in Sinai.*)

The constant recurring changes of the moon caused this to be accepted as the ruler of times and seasons by the huntsman and the herdsman generally. The Hebrews came from a stock of moon-worshippers. It was from Ur of the Chaldees, a centre of moon-cult, that Terah and Abraham migrated to Haran on the way to Canaan about B.C. 2100.[1] The Arab writer Al Biruni (c. A.D. 1000) in his *Chronology of the Ancient Nations,* noted the connection of Haran with the moon-cult, and stated that near it was another place called Selem-sin, its ancient name being Saram-sîn, *i.e. Imago lunae,* and another village called Tera-uz, *i.e. Porta Veneris.*[2]

The acceptance of moon-worship among the ancient Hebrews is confirmed by Artapanus, some of whose statements were preserved by Alexander Polyhistor (B.C. 140). Artapanus described the Syrians who came to Egypt with Abraham as " Hermiouthian " (*i.e.* worshippers of Hermes), and stated that Joseph's brethren built Hermiouthian sanctuaries at Athos and Heliopolis.[3] Heliopolis, the city On of the Bible (Gen. xli. 45), was near the present Cairo ; followers of Abraham were held to have settled there. Athos has been identified as Pithom. More probably it was Pa-kesem, the chief city of Goshen. The word Hermiouthian indicates moon-worshippers, as Hermes, the Greek god, was reckoned by the classic writers the equivalent of the Egyptian moon-god Thoth, as is shown by the place-name Hermopolis, (*i.e.* the city of Thoth), in Lower Egypt.

Another name for the moon-god was Ea or Yah, who was accounted the oldest Semitic god in Babylonia, to which his devotees were held to have brought the cultivation of the date-palm, an event that marked a notable step in civilisation.[4] The emblem of Sin was the crescent moon, the emblem of Ea was the full moon, who, in the Assyrian Creation story is described as " Ea the god of the illustrious (*i.e.* lustrous) face."[5] On Babylonian seal cylinders Ea is shown standing up as a bull, seen front face, with his devotee Eabani (*i.e.* sprung

[1] Jastrow, M. : *The Religion of Babylonia and Assyria,* 1898, p. 76.
[2] Al Biruni (Muhammad Ibn Ahmad) : *Chronology of Ancient Nations,* transl. Sachau, 1879, p. 187.
[3] Cited Eusebius, *Evang. Præp.,* bk. ix. c. 18, c. 23.
[4] Barton, G. A. : *A Sketch of Semitic Origins,* 1902, p. 198.
[5] Birch, *Rec. Past,* N.S., I. 145.

Sandstone Baboon from Serabit

Glazed Baboon from Hierakonpolis   Glazed Baboon from Abydos

Fig. 2.—Figures of Baboons. (*Ancient Egypt*, a periodical, 1914, Part i.)

from Ea), a man seen, front face also, who wears the horns and hide of a bull.[1] This representation perpetuates the conception of the horned beast as a sacrosanct animal that was periodically slain. We shall come across this conception later in the emblem worn by the Pharaoh, and in the story of the Israelites and the Golden Calf.

The monuments found in Sinai contain information which points to the existence of moon-worship there at a remote period of history. These monuments consist in rock-tablets which were engraved by the Pharaohs from the First Dynasty onwards over the mines which they worked at Maghara, and of remains of various kinds discovered in the temple ruins of the neighbouring Sarbut-el-Khadem or Serabit. Maghara more especially was associated with the moon-god and was presumably the site of a shrine during the period of Babylonian or Arabic influence which preceded the invasion of the peninsula by the Egyptians (Fig. 1).

Among the Egyptians, Thoth, the moon-god, had shrines at Hierakonpolis and at Abydos in Upper Egypt, and in both these places he was worshipped under the semblance of a baboon. He was worshipped also at Hermopolis in Lower Egypt, but here he was represented as ibis-headed. In Sinai we find him represented sometimes as a baboon and sometimes as ibis-headed.

Thus the excavations of the temple-ruins at Serabit in 1906 led to the discovery of several figures of baboons. One was the rude figure some three inches high which is here represented; it was found in the cave that was the treasure-house of the sanctuary. This little figure is similar in appearance and in workmanship to figures found at Hierakonpolis and at Abydos, the centres of moon-worship in Upper Egypt. Several of these figures were found at Hierakonpolis.[2] At Abydos more than sixty were discovered in the winter of 1902 in a chamber at the lowest temple level, where they were apparently placed when the later cult of Osiris superseded the earlier cult of Thoth. This took place in pre-dynastic times.[3] The figure of the baboon who stood for the lunar divinity in Egypt, was doubtless deemed a suitable offering

---

[1] Such tablets are in view in the British Museum.
[2] Petrie, W. M. Fl.: *Hierakonpolis*, I. 1900, p. 129.
[3] Petrie, W. M. Fl.: *Abydos*, I. 1902, p. 25.

to the sacred shrine at Serabit in Sinai, because of the nearness of this shrine to the centre of moon-worship of the country. If the figure was carried to Sinai at the time when similar figures were offered in Egypt, the establishment of the moon-cult in the peninsula dates back to the pre-dynastic days of Egypt.[1]

Fig. 3.—Sneferu ravaging the land. (*Ancient Egypt*, a periodical, 1914, Part i.)

Another baboon, carved life-size in limestone with an inscription around its base, came out of one of the chambers of the adytum to the sacred cave at Serabit, the work and inscription of which dated it to the Middle Kingdom of Egypt. The presence of this figure suggests that the Egyptians

[1] On the dating of the dynasties of the Egyptian kings, see p. v.

associated their moon-god with the moon-worship of the peninsula.

The chief shrine or sanctuary of the moon god in the peninsula probably lay in Wadi Maghara where mining on the part of the Arabs preceded that of the Egyptians, for the

Fig. 4.—Khufu smiting the Anu before Thoth.

Egyptians here fought for the possession of the mines. This is shown by the tablets carved in the living rock, which commemorate the Pharaohs from King Semerkhet (I 7) of the First Dynasty onwards. They are represented as smiters of the enemy above the mines which they worked. One of these tablets represents Sneferu, the ninth king of the Third

Dynasty, who wears a head-dress that consists of a double plume which rises from a pair of horns as is seen in the illustration. The double plume is well known, but the horns are foreign to Egypt, and recall the lunar horns that are worn by Eabani, the devotee of the moon-god Ea or ancient Babylonian seal cylinders. The adoption of horns by the

Fig. 5.—Amen-em-hat III, Thoth and Hathor. Maghara. (Petrie : *Researches in Sinai.*)

Pharaoh of Egypt seems to indicate that he has usurped the authority of the earlier ruler of the place (Fig. 3).

Other monuments found at Maghara point to the same conclusion. Thus one rock-tablet represents King Khufu (IV 2), the great pyramid builder, smiting the Anu in front of the ibis-headed figure of Thoth who stands holding out his sceptre facing him (Fig. 4). Other Pharaohs are represented as smiters. But after the Fifth Dynasty the opposition which the Pharaohs encountered in Sinai must have come to an end, for later Pharaohs were no longer represented as smiters, but are seen in the double capacity of lord of Upper and of Lower Egypt standing and facing the ibis-headed figure of the moon-god Thoth, who now holds out to them his sceptre supporting an *ankh* and a *dad*, the Egyptian emblems of life and stability. Among the Pharaohs so represented was Amen-em-hat III, sixth king of the Twelfth Dynasty, who is shown facing the god Thoth behind whom the goddess Hathor is seen (Fig. 5) The interpretation is that the Pharaoh is now acting in complete agreement with the divinities of the place. Of these Thoth stands for the moon-god who originally had his shrine at Maghara, and Hathor stands for the presiding goddess who had her shrine at Serabit. This shrine or sanctuary at Serabit is of special importance in the religious associations of the peninsula.

CHAPTER III

THE SANCTUARY OF SERABIT

THE existence of the sanctuary at Serabit in Sinai was unknown to Europeans till the year 1762, when it was chanced upon by Carsten Niebuhr, who did not, however, record its name. Seetzen who visited it between 1809 and 1810 noted this as Serrabit-el-Chadem.[1] *Sarbat* is Arabic for height, *khadem* signifies slave. But Prof. Sayce claims for the name a different derivation. In ancient Egyptian *ba*, plur. *bit*, signifies hole or mine, *khetem* signifies fortress. Serabit el Khadem thus signifies mine fortress, with the prefix *sar*, which probably stands for exalted.

Other place names in the district probably date from the ancient Egyptians also. Thus the valley leading up from the coastal plain of El Markha to the mine district is called Wadi Baba, *i.e.* mine valley. Again, a tributary of the Baba, with its valley head close to Serabit, is the Wadi Bateh, a name which probably includes the word for mine also.

The sanctuary of Serabit[2] at the outset consisted of a cave, or rather of two caves adjacent to one another, of which the larger, which has been squared, measures 20 by 10 feet, the smaller one measures 6 by 4 feet with three steps leading up to a round-headed apse or recess (Fig. 9).

These caves have separate entrances and lie in a knoll facing a plateau in the midst of wild, upland scenery. The plateau lies some 2680 feet above sea level, and is difficult of access on all sides (Fig. 6).

To the north it communicates with the Wadi Suweig along the steep and tortuous Wadi Dhaba, which is marked number 6 on the map. The word *dhaba* signifies panther, probably in

---

[1] Cf. Weill, R.: *La presqu'ile de Sinai*, 1908, p. 302.
[2] Petrie: *Res. Sinai*, p. 72 ff.

allusion to the feline animal which was at one time associated with the presiding female divinity at Serabit.   Another valley, marked number 7 on the map, leads up to the temple ruins, with a path passing the mines which contain inscriptions in an early Semitic script.   But it was not along these gorges, but along a path leading up from the plain El Markha along the Wadi Baba and the Wadi Nasb that the ancient Egyptians approached the sanctuary.   This path has been included in the Ordnance Survey of 1871.   A rock tablet marked P on the map, which commemorates the Pharaoh Amen-em-hat IV (XII 7), lies near the watershed, and this shows that the Egyptians passed here.   A small Egyptian shrine (Q) was also discovered at the western end of the plateau.

To the south of the plateau, and separated from it by several ravines and valley heads, extends the Wadi Umm Agraf which is comparatively remote from the valleys communicating with the Wadi Suweig and the Wadi Baba, and relatively close to the sanctuary.   The approach to the temple from this side was unknown to Europeans till the winter of 1905–6, when Prof. Flinders Petrie and his party, who worked at excavating the temple ruins, pitched their tents here.   A path was constructed from the camp up the mountain side to the temple by clearing away the stones.   In parts an old path was re-used, the existence of which showed that there was at one time frequent intercourse between the sanctuary and the Wadi Umm Agraf.   Some way down the Wadi Umm Agraf the valley floor is crossed by a wall made of rough stones piled together, the purpose of which was to mark off the upper reaches of the Wadi as is seen by a glance at the map.   These upper reaches evidently constituted a tract of land the use of which was reserved to the sanctuary.   A copious supply of good water is obtainable at a well some miles down the valley.   The separation wall across the valley is undoubtedly old.   A similar wall crosses the Wadi Maghara, which was dated by Prof. Petrie to at least the Fourth Dynasty.   Its purpose, like that near Serabit, was to mark off the upper reaches of the valley, which in this case may have represented the *hima* or tract of land that was originally appropriated to the sanctuary of the moon-god.

The plateau of Serabit falls away abruptly on its southern and western edge, and the stratum here appears which anciently

Steles A Amenemhat II
      B Amenemhat III
      C   ,,   ,,
      D   ,,   ,,
      E Tahutmes IV
      P Amenemhat IV
      Q Rock Shrine
Mines F to N
      x Watersheds
      ⬤ Haematite Bed
.... Ancient Path
- - - - - Modern Path

Scale 1 25000

VALLEYS OF SERABÍT EL KHADEM

Fig. 6 —Sanctuary surroundings at Serabit. (Petrie: *Researches in Sinai.*)

yielded turquoise. The wish to control access to this turquoise no doubt originally led to the permanent occupation of the caves, and we shall probably not be far wrong if we imagine this in the possession of a clan or hereditary priesthood, who, in return for offerings brought to their cave, gave turquoise or the permission to work it inside the appropriated area. The offerings brought to the cave naturally led to a sacrifice and feast which, in the course of time, would hallow the precincts of the place. Prof. Robertson Smith remarked that almost every sacred site in Palestine had its cavern or grotto which served to store the vessels and utensils that were used at the sacrifice that took place near it. No religious significance originally attached to the cave. But the holiness of the sacrifice reflected on it, and in the course of time it was identified as the abode of the divinity.[1]

The plateau in front of the caves at Serabit served as a High Place of Burning. Such high places were in use in Canaan before and after the Exodus. Prof. Robertson Smith showed how the barren and unfrequented hill top would be one of the most natural places chosen for the holocaust, and in this connection recalled the proposed sacrifice of Isaac on the mountain.[2] We read in the history of Samuel how he was called upon to sanctify the sacrifice on the height, of which the people would not partake until it had received his blessing (1 Sam. ix. 12); also that Solomon visited Gibeon, where he burnt sacrificial flesh and offered a thousand burnt offerings upon the altar (1 Kings iii. 4). In consequence of the building of the Temple at Jerusalem efforts were made to draw to it all the offerings, but the High Places seem to have continued till the Captivity. They finally came under the ban of the ceremonial law.[3]

The use made of the plateau of Serabit as a High Place of Burning was shown by the excavations. In front of the caves, beneath the stone floor of the Temple buildings that were erected by the Egyptians after their appropriation of the site, there was found a continuous bed of wood-ashes which extended all across the temple area and out as far as the buildings and stone walls on the south, in all fifty feet in breadth.

---

[1] Smith, W. Robertson : *The Religion of the Semites*, Ed. 1901, p. 197.
[2] *Ibid.*, p. 490.
[3] Hastings : *Dictionary of the Bible*, art. " High Places."

Outside the area covered by the stone floor the ashes would
be carried away by wind and rain. In the words of Prof.
Petrie : " We must therefore suppose a bed of wood ashes at
least 100 by 50 feet very probably much wider, and varying from
3 to 18 inches thick, in spite of all denudation that took place
before the XVIII dynasty. There must lie on the ground
about 50 tons of ashes, and these are probably the residue of
some hundreds of tons of ashes. The ashes are certainly
before the XVIII dynasty." In further explanation of the
way in which the sacrifice was treated, Prof. Petrie tells us
that " the fires were not large, as the ash is all white, and no
charcoal of smothered fire remains. No whole burnt sacrifice
was offered, as no calcined bones were found ; and some kind
of feeding at the place is suggested by the finding of a few
pieces of pottery jars and of thin drinking cups. These belonged
to the age of the XII dynasty." [1]

The space in front of the caves was fenced in by a wall
built of rough stones loosely piled together, similar in construction to the walls that cross the Wadi Umm Agraf and
the Wadi Maghara. The temple area which the wall enclosed
varied at different periods. It was finally 200 feet in its
greatest length and 140 feet at its greatest breadth. Behind
the caves across the knoll its course was doubled. It thus
enclosed a vast temenos of oblong form which included large
open spaces that were again partitioned off, besides the ground
that was covered by the Egyptian temple buildings (Fig. 11).

Outside the temenos wall and well in view of the knoll,
rough circular enclosures lie scattered here and there on the
plateau, which were made by clearing the ground of stones
and piling these together in the same way as the walls were
built up. These stone enclosures are for the most part four to
six feet inside measurement, a few are larger, and many of
them contain one stone of larger size that was set up at one
side of the enclosure and propped up by other stones. There
were also some uprights without enclosures.

Similar uprights and enclosures are found in Syria ; their
devotional and commemorative origin is apparent from incidents related in the Bible.

Thus in the story of Jacob we read how, coming from
Beersheba, he lighted on a certain place that was holy ground,

[1] Petrie : *Res. Sinai*, p. 99.

and tarried all night because the sun was set. "And he took of the stones of that place and put them for his pillows " (Gen. xxviii. 11 ; LXX at his head). In the night he had his wonderful dream and on the following morning he set up the stone and poured oil on it and called it Bethel (*i.e.* house of El), saying, "And this stone which I have set for a pillar (*mazzebh*) shall be God's house " (Gen. xxviii. 22). On another occasion he made a covenant with Laban in ratification of which he took a stone and set it up for a pillar (*mazzebh*), and called his brethren to take stones and make an heap (perhaps an enclosure), "and they did eat there upon the heap " (Gen. xxxi. 45, 46). Again when the Israelites camped in Sinai, Moses erected an altar, and set up twelve pillars (*mazzeboth*), and when they crossed the Jordan, Joshua took twelve stones from the river which he set up at the place which was known as Gilgal (Joshua iv. 1–9, 19–20). The name Gilgal in this case was associated with "rolling" away the reproach of Egypt (Joshua v. 9). But the word Gilgal signifies "circle of stone." [1] In the Septuagint the word generally stands in the plural Galgala (Joshua iv. 19, 20, etc). If the single stones (*mazzeboth*) were set up inside circular stone enclosures, this would correspond with the way the uprights were set up at Serabit.

In the course of the Twelfth Dynasty, the Egyptians secured a foothold in Serabit where they erected inscriptions and steles, and commemorated the female divinity of the place under the name of Hathor. A statuette of Hathor was the usual gift to the shrine of the Pharaohs of this dynasty. Her cult was at first coupled with that of the moon-god Thoth as the representative of the neighbouring Maghara, later she appears alone or associated with the local divinity Sopd.

At Wadi Maghara Hathor appears on one tablet following the ibis-headed Thoth, who faces the Pharaoh Amen-em-hat III (XII 6), as already mentioned (Fig. 5). On a corresponding tablet found at Serabit she is seen holding out to the same king a sceptre which supports the *ankh* and the *dad*. There were many Hathors in Egypt, for Hathor here took the place of earlier mother-divinities in much the same way as the Virgin Mary took the place of local mother-divinities in Europe. The goddess Hathor in Sinai was generally represented wearing

---

[1] Hastings: *Dictionary of the Bible*, art. "Gilgal."

a head-dress that consists of a pair of horns which support the orb of the full moon, and she is described as mistress of the turquoise land, and later simply as mistress of turquoise (*mafkat*). Hathor stands for the unwedded mother-goddess

Fig. 7.—Figure with Semitic Script. (Petrie: *Researches in Sinai.*)

who appears as Ishtar in Babylonia, as Ashtoreth in Canaan, and as the Queen of Heaven generally. At Serabit her name appears in script which may be Semitic. One of these inscriptions is on a figure of the usual squatting type that came out of the sanctuary (Fig. 7). Another is on a peculiar sphinx that is now in the British Museum. Others are on much-battered steles that were carved on the rock in the mine along the valley marked number 7 (Fig. 6). The name consists of a sequence of four signs, which Dr. Alan Gardiner reads as Ba-alat : " Almost every Egyptian inscription from Serabit names the goddess Hathor, and there could not possibly be a better equivalent for the name of this goddess than Ba-alat." [1]

The name Ba-alat recalls Alilat whom Herodotus (c. B.C. 450) named as the chief divinity of Arabia (iii. 8), and who re-appears as Al-Lat in the Koran (c. A.D. 630). Al-Lat had her sanctuary at Taïf, about forty miles north-north-east of Mecca, which consisted of a cave in an upland plain in which clothes, jewels, incense, silver and gold, were stored. The goddess was held to be incarnate in a white rock that was afterwards seen lying under the mosque, and which was described by Hamilton and by Doughty as a mass of white granite now shattered with gunpowder and shapeless.[2] Appropriated to the sanctuary at Taïf was a guarded and reserved tract of land, the *hima*, where no *idah*-tree might be cut and no animal hunted, and the reluctance of Mohammad to dislodge the goddess was shared by the Taïfites, to whom the gatherings near the shrine were a source of wealth.

Another cave sanctuary at El Nakhl, not far from Mecca, which was associated with El Uzza, likewise consisted of a cave with accumulated wealth and owned a reserved tract of land or *hima*.[3] The arrangement at Serabit was apparently the same, and proves the Arabian or Semitic origin of the place.

The excavations at Serabit, moreover, led to the discovery of temple furniture such as served the " Queen of Heaven " elsewhere.

Thus several short stone altars were found, of which one, broken in half, was 22 inches high with a cup hollow on the top, 3½ inches wide and one inch deep. Another was described as " well finished, and on the top the surface was burnt for about a quarter of an inch inwards, black outside and dis-coloured below. This proves that such altars were used for

[1] Gardiner, Alan : *Journal of Egyptian Archæol.*, 1916, vol. 3, p. 1.
[2] Smith, W. Robertson : *Lectures and Essays*, 1912, p. 554.
[3] Wellhausen : *Reste Arabischen Heidenthums*, 1897, pp. 30, 39.

burning, and from the small size, 5 to 7 inches across, the only substance burnt on them must have been highly inflammable, such as incense." [1]

Two rectangular altars cut in stone were also found, each with two saucer-like depressions, ten inches wide all over, and seven inches across inside, which " might well be for meat offerings, or cakes of flour and oil, a kind of pastry." [2] According to a passage in Jeremiah, the Israelite women, who repudiated visiting the sanctuary of the Queen of Heaven without their husbands, which was forbidden to them, said, " And when we burned incense to the queen of heaven, and poured out drink-offerings unto her, did we make her cakes to worship her, and pour out drink-offerings unto her, without our men ? " (Jer. xliv. 19). The utterance shows that offerings in food and drink as well as incense burning was customary in the cult of the Semitic goddess.

Offerings that consisted of cakes continued in Arabia into Christian times. For Epiphanius of Cyprus († 403), in his book, *Against all Heresies*, denounced certain Christians as Collyridians, from the cakes which they placed under an awning and offered in the name of the Virgin. [3]

Hathor, however, was not the only divinity whose cult was located at Serabit. While the larger of the two caves was appropriated to her, the smaller adjacent cave was associated with Sopd, who was repeatedly named here from the reign of Amen-em-hat III (XII 6) onwards. One inscription of the sixth year of this king named him together with Hathor. Another of the forty-second year mentioned Sebek-didi who set up an inscription and described himself as " beloved of Hathor ; mistress of the *mafkat*-country ; beloved of Sopd, lord of the east ; beloved of Sneferu and the gods and goddesses of this land." [4]

The special association of Sopd with the Pharaoh Amen-em-hat III is shown by an open hall that was erected outside the temple at Serabit in the course of the Eighteenth Dynasty, the decoration of which caused Prof. Petrie to call it the hall of the kings. On the inner wall of this building are the

[1] Petrie : *Res. Sinai*, p. 133.
[2] *Ibid.*, p. 134.
[3] *Hær.* 79 in Migne : *Patr. Græc.*, xlii, 742.
[4] Breasted, J. H. : *Ancient Records of Egypt*, i. 722.

figures of the divinities and the kings who were especially associated with Serabit. Among them is Sopd who is seen holding in one hand an *ankh*, in the other a staff of justice, and who follows the Pharaoh Amen-em-hat III.[1] Sopd during the Eighteenth Dynasty was reckoned the equal of Hathor. For the entrance to a mine that was opened conjointly by Queen Hatshepsut and her nephew Tahutmes shows Tahutmes offering incense to Hathor and Hatshepsut in a corresponding scene offering incense to Sopd.

The divinity Sopd has no place in the older Egyptian pantheon, and is to all appearance an Egyptianised divinity of Semitic origin. He is named among the gods who are favourable to the Pharaoh Sen-usert I (XII 2) in the so-called *Tale of Sanehat*, which describes an incident of the time and is looked upon as a genuine historical account.[2] The cult of the god seems to have gained a firm foothold in connection with the forced retreat of the Mentu people. For it says in a nome text of Edfu, " Shur is here Sopd, the conqueror of the Mentu, lord of the east country, and in Edfu golden Horus, son of Isis, powerful god Sopd."[3]

One mention of Sopd in Egypt is on a tablet of Sen-usert II (XII 4) that was found in the temple of Wadi Qasus in the desert of Kossayr on the borders of the Red Sea. On it Sopd is described as " lord of the eastern foreigners (*sut*), and of the east (Neb-Apti)."[4]

The description " lord of the east," refers to the cult of Sopd in the land of Goshen, the twentieth nome of Lower Egypt, the capital of which, Pa-kesem, was known also as Per-Sopd, *i.e.* the House of Sopd. The amulet of Sopd at Per-Sopd was of turquoise, which bore out his connection with Sinai. An Egyptian text, moreover, described Sopd as " noblest of the spirits of Heliopolis."

Now the Syrians or Hebrews, as already stated, had a foothold at Heliopolis since the days of Abraham, while the land of Goshen, as we know, was allotted to the Israelites. The inference is that Sopd who had a sanctuary in Sinai, had sanctuaries in Heliopolis and in the land of Goshen also.

[1] Petrie: *Res. Sinai*, fig. 98.
[2] Petrie: *Egyptian Tales*, I. 1895, p. 116.
[3] Brugsch, H.: *Religion u. Mythologie der alten Egypter*, 1888, p. 568.
[4] Wilkinson: *Ancient Egypt*, ed. 1878, vol. 3, 234-6.

The study of these sanctuaries shows that they had features
in common with some of the early sanctuaries in Palestine.

The ancient city Per-Sopd in Egypt, known as Phakusa
in Greek, and as Kesem in the Septuagint, is now called Saft-
el-Henneh. The change from Sopd to Saft suggests a possible
origin of certain place names in Palestine, including Tell-es-
Safi, which is situated between Jerusalem and Gaza, and
Safed, which is situated north of the Sea of Galilee. Both of
these were hallowed by ancient religious associations.

Modern Safed occupies a conspicuous position on the
summit of a mountain. Together with Jerusalem, Hebron
and Tiberias, it ranked as a holy city of Palestine.[1] It is

CAVE OF HATHOR.   CAVE OF SOPDU.

Fig. 8.—Caves at Serabit. (*Ancient Egypt*, a periodical, 1917, Part iii.)

named Tsidphoth in the *Travels of an Egyptian Mohar*,[2] and
is Tsapheth in the Talmud, and Sephet in the Vulgate of Tobit.

On the other hand Tell-es-Safi, situated between Jerusalem
and Gaza, was identified as a High Place of Burning by recent
excavations. Possibly it was Gath of the Bible, one of the
five holy cities of Palestine. The excavations at Tell-es-Safi
led to the discovery of features which recall the arrangements
at Serabit in Sinai. At a depth of 11 to 21 ft. the pre-Israelite
ground was reached, on which stood several pillars (*mazzeboth*),
some of which were enclosed in the largest of several chambers

[1] Murray: *Palestine and Syria*, 1903, p. 259.
[2] Birch: *Rec. Past*, ii, p. 111.

that were built on slightly higher level. The long wall of the chamber which included the uprights, had a break, roughly in the form of an apse that was 4 feet 5 inches wide and 2 feet 4½ inches deep. A rude semicircle built of stone stood 20 inches high from the ground a distance of a few feet, facing it.[1] This apse corresponds with the recess at the back of the cave of Sopd in Sinai.

The likeness between the place names Per-Sopd, modern Safet in Egypt, and the place names Sephet, modern Safed, and Safi in Palestine, suggests that the cities in Palestine also were the site of a shrine of the Semitic divinity who figures in Egypt and in Sinai under the name Sopd. It is possible that Sopd is the verbal equivalent of the Hebrew word *shophet*, Phœnician *sufet*, which signifies judge. Among the early Semites the sanctuary was the seat of justice, and the priests were its administrators, who, in this capacity, gave out the pronouncements. As such they were sacred and, with reference to the joint divinities (El) of the tribes, they were at first called Elohim, later Kohanim. The word shophet itself indicates the Supreme Judge, as in the passage, " Shall not the Judge (shophet) of all the earth do right ? " (Gen. xviii. 25), while the relation between the Judge and His administrators is indicated by the words, " And the heavens shall declare his righteousness, for Elohim is Shophet himself " (Psa. l. 6).

The shrine of Sopd in Sinai and the one at Per-Sopd in Egypt, perhaps the one at Heliopolis also, served the same purpose as the shrine at Tell-es-Safi. The priest would stand in the recess with his face towards the suppliant, who, at Safi, stood in the low semicircle.

In Sinai the cave of Sopd was adjacent to that of the moon-goddess (Fig. 8). According to information already cited, a shrine at Heliopolis where Sopd was "noblest of spirits" dated from the " Hermiouthians," who came there with Abraham, while Hermiouthian sanctuaries were erected in Goshen by the brethren of Joseph. We are left to infer that a shrine of Sopd, presumably a centre for the administration of justice, was connected here also with the localised cult of the moon.

Other features at Serabit confirm the non-Egyptian

---

[1] Bliss, F. G , and Macalister, R. : *Excavations in Palestine*, 1902.

character of the cult of Sopd.   Thus, on the northern approach
to the temple stood a stone tank measuring 54 by 32 inches,
with a hollow of 37 by 17 inches.   Inside the temple area, in
one of the courts which were built in the Eighteenth Dynasty,
stood a circular tank, 31 inches across with a hollow of 25
inches, and another rectangular tank, 44 by 30 inches stood in
the same court, and a further rectangular tank in the hall on
the approach to the lower cave.   The disposition of these tanks
was such that the worshipper who approached the temple from
the north, passed the tank outside and the various other tanks
on his way to the lesser cave.   The use of tanks outside and
inside the temple, is foreign to Egypt.   They are in keeping
with the *apsu* or stone tank of the Babylonian temple ; and
with the regulations of Moses regarding the laver that stood
between the entrance to the temple and the altar (Exod.
xxx. 18).   In Jerusalem in the temple of Solomon was a
"molten sea" that was round about, and there were ten lavers
of brass, five on the right and five on the left side of the house.
(1 Kings vii. 23, 38, 39).   A similar arrangement prevails to
this day in the Arab mosque.   Outside stands the well or
place for legal washings *ghusl*, and inside is the circular tank
for ablution *wazur*.[1]   The tanks at Serabit were therefore
connected with the cult of Sopd, and their presence confirms
the Semitic character of the place.

[1] Hughes, Th. : *Dictionary of Islam*, 1845, art. " Masjid."

CHAPTER IV

THE EGYPTIANS IN SINAI

I

THE monuments which the Egyptians erected in Sinai are evidence of their continued connection with the place. These were examined and studied in the winter of 1906.[1] They comprised many monuments which were carved in the living rock, and were found in the Wadi Maghara, the Wadi Nasb and at Serabit. At Serabit, moreover, there were found numerous offerings consisting of statuettes, vases, pottery, and other objects which were brought from Egypt to the sanctuary. Outside this sanctuary the Egyptians set up steles near the holy caves and on the neighbouring hillside, and they built chambers and porticoes inside the temenos, and covered these with scenes and inscriptions. Thus the buildings outside the caves went on increasing till the place assumed the appearance of a vast temple.

The baboon figure which was discovered in the temple of Serabit, and the turquoise that was found in early graves in Egypt, show that the Egyptians came to the peninsula in pre-dynastic days. The beginning of dynastic history in Egypt was dated by Prof. Breasted (1909) to about B.C. 3400,[2] and by Prof. Petrie (1914) to about B.C. 5500. Scholars are more and more inclining to accept the earlier date.

At the beginning of the First Dynasty the Egyptians had secured a firm foothold in the peninsula, as is shown by the inscriptions on the living rock of the Pharaohs of this dynasty. These rock-inscriptions are close to the mine holes in the hillside about 170 feet above the valley floor. Besides these

[1] Petrie, W. M. Flinders : *Researches in Sinai*, 1906.
[2] Breasted, J. H. : *A History of Egypt*, 1909, p. 597.

there were many inscriptions of kings of the Third, Fifth and Sixth Dynasties. They were known to Europeans in the eighteenth century, and some were drawn and described. But their importance was not fully recognised and many perished in the blasting, when the search for turquoise was renewed in the nineteenth century. Among those which were ruthlessly destroyed was the great tablet of King Khufu (IV 2), here reproduced. A full record was therefore made of those which remained in 1906, and, in order to save the tablets, they were removed to the Museum in Cairo. One only was left *in situ*. It was the oldest of all, dating from King Semerkhet (I 7), seventh king of the First Dynasty, which is engraved on the rock 394 feet above the valley floor in a position which seems to guarantee its safety.

The earliest tablets in the Wadi Maghara represented the Pharaoh under three aspects : as king of Upper Egypt, as king of Lower Egypt, and as smiter of the enemy who crouches before him. There is, at first, little wording beside the names and the titles of the king. As a smiter the king holds a mace in one hand and a staff in the other, and the enemy has a bold cast of countenance, abundant hair, a peaked beard, and wears a loin-cloth. The Pharaoh holds him by the top-knot, together with a carved object which he seems to have taken from him. This may be a feather ; possibly it is a boomerang or throwstick.

The rock inscription of Semerkhet was worked by cutting away the face, and leaving the figures and the hieroglyphs standing in relief. A little in front of the scenes, and worked on the same scale, was the general of the expedition, who wears no distinctive dress, but the word *Mer-meshau* (leader of troops), written in hieroglyphs, is before him. He is without head-dress and carries arrows and a bow of the double-curved Libyan type.

Semerkhet was probably not the first Pharaoh who worked in Sinai. For a small plaque found at Abydos represents Den-Setui, an earlier king of the First Dynasty, who is seen in the same attitude as the Pharaohs on the Sinai rock tablets, and the cast of countenance of the enemy is also the same.[1]

Little is known of King Semerkhet outside Sinai. It is

[1] Breasted : *A History*, fig. 26, p. 42.

supposed that the First Dynasty at his time was weakening. No records in Sinai mention kings of the Second Dynasty, who were indigenous to the Nile valley, and whose energies were devoted to reconstructing the older elements of government at home.

A new spirit arose with the kings of the Third Dynasty, of whom Sanekht (III 1) was represented at Wadi Maghara in the usual scenes with the addition of the jackal-nome standard, one of the earliest represented in Egypt, which may refer to the troops that accompanied his expedition. The face of Sanekht is strongly Ethiopian in character, not unlike the present Sudanys. The jackal-nome standard appears also on the tablet of Zeser (III 2), the next Pharaoh recorded, who was seen in the regular group of smiting with the addition of the familiar titles, " giver of purity, stability, life, gladness for ever." [1]

The intercourse between Egypt and Sinai found a new development under Sneferu (III 9), who was represented wearing the horned head-dress mentioned above, and the wording of his tablet described him as " Great god ravaging the lands," here reproduced. Sneferu worked not only at Maghara, but was in contact also with the sanctuary at Serabit. To this he presented the figure of a hawk, his favourite emblem, worked in grey limestone, which was discovered in the winter of 1906 in the sacred cave itself. Its work and inscription mark it as a contemporary monument. It is now in the British Museum. Later ages looked upon Sneferu as especially connected with Sinai, reckoning him as one of the protecting divinities of the place, and his haul in turquoise was referred to in the Twelfth Dynasty as exceptional. " I obtained more turquoise than any man since Sneferu." [2] The value which was set on turquoise in Egypt during his reign is shown by one of the so-called *Tales of the Magicians*, which relates how the damsels of the harim of Sneferu went rowing on the lake. One dropped her jewel of " new turquoise " into the water, which was recovered by magical means.[3]

The next Pharaoh who was commemorated at Maghara

[1] Petrie : *Res. Sinai*, fig. 49.
[2] Breasted : *Rec.*, i. 731.
[3] Petrie : *Egyptian Tales*, I. p. 18.

was Khufu (IV 2), the great pyramid builder, who, as already mentioned, was figured smiting the enemy before the ibis-headed figure of the god Thoth. At Maghara several tablets recorded him, which were of large size and of excellent workmanship. The chief one had fortunately been drawn and photographed before it was entirely smashed during the recent blasting. On this tablet, the Pharaoh, here named Khnumu-Khufu, was described as a smiter of the Anu, a word written with three pillar signs, with a man as a determinative (Fig. 4).

Next in date at Maghara was the tablet of Sahura (V 2), which was framed by a colossal *Uas*-sceptre on either side and a row of stars along the top. Sahura was described in the wording as "smiter of the Mentu." The same words were used to describe Ra-en-user (V 6), whose tablet at Maghara measured 63 by 102 inches, and was the largest of all. This tablet has the additional feature of an enormous vase supported by two *ankhs* with the words : "The lord of foreign lands (*neb Setui*) gave coolness," which suggests that a water supply was made accessible by some local sheykh.

The Pharaohs at Maghara, between the First and the Fourth Dynasties, were always represented as smiters. The tablets of the Fifth and Sixth Dynasties are for the most part broken or destroyed, but what is left of them points to more peaceful relations, and records the mining expeditions with additional detail.

Thus the tablet of Dadkara (V 8) states that the expedition (*upt*) was sent in the year after the fourth cattle census, which dates it to the eighth or ninth year of the reign of this king. Again, a tablet of Pepy I (VI 3) was dated by "the year after the eighteenth cattle census" These tablets, moreover, mention some of the dignitaries who took part in the expedition. That of Dadkara named the ship-captain Nenekt-Khentikhet ; that of Pepy I the ship-captain Ibdu ; a further one of Pepy II (VI 5) the ship-captain Benkeneph.[1] This shows that the Egyptians approached the mine-land by water. There is mention on these tablets also of princes, of scribes, of a commander of recruits (*hez-uz-neferu*), of inspectors (*uba*), of interpreters of princes (*sehez-saru*), of the

[1] Weill, R. : *Recueil des Inscriptions*, 1904, 120 ff.

seal-bearer to the god (*neter sahu*), of a chief of the land (*mer ta*), of a chief of the storehouse (*mer ab*), of a chief of the elders (*mer uru*), and of others, which shows how carefully the expeditions were organised. The tablet of Dadkara, moreover, mentions for the first time the *Fkat* country, *fkat* being short for *mafkat*, the ancient Egyptian word for turquoise. These is always a difficulty in reading aright the names of precious stones. *Mafkat* was often rendered as malachite, and it needed the turning over of the rubbish heaps at Serabit and the discovery of turquoise, in order fully to establish the nature of the stone that was the product of the area appropriated to " Hathor of Mafkat."

The close of the Sixth Dynasty brought ·a break in the relations between Egypt and Sinai, which is attributable, no doubt, to changes in Egypt itself, of which we know little at this period. Perhaps there were movements among the people of the east. Among those who threatened Egypt from this side were the Mentu, who were Asiatics, and whose successful defeat was achieved, as mentioned above, with the help of the devotees to Sopd.

The Egyptians probably resumed work in Sinai during the Eleventh Dynasty, since workmen's pots, found in the Wadi Maghara, are dated to this dynasty by their style.[1] The reign may have been that of Mentu-hotep III (XI 7), for a group of four kings seated at a table carved in stone was discovered at Serabit; with the names of the kings along the edge of the table on which their hands were placed. They were Sneferu (probably), Mentu-hotep III (XI 7), Amen-em-hat I (XII 1), and his son Sen-usert (XII 2), who was probably the donor of the group.[2]

When work was resumed in Sinai in the Eleventh Dynasty, the attitude of the Egyptians towards Serabit had undergone a marked change. In early days they had approached the sanctuary as quasi-worshippers, presenting offerings such as the baboon and the hawk. Now the sanctuary itself was drawn within the sphere of their influence, and they erected uprights or *mazzeboth* on the approach to the cave on which they recorded their mining expeditions.

Uprights of this kind are entirely unknown in Egypt.

[1] Petrie: *Res. Sinai*, p. 52   [2] *Ibid.*, p. 123.

The *mazzeboth* erected by the Egyptians in Sinai were therefore set up in deference to the custom of the place. They were worked in red sandstone which was quarried on the north side of the temple height judging by a great square cutting that remains there, and the work of inscribing them was done *in situ* by Egyptian stone-cutters who were attached to the expeditions. These steles are for the most part 6 to 12 feet high, 2 to 4 feet broad, and 6 to 8 inches thick. Their tops are rounded, which gives them the appearance of gravestones, and this led some of the earlier travellers to describe the height of Serabit as a place of burial.

The oldest of the *mazzeboth* were erected on a prominent spot outside the temenos within sight of the sanctuary; later these steles were placed along the approach to the cave, more and more crowding the adytum. These Egyptian inscribed *mazzeboth* all have a flat stone at the base which suggests a place of offering, and their purpose seems to have been to recommend the members of the expedition who set up the stone to the good graces of Hathor of Mafkat.

In keeping with this, a statuette of Hathor was presented to the shrine by the Pharaohs of the Twelfth Dynasty, every one of whom organised one, if not several, expeditions to Sinai, in order to secure turquoise. Several of these statuettes, varying in size and in workmanship, were discovered inside the temple area during the winter of 1906; most of them were sadly mutilated.

One statuette was the gift of Amen-em-hat I (XII 1), the founder of the dynasty, who erected a portal outside the lesser cave as was shown by a stone lintel bearing his name, which was found here. His successor, Sen-usert I (XII 2), added to this portal as was shown by a piece of limestone bearing his name. The larger cave about this time was squared, its walls were smoothed and a slab was fixed inside, on which were placed the more important Egyptian offerings, including the hawk presented by Sneferu, and the statuettes of Hathor. It served also to hold a hawk worked in sandstone that was presented by Sen-usert himself, which named him, his queen Khent, their daughter Sebat, and Ankhab, chief or overseer of the north land.

The same Ankhab also set up a tablet of his own, inside the cave on which he was represented offering loaves to Amen.

Of the next king, Amen-em-hat II (XII 3), there was found the usual statuette of Hathor, which was presented by the ship-captain Sneferu. Inscriptions on a hill at some distance from the caves showed that the Egyptians now worked turquoise mines at Serabit on their own account on land which they had acquired. One inscription was of the seventeenth year of Amen-em-hat II, another of his twenty-fourth year. The latter mentioned the " mine chamber which Men, born of Mut, triumphant and revered, excavated." Two steles erected in the approach to the sanctuary likewise recorded the seventeenth and the twenty-fourth year of the reign of the same king.

The next kings, Sen-usert II (XII 4) and Sen-usert III (XII 5), made the usual gift of a statuette of Hathor. The latter was presented by five officials, including Merru, two inspectors, a scribe of the cattle, and an Amu or Syrian named Lua or Luy, " a name which corresponds to the Semitic Levy."[1] This shows a Semite in actual contact with the place. A stele of the same Pharaoh stood in a knoll of hæmatite on the plateau, the exposed position of which caused it to fall and crumble long ago ; its remains strew the ground.

The reign of the next Pharaoh, Amen-em-hat III (XII 6), marked a climax in the intercourse of Egypt and Sinai. Of the forty-four years of his reign, at least fourteen witnessed expeditions to Sinai, which were commemorated by inscriptions set up in Wadi Maghara, in Wadi Nasb, and at Serabit.

A great inscription of the second year, mentioned above, stands on a boulder at the entrance to Wadi Maghara, which shows the king facing the ibis-headed Thoth and Hathor, and the accompanying wording mentions Khenti-hotep Khenemsu, who was commissioned to fetch turquoise and copper, and who had with him 734 men. Another inscription was set up by Harnakt, who " crossed the sea and secured stones of great excellence." [2]

At Serabit also Amen-em-hat III was commemorated by many inscriptions. Large stone steles, set up on the plateau, recorded the 4th, 8th, 13th, 23rd, 30th, 44th, and 45th year of this reign. Several of these steles mention by name the Retennu people, of whom we now hear for the first time in Sinai.

[1] Petrie : *Res. Sinai*, p. 124.
[2] Breasted : *Rec.*, i. 713, 717-8.

The stele of the fourth year contained in two columns the

Fig. 9.—Upper half of Stele of Amen-em-hat III. (Petrie: *Researches in Sinai.*)

names and titles of over a hundred persons who took part in

the expedition. The names start in fairly large hieroglyphs at the top, and diminish in size lower down. A few additional names were roughly inscribed along the edge of the stele as the result of an afterthought. This splendid stele stood about ten feet high in the approach to the temple, but, worn through at the base by the continued action of wind and rain, it fell, and snapped in two in the falling (Fig. 9).

Not far from this stele stood one that was set up by Horoura, describing an expedition which reached the mines in hot weather. " The desert burnt like summer ; the mountains burnt like fire ; the vein seemed exhausted ; the overseer questioned the miners ; the skilled workers who knew the mine replied, There is turquoise to all eternity in the mountain, and at that moment it appeared." [1]

The reference is to the turquoise mines opened by Amen-em-hat II, which were now further developed. The neck of rock which contained the turquoise had hitherto been worked from the north. This neck of rock was now attacked from the south, and, as the work became complex, a shaft of about ten feet square was sunk from above, which brought light and air into the passages. This shaft was wrongly described by some travellers as a reservoir. The passages eventually extended about 220 feet into the rock. A great inscription on the rock, near the chief opening, gives an idea of the offerings which the Egyptians made at the sanctuary at this time ; evidently in return for the permission to work here. It mentions " a thousand loaves, jars of beer, cattle, fowls, incense, ointment, and everything on which the gods live." The offerings in this case were presented by Sebek-her-heb, chief chamberlain, who declared, " I excavated a mine-chamber for my lord, the workmen came in full quota, never was there any neglect." [2]

The same Sebek-her-heb erected the stele of the 44th year of Amen-em-hat III on the plateau. It is inscribed on one side only and stands in a rough stone enclosure with a flat stone at the base. The inscription runs " a royal offering to Hathor, mistress of turquoise (*mafkat*), for the family spirit (*ka*) of the chief chamberlain Sebek-her-heb, and the

[1] Breasted : *Rec.*, i. 735-6.
[2] *Ibid.*, pp. 725-7.

ka of the seal-bearer, deputy of the overseer of seal-bearers, Kemnaa, born of Ka-hotep." [1]

Another inscription of the 45th year of Amen-em-hat III, named Ptahwer, triumphant, who described himself as " delivering the Anu Sut (eastern foreigners) to the Pharaoh, and bringing the Mentu to the halls of the king." [2]

During the reign of Amen-em-hat III the caves at Serabit were re-modelled to their present shape. The larger cave, without the recesses, now measures 20 by 10 feet. A square pillar of rock was left standing in its centre as a support to the roof. On one side of this pillar the Pharaoh was represented facing the goddess Hathor, wearing a high head-dress, who held out to him a sceptre. Beneath this scene Khenum-su, Ameny-seneb, seal-bearer, and other officials were seen.[3] The walls of the cave at the same time were smoothed and inscribed with mortuary prayers. But their surface for the most part has crumbled away, perhaps owing to intentional desecration, and the inscriptions are lost.

Ameny-seneb who was represented on the squared pillar, also set up in the cave an altar in the name of his king. This altar measured 40 by 26 inches, and probably stood at the back of the cave in a recess of corresponding dimensions. It was found in another part of the cave. This altar had the ordinary appearance of an Egyptian altar and was worked in the red sandstone of the place. It apparently took the place of an earlier stone or altar of different appearance, fragments of which were also found inside the cave. The smashing of this altar also points to an intentional desecration of the place.

The smaller cave which was appropriated to Sopd, was probably re-arranged at the same time. There was here no sign of inscription or tablet. It was simply a rounded apse with three steps leading up to it.

The other work which was done during the reign of Amen-em-hat III included mining in the Wadi Nasb, where an inscription at the head of the valley recorded his 20th year.[4]

The head of the valley floor of the Wadi Nasb is covered

[1] Petrie: *Res. Sinai*, p. 66.
[2] Breasted: *Rec.*, i. 728 ; Petrie: *Res. Sinai*, p. 156.
[3] Breasted: *Rec.*, i. 716.
[4] Petrie: *Res. Sinai*, p. 27.

with an enormous mass of slag, which points to extensive
copper smelting.   The mass of slag is 6 to 8 feet deep, 300 feet
wide, and extends about 500 feet down the valley.   It " may
amount to 100,000 tons."   The provenance of the copper
that was smelted here is insufficiently known.   It can hardly
have been brought up from the mines in the Wadi Khalig.
But even at Serabit, now entirely denuded of trees, a crucible
was found.

 After the long reign of Amen-em-hat III came the short
reign of Amen-em-hat IV (XII 7), the last king of his dynasty.
An inscription in the Wadi Maghara recorded work done there
in his sixth year, and, at Serabit, the small rock tablet mentioned above, was set up on the western side of the plateau.
A portico-court about 10 feet square was also built by him
outside the larger cave.   This court was roofed over with
slabs of stone, the roof being supported by two fluted
columns which, like the rest of the building, were worked
in the red sandstone of the place.   The walls of this portico
were inscribed, the subject being Hathor seated with the
Pharaoh offering to her, and a long row of officials behind
him.   The same scene reversed was represented on the other
side of the entrance.   But the surface of the wall has crumbled
so that the general character only of the scenes is visible
and the names of the officials have gone.

CHAPTER V

EARLY PEOPLE AND PLACE NAMES

THE ancient peoples and place names of Sinai claim separate attention.

The earliest Egyptian rock inscription at Maghara represents the Pharaoh as a smiter, and describes him as such with the signs of a hand, an eagle, and the determinative of hills. The term is held to apply to no people in particular, and is therefore rendered as " barbarians."

King Khufu (IV 2), in addition, is described as a smiter of the Anu ; the word is written with the pillar sign. The word Anu was applied in Egypt to cave-dwellers generally, more especially to those of Nubia. The Anu are first mentioned on the Palermo Stone in connection with a king of the First Dynasty whose name is broken away but who was probably King Den-Setui.

In the estimation of the historian Josephus (c. A.D. 60), the inhabitants of Sinai at the time of Moses were cave-dwellers, for he stated that Moses, in going to Sinai, went among the " troglodytes " (*Antiq.*, ii. 11).

Among the early inhabitants of the peninsula were the Horites. The Babylonian kings who fought against the four kings of southern Syria who revolted in the time of Abraham, " smote the Rephaims in Ashteroth Karnaim, and the Zuzims in Ham, and the Emims in Shaveh-Kiriathaim, and the Horites in their mount Seir unto El Paran, which is by the wilderness " (Gen. xiv. 5–6). This associates the Horites with Mount Seir, which extended along the depression between the head of the Gulf of Akaba and the Dead Sea.

In the estimation of Prof. Robertson Smith the Horites of the Bible were troglodytes, which would bring them into line with the Anu of the Egyptian inscriptions. These

Horites were accounted of low stock by the Hebrews, and were
probably in the stage through which the Israelites had passed
before they formed a confederacy. Prof. Robertson Smith
pointed out that the list of their so-called dukes (Gen. xxxvi. 20)
is not a literal genealogy, but an account of their tribal and
local division, since five of the names are animal or totem
names.[1] The view that the Horites were cave-dwellers was
based on the likeness between the name Horite and the Hebrew
word *hor*, which signifies mountain. The connection between
the names is now denied, and the Horites of the Bible are
identified with the Kharu or Khalu of the Egyptian texts.
The Kharu appear in the *Annals* of Tahutmes III (XVIII 6)
and of Amen-hotep IV (XVIII 10), among the people against
whom the Egyptians fought on the way to Naharain *i.e.*
Mesopotamia.[2] But the word Kharu on the Egyptian side
has been interpreted as "mixed multitude."

The next people who are mentioned on the Egyptian
monuments in Sinai are the Mentu. King Ra-en-user (V 6)
was described as "great god of the smiting countries and
raider of the Mentu." Again, the tablet of Men-kau-hor,
mentioned a royal expedition to the Mentu; and Ptahwer
in Sinai of the Twelfth Dynasty was described as "bringing
the Mentu to the king's heels."

The Mentu took part in the great Hyksos invasion of Egypt
between the Twelfth and the Eighteenth Dynasties. For when
the tide of foreign nations was rolled back, they were among
the conquered. King Aahmes I (XVIII 1), after seizing the
foreign stronghold Avaris, "made a slaughter of the Mentu
of Setiu, and going south to Khent-hen-nefer, he destroyed
the Anu-Khenti."[3] Among the conquered people who were
represented around the throne of Amen-hotep II (XVIII 7)
are the Mentu, who have the appearance of true Asiatics.
An Edfu inscription, as mentioned above, stated that the
Mentu were thrown back with the help of the devotees of
the god Sopd.

The people who figured most prominently in the Egyptian
annals of Sinai were the Retennu, who were mentioned again
and again on the steles which were set up at Serabit in the course

[1] Smith, W. Robertson: *Lectures*, p. 471.
[2] Petrie: *Hist.*, ii. 105.
[3] *Ibid.*, ii. 22.

of the Twelfth Dynasty. On three separate steles it says that the Egyptian expedition was sped across the desert by the brother of the sheykh (*sen-heq-en*) of the Retennu country, whose name was Khebdet or Khebtata, and who is represented riding on an ass which is led by a man in front, with a servant carrying his water flask behind him. On one stele six Retennu are named.[1]

These Retennu who figure in the annals of the Sinai in the Twelfth Dynasty are mentioned as dwelling in southern Syria in the Egyptian *Tale of Sanehat*, otherwise *Sinuhe*. This tale describes how a high-born Egyptian fled when news reached him of the death of King Amen-em-hat I (XII 1). He was at the time on the western Delta and by way of the Wadi Sneferu (unknown) reached the quarries of Khri Ahu (perhaps Cairo), crossed the Nile and passed the domain of the goddess Hirit, mistress of the Red Mountain (possibly Gebel Ahmar), and the wall which the prince had constructed. He reached Keduma (or Aduma) where Amu-anshi, sheykh of the Upper Tennu, took him for a sojourner or son-in-law, and settled him in the adjoining Ya-a country, a land of honey and figs, where wine was commoner than water. Sanehat remained here many years till the death of the Pharaoh caused him to petition his successor Senusert 1 (XII 2) for return to Egypt.[2] The name of the land to which Sanehat fled was read either as Aduma which would be the equivalent of Edom, but more probably (cf. Maspero and Dr. Alan Gardiner) as Keduma, and is probably the land Kedem, *i.e.* the east country, to which Abraham sent the sons of his concubines (Gen. xxv. 6). But the Retennu, who were peaceful neighbours of the Egyptians during the Twelfth Dynasty, were among the peoples against whom they afterwards waged war. Tahutmes I (XVIII 3) fought the Retennu on his way from Egypt to Naharain, *i.e.* Mesopotamia ; Tahutmes III (XVIII 6) again and again ravaged their country ; and Sety I (XIX 2), whose objective was Kadesh on the Orontes, was represented in his temple at Karnak dragging after him the great sheykhs of the Retennu, whom he is shown holding by the hair of their heads.[3] Again, Ramessu III (XX 1) mentioned the tribute

[1] Petrie: *Res. Sinai*, p. 118.
[2] Petrie: *Egyptian Tales*, i. 97–127.
[3] Petrie: *Hist.*, ii. 101 ; iii. 3.

which was brought by the Retennu, in the great inscription of his temple at Medinet Habu.[1]

The Retennu and their name survived in Sinai, for Ptolemy, the geographer, named as its inhabitants the Pharanites, the Raithenoi and the Munichiates. Again, in the year 1816 the traveller Burckhardt noted that, attached to the mosque that stood inside the convent precincts, there were certain poor Bedawyn "called Retheny," whose duty it was to clean the mosque. One of them had the dignity of *imam*, a leader in prayer, and was supported by offerings.[2]

And not only did the Retennu continue, the language which they spoke seems to have continued likewise. The sheykh who befriended Sanehat about two thousand years before our era, was named Amu-anshi, as recorded in the *Tale of Sanehat*. About the year A.D. 440 the Christian community of Pharan in Sinai, in consequence of outrages committed by the Arabs, lodged a complaint with their sheykh who stood in the relation of phylarch to the Romans, and who dwelt at a place described as twelve days' journey from Pharan. The sequel of the account makes it probable that it was Petra. The name of the sheykh was Ammanus, which is the Latinised equivalent of Amu-anshi.

Another people who were associated with Sinai were the Rephaim who are mentioned in the Bible among the people who were raided by the Babylonian kings about B.C. 2100. "They smote the Rephaims in Ashteroth Karnaim" (Gen. xiv. 5). The word Rephaim is related to Raphaka or Raphia of the annals of Sargon II (B.C. 722–50).[3] It lies on the high road from Syria to Egypt on the Mediterranean. Its modern name is Rafa.

The Rephaim of the Bible were accounted giants. In Arabian tradition we also hear of giants or tyrants, the Jaba-bera. They were accounted descendants of the Aulad bin Nuh (children of Noah), or Amalikah, from their ancestor Amlah bin Arfexad bin Sam (Shem) bin Nuh. Masudi spoke of the giants of the race of Amalekites who ruled in Syria at the time of Moses.[4]

[1] Breasted : *Rec.*, iv. 28.
[2] Burckhardt : *Travels in Syria*, ed. 1822, p. 544.
[3] Birch : *Rec. Past*, vii. 26.
[4] Masudi : *Prairies d'Or*, c. 4, trad. *Société Asiatique*, vol. i. p. 98.

According to Arab belief the Amalekites were inspired with a knowledge of the Arabic tongue, and settled at Medina, and were the first to cultivate the ground and plant the date palm. In the course of time they extended over the whole tract towards the Red Sea (El Hedjaz), and the north-western part of the Indian Ocean (El Omar), and became the progenitors not only of the Jababera, but also of the Faraineh (*i.e.* the Pharaohs) of Egypt.

In the Biblical genealogy Amalek appears as a descendant of Esau, his mother, Adah, being a Hittite (Gen. xxxvi. 2, 12). But scholars generally are agreed in assigning a high antiquity to the Amalekites. The prophet Balaam, inspired by Jehovah, uttered the words, " Amalek was the first of the nations " (Num. xxiv. 20).

Whatever their origin, the Amalekites were in the possession of Sinai when the Israelites came there, since they opposed their entrance and harried them on their way to the holy mount, and later attacked them in Rephidim, where the Israelites carried the day (Deut. xxv. 17 ; Exod. xvii. 8-16). Later, acting in concert with the Canaanites, they smote the Israelites on their way to Hormah (Num. xiv. 25–45), and in the time of Saul they still occupied the land " from Havilah unto Shur " (from Arabia to the Wall of Egypt), which, according to another account, was allotted to the sons of Ishmael (Gen. xxv. 18). Saul waged a fierce war against them.

The connection of the Amalekites with Sinai continued in the mind of the Arab, for Makrizi († 1441) speaking of Pharan, the city of Sinai, described it as a city of the Amalekites.[1]

The Amalekites of the Bible and of Arab tradition are probably the Milukhkha of the ancient annals. As mentioned above, they appear on the statue of Gudea of about the year B.C. 2500, and in the Assyrian fragment of geography of about B.C. 600.

Pharan, which the Arab writers described as a city of the Amalekites, was from early times a place-name in Sinai. According to the Bible, the Babylonian kings (*c.* B.C. 2100) pressed the Horites as far as " El Paran, which is by the wilderness," a phrase which the Septuagint rendered as

---

[1] Makrizi : *Description de l'Egypte,* 1900, ii. 27, p. 543.

"the terebinth of Pharan," as though it were a site marked by a tree. Pharan, to all appearance, was a general name given to the peninsula of Sinai. It is like the name Pharaoh, and this is apparently the reason why the name "Bath of Pharaoh," Gebel Hammam Faraun, is given to a hill near the west coast, and the name Giziret el Faraun to the island near Akaba, the idea of the Pharaoh leading to various localised legends.

In the Bible we read that the Israelites, after leaving the Holy Mount, passed through "the wilderness of Paran" on their way to Edom, which would locate it to the Badiet Tîh. Again, King Hadad (c. B.C. 1156), on his way from Midian to Egypt, passed through Paran (1 Kings xi. 17).

The Septuagint and the classical writers rendered Paran, as Pharan, and Ptolemy, the geographer, named a village (κώμη) Pharan, the position of which corresponds with the seat of the later Christian bishopric in the Wadi Feiran. He also named the southernmost point of the peninsula, the present Ras Mohammad, as the promontory of Pharan, and included the Pharanites among the inhabitants of Sinai.

Again, Pliny († A.D. 79) mentioned a variety of precious stone as *sapenos* or *pharanites*, so called from the country where it is found (xxvii. 40). Perhaps turquoise is meant, in which case Sapenos, a word otherwise unknown, may be connected with the name Sopd; Pharanites would refer to Pharan or to Pharaoh.

The Egyptologist Ebers was the first to suggest that the name Paran shows Egyptian influence, and may be the place-name Rahan *plus* the Egyptian article *Pa*, in the same way as Pa-kesem is the land of Kesem, *i.e.* Goshen.[1]

The word Rahan occurs in an Egyptian inscription of the Twelfth Dynasty, according to which an envoy coming from Egypt crossed Desher to the Rahan country.[2]

The word Raha as a place continues in different parts of the peninsula to the present day. The north-western part of the Tîh is called Gebel er Raha, and the wide sandy plain that extends north of the Gebel Musa is the Plain of Raha.[3]

According to the Bible, Ishmael "a wild man and an

[1] Ebers: *Durch Gosen zum Sinai*, 1872, p. 288.
[2] Lepsius: *Denkmäler*, ii. 150, a. 12.
[3] Keith Johnson: *General Atlas*.

archer," dwelt in the wilderness of Paran, and his mother, who was an Egyptian, " took him a wife out of Egypt." The Septuagint rendered this as " out of Pharan of Egypt " (Gen. xvi. 12 ; xxi. 21). The Ishmaelites in the Bible are referred to Abraham himself, which shows that they were regarded as an allied stock by the Hebrews, a certain inferiority being implied by their having Egyptian blood in their veins. The acceptance of a joint divinity El seems to have made a bond of union between the twelve tribes of Ishmael, as it did between the tribes of Israel. According to Genesis the Ishmaelites dwelt from Havilah unto Shur, " living in houses and castles," or rather in " tents and booths," as the Septuagint rendered the passage (Gen. xxv. 16).

While Paran in the Bible was associated with Ishmael the adjoining land of Edom was connected with Esau, the incidents of whose story are more or less mythical, but a clue to them is yielded by the word Edom which signifies red in Aramaic.

Esau was red-haired at birth. " And the first came out red, all over like a hairy garment ; and they called his name Esau " (Gen. xxv. 25). Again, Esau, in exchange for his birthright, *i.e.* herds and flocks and precedence after his father's death, took " very red food," literally the " red, red thing," which the Septuagint rendered as " fiery red " ($\pi\nu\rho\rho\sigma\hat{\nu}$). In the further development of the story, the red thing is described as a pottage of red lentils. " And Esau said to Jacob, Feed me, I pray thee, with that same red pottage ; for I am faint : therefore was his name called Edom " (Gen. xxv. 30). The hairiness of Esau has been connected with Mount Seir, a word signifying rough ; [1] on the same basis the idea of redness conveyed by the word Edom, is referable to the red sandstone of the district.

The Edomites, according to the Bible, took possession of the land of Uz (Lam. iv. 21), which was the land of Job (Job i. 1). Uz was described as the son of Aram, the son of Shem (Gen. x. 23), or, according to Masudi († 957), " Aud, the son of Aram, the son of Shem." [2]

Uz and Aud are thus identified, and in keeping with this, Septuagint described Job as dwelling in the land "Ausitis."

[1] Hastings : *Dict. Bible*, art. " Esau."
[2] Masudi : *Prairies*, c. 3, vol. i. p. 77.

Aud was a divinity by whom a group of Arabs took their oath, and the people of Ad or Uz were among the great people of the Arab legendary past, who were smitten by misfortune. The calamities which befell them are, perhaps, reflected in the story of Job.

In the Koran the utterance was put into the lips of Moses, " Hath not the story reached thee of those who were before thee, the people of Noah and Ad and Themud " (xiv. 9).[1] " And unto Ad we sent their brother Hud . . . and unto Themud we sent Saleh, but the people received them not as their prophets, and they were destroyed " (vii. 63). " And we destroyed Ad and Themud " (xxix. 38). According to Masudi († 957) Aud, who was sent to the Adites, and Saleh, who was sent to the Thamudites, lived immediately after the Flood, before Abraham.[2]

Many stories were current among the Arabs concerning the wealth and influence of the Adites. They were said to have lived twelve hundred years, when their sons the Shaddad, subjected the country of the Egyptian, and in this they remained two hundred years, and built the city Aour or Awar.[3] The reference is to the great fortress of the Hyksos, the Hatuar of the Egyptians, the Avaris of Manetho-Josephus, situated about twenty miles north of Cairo. If the Adites were instrumental in erecting this city, they must have taken part in the great Hyksos invasion which happened during the Fourteenth Dynasty of Egypt, *i.e.* about B.C. 2500.

According to Makrizi († 1441), the Adite king who marched against Egypt was Shaddad ben Haddad ben Shaddad ben Ad, and the Pharaoh whom he conquered was Ashmoun ben Masir ben Beisar, son of Cham, son of Noah, whose buildings he destroyed and in his turn he raised pyramids (probably pillars), traced Alexandria and then left for the Wadi el Korah between El Nabouyah and Syria. He built a series of square reservoirs, which resulted in many kinds of cultivation, which extended from Raïah (*i.e.* Raithou) to Aila (at the head of the Gulf of Arabia) to the western sea (*i.e.* the Mediterranean). His

[1] Smith,W. Robertson: *Kinship and Marriage in Early Arabia*, 1885, p. 260.
[2] Masudi : *Prairies*, c. 37, vol. 3, p. 78.
[3] Caussin de Perceval, A. P. : *Essai sur l'historie des Arabes avant l'Islam*, 1847, i. 13.

peoples' dwellings covered the district between El Dathmar, El Arish, and El Goufar, in the land of Shaleh (along the Mediterranean sea-board in northern Sinai), where there were wells and fruit-trees, and cultivation including that of saffron of two kinds and of the sugar-cane. This land was occupied by Khodem ben El Airan, when God, because of the over-bearing of the Adites, raised a storm, and sand of the desert covered the land they inhabited. Hence the words of the Koran, " And in Ad : when we sent against them the desolating blast, it touched not aught over which it came, but it turned it into dust." [1]

The Adites at one period controlled the gold and incense route from Inner Arabia to Syria, and the Koran credited them with erecting pillars, probably *mazzeboth*, in high places. " Hast thou not seen how the Lord dwelt with Ad at Iram, adorned with pillars whose like have not been raised in these lands " (lxxxix. 6). And again, " Build ye land-marks on all heights in mere pastime " (xxiv. 128). Ptolemy, the geographer (A.D. 140), located the Oaditæ to the east of the Gulf of Akaba, and named as their chief city Aramava, which was an important watering station on the way between Petra and Mecca. Aramava is perhaps Iram of the Koran. [2]

The Adites as traders were succeeded by the Thamudites, who, according to the Koran, " hewed rocks in the valley " (xxxix. 8). The reference is possibly to Petra. According to tradition they occupied Aila. [3]

A prophet of the Thamudites was Saleh, who has a special interest for southern Sinai, since the Benu Saleh, who claim descent from him, are among the oldest and most powerful tribes of the peninsula. Saleh in the Biblical record is named as third in descent from Shem, and as the progenitor of Eber (Gen. x. 24).

The remembrance of the Thamudites survives in the present Diar (or land of) Themoud, in north-western Arabia, which includes the great Wadi El Korah which is followed by the pilgrims from Damascus to Mecca. In the Wadi El Korah lie the Medaïn (cities of) Saleh, and some distance south of these, is the pass which is associated with the destruction

---

[1] Makrizi : *Descrip.*, ii. 21, p. 523.
[2] Sprenger : *Alte Geographie Arabiens*, 1875, no. 207, p. 144.
[3] Makrizi : *Descrip.*, ii. 27 ; *De la ville d'Eilah*, p. 530.

of the she-camel, the creation of Saleh. For the people of Themoud to whom Saleh was sent, did not accept him. They asked for a sign, whereupon he produced from the rock the Naga or she-camel that gave milk. " Let her go at large," was his command, " and feed on God's earth, and do her no harm. Drink there shall be for her and drink there shall be for you, on a several day for each ; but harm her not, lest the punishment of a tremendous day overtake you. But the Thamudites hamstrung her, and repented of it on the morrow, for the punishment overtook them."

This story of the she-camel preserves the tradition of man's right to the free use of an animal, which was indispensable to the well-being of the man of the desert. According to the Koran, it will be the end of all things when "the sun is folded up, the stars fall, the mountains rock, the she-camel is abandoned and the wild beasts are gathered together" (lxxxi. 1).

In the year 1873 Doughty, coming from Damascus, stayed at the Medaïn Saleh, where he saw and described the well, now enclosed in a tower, where the she-camel was watered. He also visited the pass some way further along the road, the Mubrak en Naga, where the she-camel was killed.[1]

According to one tradition this was done by Codar el Ahmar (i.e. the Red), a name in which Caussin de Perceval, saw a likeness to Chedorlaomer of the time of Abraham.[2] This agrees with Masudi's statement that Saleh came to the rescue of the Thamudites when their existence was threatened by a descendant of Ham.[3] Saleh and King Djundu fled to Sinai where they became hermits, and Saleh died and was buried in El Ramlah. The tomb of Nebi Saleh is located in the present Wadi Sheykh near the Gebel Musa, and is the site of the great annual encampment of the Arabs of southern Sinai.

In the newly discovered annals of King Sargon of Assyria (B.C. 722–705), the people of Tamud are named among " the Arabians living at a distance in the desert of whom the Wise Men and the Magi knew nothing, who never brought tribute to (my father) the king, whom I overthrew, and the remainder

---

[1] Doughty : *Travels,* ed. 1888, i. p. 81, etc.
[2] Caussin : *Essai,* i. 26.
[3] Masudi : *Prairies,* c. 38, vol. 3, p. 90.

I carried off into Palestine." [1] This transportation explains the re-appearance of the Thamudites in different localities. Ptolemy knew of Thamuditæ who dwelt along the Gulf of Akaba, and of Thamudenæ who dwelt further inland.[2] Diodorus Siculus (c. B.C. 50) mentioned Thamideans living in Arabia.[3] As late as about A.D. 452-3 a *Notitia Dignitatum* mentioned *equites Thamudeni*, who were in the service of Rome, of whom one division, the *equites Saraceni Thamudeni* camped on the frontier of Egypt, another, the *equites Thamudeni Illyriciani*, were stationed in Judæa.[4] The present Bir Themed, in Sinai, situated halfway between Akaba and Kala'at en Nakhl, recalls the connection of the Thamudites with the peninsula.

[1] Delitzsch : *Wo lag das Paradies*, 1881, p. 304.
[2] Sprenger : no. 314, p. 192.
[3] Diod. Siculus : *Bibliotheca*, iii. 3, trans. 1814, p. 185.
[4] Caussin : *Essai*, i. 27.

CHAPTER VI

II

AFTER the close of the Twelfth Dynasty, the Egyptians ceased for centuries to come to Sinai. The reason was that foreigners, for over a hundred years, ruled in the Nile valley whom the Alexandrian writers called Arabians or Phœnicians. The Egyptians themselves called them Hyksos. To this period probably belong the inscriptions in Semitic script that were set up in some mines in the Wadi Dhabah near Serabit, and the offerings of a squat figure and of a sphinx inscribed in the same Semitic script which were presented before the shrine of the goddess. These inscriptions again and again mention the goddess of the place in lettering which may be Ba-alat, and the script itself is considered of the highest interest in the study of Semitic characters generally.

After throwing back the foreign invaders of Egypt, the Pharaohs of the Eighteenth Dynasty once again sent expeditions to Sinai, where, as we learn from the inscriptions and monuments, they worked both at Maghara and at Serabit. At Serabit building was now continued on an extensive scale outside the caves of the sanctuary. Halls, courts, a pylon, and a long row of chambers were erected on the plateau inside the temenos, which gave the sanctuary the appearance of a vast temple. The buildings were all constructed of the red sandstone of the place, which was quarried on the hill slope just below the temple on the north side, where great quarries remain (Fig. 11).

The offerings which the Egyptians now made to the shrine were smaller, more numerous and, with few exceptions, of less importance than those of the Twelfth Dynasty. They included figures, bowls, cups, vases of alabaster and glaze, ring-stands, *sistra* or rattles, *menats* or pendants, besides wands for temple use, and rows upon rows of beads. Most of these objects are similar to those which were in use in Egypt in connection with the cult of the goddess Hathor, but many bear a character which show that they were made in deference to the local associations of the place.

Thus, on some of these offerings, beginning with the

Fig. 10.—Temple ruins at Serabit.

reign of Hatshepsut (XVIII 5), a feline animal appears, which is sometimes a cheetah and sometimes a serval, and which was directly associated with the goddess Hathor, as was shown by a ring-stand on which the head of the goddess appeared with a cat on either side.

This animal, considering its varying form, can hardly be intended for an Egyptian nome-animal, such as the cat of Bubastis. Rather should we look upon it as intended for a local animal associated with the temple.

In other parts of the world, the early totem animal was sometimes associated by a later age with the mother-divinity. Possibly the animal in the offerings in Sinai was of this kind. No traditions on the subject are preserved, but the chief gorge along which the plateau of the temple is approached from the north is called the Wadi Dhaba, a word which signifies wild beast or panther in Arabic.

Of the smaller cult objects which now accumulated in the sanctuary, many were carried off before the winter of 1906, and are scattered in various museums. But the mass of the objects that remained was so great that their fragments covered the ground of the sanctuary and the portico in front of the larger cave, in a layer two or three inches thick. Fragments also strewed the ground outside the temple precincts. Of these fragments several hundredweights were conveyed from the temple to the camp, where they were laid out and fitted, but although days and weeks were spent in fitting them, and many objects had a distinctive appearance, no complete specimen of any kind was recovered. The explanation is that the objects were intentionally smashed, and their fragments scattered outside the cave where they gradually disintegrated. It was doubtless done from the same lust of iconoclastic zeal which caused the smashing of the statuettes of Hathor, but whether during some ancient upheaval or by the Moslim, who can tell ?

Among the masses of fragments as many as 447 bore cartouches of the Pharaohs, and this enables us to date them.

Thus Aahmes (XVIII 1), first ruler of the Eighteenth Dynasty, was named on a *sistrum* and on *menats ;* his daughter Merytamen was named on a *menat ;* and his successor Amen-hotep I (XVIII 2) was named on a *sistrum,* a *menat* and a plaque of Hathor. The same Pharaoh's queen, Aahmes Nefertari, was named on a *menat.*

Of these kings, Amen-hotep I restored the portico of the cave of Hathor, as was shown by a perfect lintel slab with a cavetto cornice, 22 inches high and 50 inches long, bearing his name which was found in front of the entrance. His successor, Tahutmes I (XVIII 3) gave a *menat* of himself and his queen, a wand, and an alabaster vase, and pottery vases. There was no mention of Tahutmes II (XVIII 4).

Great activity was shown during the reign of the next

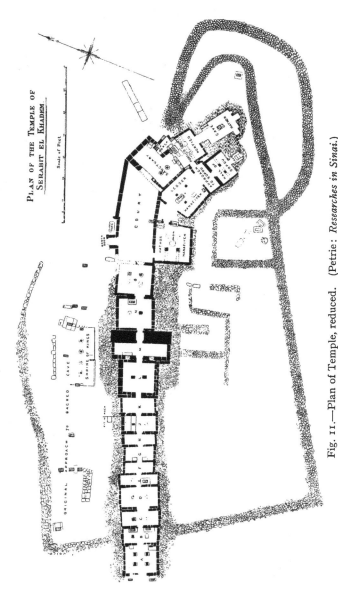

PLAN OF THE TEMPLE OF
SERABIT EL KHADEM.

Scale of Feet

Fig. 11.—Plan of Temple, reduced. (Petrie: *Researches in Sinai*.)

rulers, Hatshepsut (XVIII 5) and her nephew Tahutmes III (XVIII 6), and their names appear on a large number of small offerings, including several which show the feline animal. These rulers jointly worked the mines at Serabit which had been opened in the Twelfth Dynasty, and at Maghara a tablet dated to their 16th year stands inside the entrance to a mining gallery that is about 24 feet long, 60–70 inches wide, and about 100 inches high. It is on this tablet that Hatshepsut is seen offering incense to the god Sopd, while Tahutmes offers incense to the goddess Hathor. The large rubbish heaps outside this mine contained much discoloured turquoise.

A new era now began in the history of the sanctuary at Serabit. The Egyptians built porticoes, halls, and chambers across the High Place of Burning, which disappeared beneath them. These buildings were all worked in the red sandstone of the place, and were decorated with figures and hieroglyphs in the formal style of Egypt. The arrangement and the disposition of the buildings have nothing in common, however, with the temples of Egypt. Like the Twelfth Dynasty steles, which were erected in conformity to Semitic usage, the temple buildings of the Eighteenth Dynasty reflect a non-Egyptian influence.

A small hall was now erected outside the lesser cave, the roof of which was supported by two pillars, and the wall bore an inscription commemorating its building and naming the god Sopdu. In this stood the rectangular tank alluded to above (compare plan).

On the approach to this hall was another hall, measuring about 20 feet square, which in its complete state must have been an imposing structure. Four great square pillars surmounted by the head of Hathor supported the roof, with long roof beams from the pillars to the walls, and short roof beams between the pillars that carried the roofing slabs. These great pillars were standing when Rüppell visited the place in 1817, now only two are left. The colossal head of the goddess surmounted the pillars, and is full of dignity and strength. In the centre of the hall, surrounded by these four pillars stood a great circular stone tank, now broken across. There was, moreover, a rectangular tank built into the wall in one corner of the same hall.

Inside the north entrance on the way to the sanctuary,

Queen Hatshepsut also erected a hall which was roofed over and open at one side. The roof, in this case, was carried by four fluted columns, one of which remains standing. The inside walls of this hall were covered with figures and writing, which gave an account of its building, and a recital of the offerings that were made for it. Among the figures represented were Sneferu, Amen-em-hat III, Sopd, Queen Hatshepsut, and Hathor. The position of this hall suggests that it served for the formal reception of worshippers who entered the temple precincts from the north. It has a wide outlook over the gorges below.

The building activity of Tahutmes increased, if anything, after the queen's death. He set up two small sphinxes in the court between the approach to the larger and the lesser cave, one of which was found *in situ*. They were too large to convey, and were re-buried. He also built a great pylon with a forecourt (M), over the doorway of which, was an inscribed lintel with mention of him. This pylon, which stands up high among the ruins, at this period formed the entrance to the temple from the west. It was flanked by two steles of the fifth year of the king's reign. An outer court (L) was perhaps his work also.

Outside this entrance the next king, Amen-hotep II (XVIII 7) added two small chambers (I H), which were again so constructed that their western side formed a front to the temple. He also presented *menats* and vases to the sanctuary. Later rulers built additional chambers, pushing the temple front out further west. These chambers measured about 6 by 10 ft. each, with a seat on either side, and they eventually extended in one long line from the pylon along the whole length of the temenos, a distance of about 200 feet. They had been built under shelter of a break in the hill and were roofed over. Loose stones were piled up against their walls from outside along the whole length, which concealed them from view and gave them a subterranean character. Their purpose is a matter of conjecture. Probably they housed the guardians of the sanctuary, and served as an adytum to the cave of Hathor. The worshipper who approached the sanctuary from the west, and entered the outermost chamber, would feel himself in proximity to the cave while he was in reality a long way off. As the treasures which were stored in the cave multiplied, the device would help to ensure their safety.

The erection of these buildings across the bed of wood-ashes put an end to the use of this space as a High Place of Burning. The site for offering the holocaust was therefore removed, probably to a site on the north side of the temple which had been squared in the course of quarrying stone for temple buildings. Corn was growing on this site in the winter of 1906, which prevented its being dug down to the rock. But the peculiar fertility of the accumulated soil which rendered the growing of corn possible, suggested that, here also, there might be an accumulation of wood ashes due to extensive burning.

His successor, Tahutmes IV (XVIII 8), further extended the mines of the Twelfth Dynasty, and recorded his doing so by a tablet which is dated to the fourth year of his reign. Tablets of the fifth and the eighth years of his reign have also been mentioned by travellers, but these were sought for in vain in the winter of 1906.

The next Pharaoh, Amen-hotep III (XVIII 9), also added further chambers to the temple approach (G.F), and flanked the new entrance with two steles which record mining expeditions of his 36th year.

The fragments of many beautiful objects which dated from this reign were found in and near the cave of Hathor. They included *menats* and wands, and some cups in lotus form of alabaster of exquisite workmanship. There were also pieces of glazed inlay of two colours—an ancient art of Egypt which was revived at this time. A find of considerable importance was the relief, here reproduced, on which Amen-hotep III is seen offering to the god Sopd who faces him wearing the double plume ; in his one hand the staff of royalty. This shows that special significance was attached to the god of non-Egyptian origin at the court of a Pharaoh who had strong Syrian affinities. The connection was further emphasised by the discovery of the head of a statuette of Queen Thyi, the consort of the magnificent monarch Amen-hotep III. This, in some ways, was the greatest find of all. In the words of Prof. Petrie, " It is strange that this remotest settlement of Egypt has preserved her portrait for us, unmistakably named by her cartouche in the midst of her crown.

The material is dark-green schistose steatite, and the whole statuette must have been about a foot in height. Unfortunately no other fragment has been preserved. The haughty dignity of the face is blended with a fascinating

Fig. 12.—Amen-hotep III (XVIII) offering to Sopd. (*Ancient Egypt*, a periodical, 1917, Part iii.)

directness and personal appeal. The delicacy of the surfaces around the eye and over the cheek show the greatest care in handling. The curiously drawn-down lips with their fulness and delicacy, their disdain without malice, are evidently

modelled in all truth from life." [1]   The reader will recall that
Queen Thyi also was of Syrian origin, and that Amen-hotep III
and Thyi were the parents of Amen-hotep IV (XVIII 10),
better known as Akhen-aten, the great religious reformer of
Egypt.   Signs of a connection of Sinai with the reforming king
himself were not wanting, for among the work found inside
the temenos of the temple was an inscribed limestone tablet,
partly broken, which showed a figure carefully wrought in
the peculiar style of art which was favoured by Akhen-aten
as we know it at Amarna.   The figure was Ramessu I, the
founder of the Nineteenth Dynasty, who was described on the
tablet as " prince of every circuit of the Aten," a title which was
introduced by the religious reformer.[2]   The use of the term
is therefore relatively late, and suggests that the adherents
of the religious reformer after his downfall sought and found
a refuge at the relatively remote centre of Serabit.

In the estimation of the present writer, the Exodus of the
Israelites was connected with the reaction in favour of the
older Egyptian religion which followed the downfall of
Atenism, and Moses visited the sanctuary at Serabit before the
rise of the Nineteenth Dynasty.   If so he saw it as it was left
standing at the time of Amen-hotep III (XVIII 8) ; and the
account of the building activity of the later Pharaohs at the
sanctuary should therefore follow the account of the passage of
the Israelites.   But as authorities differ as to the Pharaohs who
were in contact with Moses, it seems preferable here to complete
the account of the Egyptian activity in Sinai before dealing
with the story of the Exodus.

Many small objects similar to those brought during the
Eighteenth Dynasty were presented at the shrine by the
Pharaohs of the Nineteenth and Twentieth Dynasties, who
worked extensively at the mines, where the cult of Hathor
continued.   No inscription mentions Sopd, whose cult, which
lasted from the Twelfth to the Eighteenth Dynasties, was
now at an end.

Of the kings of the Nineteenth Dynasty King Sety I (XIX 2)
made the usual small offerings, and erected a commemorative
stele on a hillock at some distance from the temple which is
still visible from afar.   He added two courts (B and A) to
the row of chambers which extended across the temenos,

---

[1] Petrie : *Res. Sinai*, p. 127.   [2] *Ibid.*

enclosing the stele which had been set up by Amen-hotep III,

Fig. 13.—Queen Thyi. (Petrie: *Researches in Sinai.*)

and carrying the row of chambers beyond the temenos wall.
These now extended wellnigh 200 feet beyond the actual cave,

the remoteness and safety of which were thereby ensured. With the work of Sety ended the growth of the temple, His successor, Ramessu II (XIX 3), rebuilt inner parts of the sanctuary, and erected several commemorative steles. He also made a large number of small offerings. Again, Meren-ptah (XIX 4) inscribed the pylon, carving his name across that of Tahutmes III, and made the usual small offerings. Sety II (XIX 6) and Ta-usert (XIX 7) made small offerings of glazed pottery also.

The last of the steles recording a mine expedition was erected by King Set-nekht (XIX 9), on the south entrance to the temple. After him Ramessu III (XX 1) appropriated to his own use steles set up by earlier kings which he re-inscribed in the way usual to him. He also made many small offerings, including two vases, cylindrical in form, with scenes in relief modelled around them in different colours, which, in their completeness, were objects of great beauty. Fragments of them only were found which made restoration impossible. One of these vases was worked in dark grey, green and light green. " The subject was the king seated, with a girl standing before him holding a bouquet of flowers. On the other side of the vase were conventional representa- tions of two tall bouquets and garlands between them, with a duck flying above the garlands. Around the top was a wreath of petals, around the base the usual arrangement of petals. The smaller vase is more elaborate. The figures are not only in relief but brightly coloured, yellow on a violet ground ; the petals at the base are green, violet, or white. The same subject is repeated on opposite sides of the vase. King Ramessu III is seated, holding the *dad ;* his cartouches are before him, while a girl stands offering two bouquets to him. . . . Such fine relief-modelling is not known on any other vases, but it belongs to the same school as the glazed tablets with figures of foreign subjects of Ramessu III found at Tell el Yehudiyeh. The art of these has a relationship to that of the finely modelled and coloured reliefs of stucco found at Knossos." [1]

The annals of Ramessu III, preserved in Egypt, bear witness to his activity in Sinai. The *Harris Papyrus*, after

[1] Petrie: *Res. Sinai*, p. 151.

mentioning the destruction of the people of Seir of the tribes of the Shashu (Bedawyn), and the expedition to Punt (Arabia), stated that he went to Atika and " the copper mines which are in this place." Part of the expedition went by water, and part took the land journey with asses. This had not been done before. Possibly Atika stands for Sinai. Ramessu also says, he sent to "my Mother Hathor, mistress of turquoise," silver, gold, royal linen, and things numerous as the sand. And they brought back to the king wonders of real turquoise in numerous sacks, such as had not been heard of before.[1] The same king built the great temple at Medinet Habu, the inscription of which mentioned as his gifts to it myrrh, silver, gold, every splendid costly stone, the impost of the Retennu as tribute, and among the stones lazuli and turquoise." (*Ibid.*, iv. 27–30). The turquoise was no doubt part of the great haul he made in Sinai.

Of later Pharaohs, Ramessu IV (XX 2) built a porch in the temple at Serabit and altered the door of the sanctuary, making the usual small offerings. Ramessu V (XX 3) was named on some small offerings, including bracelets. Ramessu VI (XX 4) inscribed the pillars of a chamber (O), and gave a cup and a bracelet. After that, no trace was found of any construction or offering made by the Egyptians in Sinai.

[1] Breasted : *Rec.*, iv. 404-9.

CHAPTER VII

THE ISRAELITES IN SINAI

I

THE passage of the Israelites through Sinai forms the most thrilling episode in the history of the peninsula. The how and when and where of this journey periodically engage attention. A hundred years ago it was a matter of common belief that Moses wrote the five books that are associated with his name. On the contrary, Biblical criticism now holds that, " regarded as a history of ancient migrations of the Israelites and their establishment as a religious and political community in Canaan, the Hexateuch contains little more than a general outline on which to depend." [1] But the study of the episode reviewed in the light of modern research, reveals an unexpected accuracy, and once more shows that tradition is of value in proportion to our power of reading it aright.

Different views were put forward regarding the date of the Exodus and of the Pharaohs who were in contact with Moses.

According to the Book of Kings it was " in the 480th (LXX 440th) year after the children of Israel were come out of the land of Egypt, in the fourth year of his reign," that Solomon began to build the Temple at Jerusalem (1 Kings vi. 1).

Solomon ruled from c. B.C. 974 to B.C. 935. His fourth year would be 970, and the Exodus, on this basis, happened either in B.C. 1450, or in B.C. 1410 according to the Septuagint.

Prof. Brugsch looked upon Ramessu II as the Pharaoh of the Exodus. Prof. Petrie endorsed the view, accepting the date of Ramessu II as B.C. 1300–1234, and of the Exodus

---

[1] Hastings: *Dict. Bib.*, art. " Hexateuch."

as *c*. B.C. 1220. One of his reasons for doing so was that
the Israelites, as stated in the Bible, worked at the "city
Raamses" (Exod. i. 11), which, as excavations have shown,
was a creation of the Ramessides. But the expression the
"land of Rameses," was used in connection with the story of
Joseph (Gen. xlvii. 11), which deals with events that were
long anterior to the Ramessides, showing that the compilers
of Exodus used expressions that were current at the time
when they wrote.

The identification of Ramessu II, a king of the Nineteenth
Dynasty, as the Pharaoh of the Exodus, clashes with the
information reaching us through Alexandrian and Syriac
sources, which suggests that Moses was befriended by Amen-
hotep IV, better known as Akhen-aten (XVIII 10), the great
religious reformer, and that the Israelites left Egypt under
one of his immediate successors. This connection between
Moses and the great reformer of Egypt strikes the imagination,
all the more as it is in keeping with the Egyptian king's Syrian
affinities. The authorities are worth recalling.

Chief among these were Demetrius Phalereus (B.C. 345)
and Manetho (*c*. B.C. 260) who were quoted by Josephus
(A.D. 80) and Eusebius (A.D. 320); and Artapanus of unknown date, passages of whose work were preserved by
Alexander Polyhistor (B.C. 140) and accepted by Eusebius
and the Chronicon Paschale. The information of Demetrius,
Manetho, and Artapanus is peculiar in that it takes no
account of Scripture. Moreover, Artapanus compared what the
people of Memphis and the Heliopolitans preserved regarding
the passage of the Red Sea. Another writer was Philo of
Alexandria (A.D. 40) who wrote a *Life of Moses*.

The *Chronicon* of Eusebius contains the Egyptian dynasties
as derived from Manetho, and in the list of kings of the
Eighteenth Dynasty, Oros stands for Amen-hotep IV (*i.e.*
Akhen-aten). Against his name stands the entry, "the Birth
of Moses." [1] In agreement with this, Epiphanius in his book
Against all Heresies, mentioned Thermuthis, the daughter
of Amenophis, who adopted Moses,[2] while the Syriac writer
Barhebræus († 1218), who had access to many sources, held
that the princess who adopted Moses was Tremothisa, in

[1] *Chron. Liber* III. Migne: *Patr. Græc.*, xix. 374.
[2] *Hær.*, 78 in Migne: *Patr. Græc.*, xlii. 745.·

Hebrew Damris, the daughter of Amunphatisus.[1] The historian Josephus called her Thermuthis, and related that she intended Moses for her father's successor (*Antiq.*, ii. 9).

On the other hand, Artapanus gave the name of the Pharaoh as Palmanothis, adding that he built sanctuaries at Kessa (perhaps Akhet at Amarna) and at Heliopolis. His daughter Merris who was childless adopted Moses. She was betrothed to Chenefres.[2] The Chronicon Paschale called him Chenebron.[3]

Various traditions point in the same direction. Thus, the Arabs held that Moses was saved by the eldest of seven little princesses, who were daughters of the Pharaoh.[4] Students of Tell el Amarna will recall the representations of the little daughters of Akhen-aten, of whom as many as six are seen with their parents on the wall sculptures of the tombs. On the Egyptian side we know that the marriage of Meryt-aten, Akhen-aten's eldest daughter, with Ra-smenkh-ka (XVIII 11) his co-regent and successor, was without issue.

According to the Artapanus Moses spent his early manhood in the service of the husband of the princess who adopted him, and led a campaign against the Ethiopians (*Praep. Evang.*, ix. 27). In keeping with this, Stephen Martyr († A.D. 36) said that Moses was well nigh forty years old before it came into his heart to look after his brethren, the children of Israel (Acts vii. 23). The exploits of Moses against the Ethiopians were described by Josephus (*Antiq.*, ii. 10).

The identification of a daughter of Akhen-aten as the princess who adopted Moses suggests another possible date for Exodus. The reign of Akhen-aten was dated by Prof. Breasted to c. B.C. 1375–1350, and by Prof. Petrie to c. B.C. 1383–1365. If Moses left Egypt during the reign of one of his immediate successors, perhaps under that of Tut-ankh-amen (XVIII 12), c. B.C. 1353–1344, the date of Exodus on the basis of the Egyptian chronology as now accepted, would be about B.C. 1350, as against the date B.C. 1410 or 1450 as stated in the First Book of the Kings.

According to the Bible, Moses slew an Egyptian who had

---

[1] Barhebræus : *Chronicon*, 1789, p. 14.
[2] Cited Eusebius : *Evang. Præp.*, bk. ix. 27.
[3] *Chronicon Paschale* in Migne : *Patr. Græc.*, xcii. 200.
[4] Weil, G. : *Biblical Legends of the Moslim*, 1846, p. 100.

smitten a Hebrew, whereupon the Pharaoh sought to slay Moses, and he fled (Exod. ii. 12–15). According to Artapanus, the Pharaoh, after the death of the princess, called upon Chanethotes (Canuthis) to kill him. Moses, warned by Aaron, crossed the Nile at Memphis, intending to escape into Arabia. Chanethotes lay in ambush, whereupon Moses, in self-defence, slew him.

Moses then dwelt in the land of Midian, where he watered the flock kept by the daughters of Reuel (called Raguel in Numb. xi. 29). Reuel befriended him and took him for a sojourner and son-in-law (Exod. ii. 21). A further passage states that Moses kept the flock of Jethro, his father-in-law, who is described also as a priest (Exod. iii. 1), and a Kenite. Artapanus named Raguel, describing him as ruler (ἄρχων) of the country, and said that he desired to make an expedition into Egypt in order to secure the crown for Moses and his daughter, but Moses refused.[1] Barhebræus says that Moses married a daughter of Jethro, and describes Jethro as a son of Raguel.[2]. This suggests that Raguel was the father of the tribe. Philo of Alexandria also refers to Moses' claim to the crown of Egypt.

In the service of Jethro, Moses led the flock to the backside of the desert, and came to the mountain of God, to Horeb (Exod. iii. 1). Here he found himself on holy ground. The presence of a priest, of a mountain of God, and of a reserved tract of land, point to an ancient sanctuary, and our thoughts naturally turn to Serabit, for many centuries a High Place of Burning, a centre of moon-cult and a shrine of the Semitic god Sopd. The wall of rough stones across the Wadi Umm Agraf marked the limit of the ground that was reserved to the sanctuary. This would be the backside of the desert from which Moses approached the mountain.

The angel or messenger of God who spoke to Moses did so from a Burning Bush inside the limit of the holy ground (Exod iii. 5). Perhaps he was set there as a guardian to the place. During our stay in Sinai the guards who were appointed to watch over our encampment near Serabit, settled near some bushes to which they added brushwood, so as to form a circular shelter, with an opening on one side, and in this they

[1] Eusebius : *Evaug. Præp.*, bk. ix. c. 27.
[2] Barhebræus : *Chron.*, p. 79.

F

spent their time, mostly sitting around a small fire. The
appearance of the shelter from outside was that of a burning
bush (Fig. 14).

The Divinity in Sinai revealed himself to Moses in the
name of Yahveh or Jehovah, and subsequently declared
himself the God of Abraham, Isaac, and Jacob (Exod. iii. 6),
" but by my name Yahveh was I not known to them " (Exod.
vi. 3). Considering the connection of Abraham and of Joseph
with Haran and the " Hermiouthian " sanctuaries mentioned
above, their God was presumably the moon-god. The word
Yahveh under which the Divinity now manifested himself,
probably represents the moon-god as Ea or Ya under a
later and more spiritualised aspect. In our Bible the term is
rendered as " I am that I am " (Exod. iii. 14), which recalls the
interpretation by the Septuagint as Ὤν, the Self-existent One.
From the Song of Deborah we gather that Yahveh " came to
Sinai from Seir and the field of Edom " (Judges v. 4), which
leaves us to infer that he had sanctuaries there also. This
explains how it was that during the later progress of the
Israelites, Yahveh spoke to Moses at Kadesh on the borders
of Edom (Num. xx. 7), at Hor (Num. xx. 23), and again in
the Red Sea, and how it was that the prophet Balaam was
inspired by Yahveh (Num. xxiv. 13). Various allusions
render it probable that the cult of Yahveh was peculiar to the
Kenites whose home lay in Edom. Jethro, who befriended
Moses, was at once a priest of Midian and a Kenite (Judges
i. 16).

The representative of the Divinity from the Burning Bush
commanded Moses to persuade the elders of Israel to bring
forth the people out of Egypt, in order to serve God on the
mountain, going three days into the wilderness in order to
sacrifice to the Lord, the women bringing with them all
available jewels of silver and jewels of gold (Exod. xi. 2, xii. 35).
The pilgrimage is called a feast (Exod. v. 1, x. 9), which may
have been similar to the modern Arab *hadj*, a word which
signifies an encampment or erection of tents. This term, and
the general claims that were advanced, show that it was
question of a pilgrimage to a well-known centre, the thought
of which caused no surprise to the Egyptians. One of its
features was the offering of animals. Such offerings among the
Hebrews were made to keep off the plague ; they forestalled

the sacrifice of the first-born, which was the means they used to stay the plague once it had begun. The Pharaoh, who was anxious to prevent the Israelites from going the pilgrimage, proposed that they should sacrifice in Egypt instead. Moses refused on the plea that their doing so might be interpreted as sacrificing the " abomination," *i.e.* tampering with a sacred-nome animal of Egypt (Exod. viii. 26). When the Pharaoh, further wrought upon, said that the people alone

Fig. 14.—Men in Burning Bush.

might go, Moses insisted that they must have wherewith to sacrifice, and that there must be cattle, since " we know not with what we must serve the Lord until we come thither " (Exod. x. 26).

This serving the Lord with animals shows that a holocaust was in contemplation, and bears out the belief that the objective of the pilgrimage was a High Place of Burning.

The pilgrimage as planned would have been undertaken in spring, for the plagues carry us through a year's course in

Egypt, with the Nile running red when it is at its lowest in April ; with frogs abounding when the inundation comes in July ; with darkness and sandstorms in the month of March. Springtime came round again before the Israelites left, after sacrificing the lamb of the Passover.

Rallying in the city of Rameses, probably at the present Tell er Rotab, in a marshy valley, they moved to Succoth, the Thuku of the ancient Egyptians, and encamped at Etham (LXX, Othom), being led by a pillar of cloud in the day and by a pillar of smoke at night (Exod. xiii. 20–22). Doughty describes how on the *hadj* of the Moslim, " cressets of iron cages are set up on poles, and are borne to light the way upon serving-men's shoulders in all the companies." [1] The burning fire at night would naturally take the appearance of a pillar of smoke in the daytime.

At Etham the Israelites turned south, making for Piha-hiroth, between Migdol and the sea, over against Baal-zephon (Exod. xiv. 2). Pihahiroth of the Bible is Pa-qahert of the Egyptian inscriptions, while Baal-zephon is a Semitic name, recalling Zephon, the god of darkness. Pihahiroth and Baal-zephon lay west and east of the branch of the Red Sea which at this time extended so far north as to include the present Bitter Lakes. Here, owing to the blowing of the east-wind (LXX, south wind), the waters went back and the Israelites crossed (Exod. xiv. 21), at a spot which should be sought some thirty miles north of Suez. They continued to move south three days, through the wilderness of Shur, stopping first at Marah, where the waters were sweetened, and then at Elim, with its twelve wells and seventy palm-trees. Elim has been identified as the Carandara of Pliny (vi. 23), the Arandara of the lady Etheria (of about A.D. 450), who described how the waters disappeared into the ground and reappeared, which applies to the present Wadi Gharandel. If this identification be correct, the fountain which Moses changed from bitter to sweet presumably lay about half-way between Baalzephon and Wadi Gharandel, where the present Ayun Musa or Wells of Moses are found; possibly it lay nearer to the Bitter Lake.

Leaving Elim, the Israelites entered " the wilderness of Sin, which is between Elim and Sinai " (Exod. xvi. 1). A

[1] Doughty : *Travels*, p. 8.

murmur arose because of the lack of food,—perhaps of food suitable for keeping the full moon festival, the movements of the Israelites being timed by the phases of the moon. For they left Egypt after keeping the Passover, a full moon festival which comes on the 14th (Exod. xii. 6) or 15th of the month

Fig. 15.—Ayun Musa.

(Josh. v. 10) ; and a month later " on the 15th day of the second month after they had departed out of Egypt," they entered the wilderness of Sin. Moses held out the promise of help, and, as they looked towards the wilderness, "the glory of the Lord appeared in the cloud " (Exod. xvi. 10). The glory of the Lord probably indicates the moon. Quails appeared between the two evenings. They were plentiful in Sinai in the days of Josephus (*Antiq.*, 88), and continue so at certain times of the year to the present day. Manna was gathered in large quantities which took the place of bread. This shows that the Israelites were moving among groves of the tamarisk, for manna is the secretion which exudes from the tamarisk, owing to the punctures of an insect during six to eight weeks, beginning in May. A year later, when the Israelites were in the desert of Paran or Zin, they again gathered manna at the same season (Num. xi. 8), and continued to do so every year during the years they spent in the wilderness (Exod. xvi. 35). Manna appears under the name *mennu* in the contemporary records of Egypt, and is still collected in Sinai and exported.

The Israelites were now in Rephidim, the land of the Amalekites and, as there was a lack of water, Moses was divinely directed to smite the rock. The waters which he raised were Massah and Meribah (Exod. xvii. 7) ; the water which he struck near Kadesh, a year later, was Meribah also (Num. xx. 13), hence the place was called Meribath Kadesh (Ezek. xlviii. 28). A technical term for water-finding seems to be meant. In ancient Egyptian *mer* signifies channel, and *ba*, as mentioned above, signifies hole, which suggests a possible derivation. For wherever water percolates the soil with hard rock beneath it in the desert, it is possible to reach and raise it by cutting into the soil to the surface of the rock. The practice is still resorted to by the Bedawyn, who are adepts at striking water when they are on the march.

In Rephidim the Israelites were attacked by the Amalekites, who harried them while they were on their way (Deut. xxv. 17). The place where the encounter took place is not specified, nor the losses which were incurred.

The number of the Israelites was tabulated in two lists of the contingents of each tribe which were drawn up, the first when they encamped before the Holy Mount (Num. i. 46), the other when they were on the point of entering the Promised Land (Num. xxvi. 51). The internal evidence is strong that these census lists, which enumerate the numbers of each tribe, are a first hand record. At the same time the numbers arrived at by listing up the contingents of each tribe, 603,550 in the one case (Num. i.

46), and 601,730 in the other (Num. xxvi. 51), and 600,000 speaking generally (Exod. xii. 37 ; Num. xi. 21), are looked upon as in excess of the population which the land of Goshen could contain, and the land of Sinai could receive. Poetic licence or a mistake of the scribe was therefore put forward as an explanation. Prof. Petrie proposed a different solution.[1] The word *alaf* in Hebrew signifies thousand, but it also signifies family or tent-settlement. If we read the census lists as preserved in Numbers taking the so-called thousands to signify families or tent-settlements, and the hundreds only as applying to the people, the census lists contain what appears to be a reasonable statement. Thus, the tribe of Judah, instead of numbering 74,600 persons, numbered 74 tent-settlements, containing 600 persons, *i.e.* about eight persons to each tent-settlement ; the tribe of Issachar, instead of numbering 54,400 persons, numbered 54 tent-settlements, containing 400 persons, and so forth. On this basis the Israelites, at the first census in Sinai, numbered 598 tent-settlements, with 5550 persons ; and at the second census, on the entry into Canaan, they numbered 596 tent-settlements with 5730 persons. The numbers 600,000 and so forth are attributable to a mistake of the scribe who added up the contingents of the census lists, reading the word *alaf* as thousand, instead of tent-settlement.

[1] Petrie : *Res. Sinai*, p. 211.

CHAPTER VIII

THE ISRAELITES IN SINAI

II

HAVING reached the goal of their pilgrimage, the Israelites encamped near the Mount of God, Har-ha-elohim (Exod. xviii. 5), a word which can also be read as height of the priests. If we identify this goal as Serabit, it follows that they encamped near the outlet of one of the gorges on the northern side of the plateau in the direction of the Wadi Suweig, probably near the outlet of the Wadi Dhaba. This was the side from which there was direct access to the cave of Sopd, and the side on which the Semitic inscriptions were found in the mines.

The physical features of the place are in closest agreement with the requirements of Scripture. For here is " a mountain with a wilderness at its foot, rising so sharply that its base could be fenced in while yet it was easily ascended, and its summit could be seen by a multitude from below." [1]

If we go from the sanctuary down in the direction of the Wadi Dhaba and turning back, look up, we see the temple ruins standing against the skyline, with the square cutting, where the holocaust at this period presumably took place, just below it to the right.

When the Israelites were encamped, Moses was sought by Jethro, the priest, who carried out the choice of an animal and " took a burnt offering and sacrifices for God " (Exod. xviii. 12). Moses himself ascended the Mount, and after his return sanctified the people, who were now called upon to practise abstinence during three days, avoiding their wives, and washing their clothes against the third day, when " the

---

[1] *Encyclopædia Brit.*, art. " Sinai."

Lord will come down in the sight of all the people upon Mount Sinai " (Exod. xix. 11). This arrangement was apparently part of a widespread Semitic usage, for in the Koran we read of similar restrictions for the three days preceding the appearance of the new moon (Koran, ii. 193).

On the third day there were " thunders and lightnings," or rather, " voices and flashes," and the sound of a trumpet (Exod. xix. 16), and the people were led out by Moses and stood on the nether part of the Mount from where they witnessed the theophany. Fire appeared first, then smoke (Deut. v. 23), which shows that they were out before daybreak. "And Mount Sinai was altogether on a smoke, because the Lord descended upon it in fire : and the smoke thereof ascended as the smoke of a furnace, and the whole mount quaked greatly " (Exod. xix. 18). The voice of the trumpet waxing louder, Moses spoke and God answered him by a voice (Exod. xix. 19), whereupon he went up and was charged to set bounds about the Mount. On his return he declared to the people the statutes and judgments (Deut. v. 1 ; Exod. xx. 1), which were vouchsafed to him.

The ceremony points to a well-established ritual which has its roots deep down in Semitic usage. For a trumpet of horn was sounded on special occasions among the Hebrews long before the Exodus. " Blow up the trumpet (*shophar*) in the new moon in the time appointed, on our solemn feast day. For this was a statute for Israel and a law of the God of Jacob. This he ordained in Joseph for a testimony, when he went out through the land of Egypt, where I heard a language that I understood not " (Psa. lxxxi. 3–5).

In the Moslim world, nowadays, it falls to the *mu-ezzin* to call the announcement or prayer (the *azan*) from the tower of the mosque in the early morning, when a man of piety may respond.[1]

The theophany on high bearing witness to the presence of the Divinity, Moses prepared for the tribal sacrifice below by erecting an altar and setting up twelve pillars (*mazzeboth*). The young men slew the oxen, and Moses sprinkled the blood on the pillars and the people. Then, taking with him three priests and seventy elders, he went up into the mountain. " And they saw the God of Israel, and there was under His

---

[1] Hughes : *Dict. of Islam,* art. " Azan."

feet as it were a paved work of sapphire stone and as it were the very heaven for clearness " (Exod. xxiv. 10, 11). And they ate and they drank there.

We read that Moses' second stay in the Mount lasted forty days and forty nights, during which he fasted (Exod. xxxiv. 28). The Moslim identified this fast as Ramadan, which, before Mohammad interfered with its date, happened during the heat of summer.[1] The Israelites at the foot of the mountain, probably observed the same fast, since Aaron's reason for making the calf was that " to-morrow shall be a feast of the Lord," *i.e.* at the conclusion of the fast, there was feasting, drinking, throwing off of clothes, dancing and much noise (Exod. xxxii. 6, 17, 25). In this case it was a question of a full moon festival, for, on a later occasion, Jeroboam made two calves of gold, one of which he set up in Bethel and one in Dan, and ordained a feast on the 15th day (1 Kings xii. 28, 32).

In the Mount, Moses was directed to make a portable sanctuary on the model of actual arrangements which he was shown. " And let them make me a sanctuary; that I may dwell among them. According to all that I show thee, the pattern of the tabernacle, and the pattern of all the instruments thereof, even so shall ye make it " (Exod. xxv. 8, 9). " And thou shalt rear up the tabernacle according to the fashion thereof which was showed thee in the Mount " (Exod. xxvi. 30). " Hollow with boards shalt thou make it ; as it was showed thee in the mount, so shall they make it " (Exod. xxvii. 8). The furniture included an ark or chest, which contained a vase and two stones, *i.e.* the standards of capacity and weight, and the " mercy seat " which was upon the ark (Exod. xxv. 17). There was also a standard of length, perhaps the rod of Aaron. The strict adherence to these standards was henceforth a matter of religious duty with the Israelites. " Ye shall do no unrighteousness in judgment, in mete-yard, in weight, or in measure. Just balances, just weights, a just ephah, and a just hin, shall ye have " (Lev. xix. 35, 36). These standards were of Babylonian origin, and confirm the presence in the Mount of strong Semitic influence.

The ark further contained the two tables of testimony,

[1] " Ramadan, the time when the heat commenced and the soil was burning hot." *Al Biruni* (c. A.D. 1000), c. 19, 1879, p. 321.

which were cut in stone, but which were so brittle that they easily broke, whereupon Moses engaged to provide others (Exod. xxiv. 12 ; xxxii. 19 ; xxxiv. 1 ; Deut. x. 1). The commandments which they contained consisted, for the most part, of a prohibition that was followed by a precept. In this they resemble the commandments that have come out of Babylonia, which contain precepts such as these, " Thou shalt not slander, speak what is pure. Thou shalt not speak evil, speak kindly." [1]

The tablets were in the " writing of God " (Exod. xxxii. 16), which raises the question as to the language and script that were used. Moses, as we know, was "learned in all the wisdom of the Egyptians " (Acts vii. 22). He was certainly familiar with hieroglyphs, and the fact that the commandments were preserved in two texts that differ (Exod. xx ; Deut. v.), suggests that they were written in a language that was not Hebrew. But the discovery of a primitive Semitic script at Serabit itself, puts a different complexion on the matter. The " writing of God " was possibly a Semitic script.

Over and above the commandments, Moses received a collection of written customs for the guidance of those who were henceforth to decide in inter-tribal disputes. They are known as judgments (Exod. xxi. 1), which is in keeping with their being given out at a sanctuary, where Yahveh was accepted as Supreme Judge. In the Yahveh cult the pronouncements were no longer subject to the decisions at local centres. They were set down in writing and associated with the holy tent, and it was by accepting the local Baals and Ashtoreths that the Hebrews fell from the covenant and lapsed into an earlier barbarism. The discovery of the Code of Khammurabi and the points of likeness between its ordinances and those of the code accepted under the name of Moses, further corroborate the Semitic or Arabian influence of the religious centres where the ordinances were received.

Moses had many communings in the Mount, and a year had gone by when the tabernacle was set up " on the first day of the first month," in order to celebrate the Passover (Exod. xl. 2 ; Num. ix. 1). On the twentieth day of the second month in the second year the fires were extinguished and the Israelites moved out of the wilderness of Sinai while a cloud

[1] Nielssen, D.: *Altarabische Mondreligion*, 1904, p. 276.

lay on Paran (Num. x. 11–12). They were led by Hobab, the Kenite. Hobab is described in one passage as "the son of Raguel the Midianite, Moses' father-in-law" (Num. x. 29), in another as "the father-in-law of Moses" (Judg. iv. 11). The Septuagint renders the term in both passages as "brother-in-law" (*i.e.* γαμβρός) of Moses. The terms of relationship are difficult to fix, but if Raguel be accepted as the tribal father, as already suggested, Jethro and Hobab may be looked upon as younger members of the tribe, perhaps his sons.

The first station was called Taberah because of the "Burning." Here manna was again plentiful (Num. xi. 8), which shows that the district was wooded. The next place was called Kibroth-Hata-avah, *i.e.* burial place of Ta-avah, because of those who died of the plague and were buried. Here again quails were plentiful, which the wind brought up from the sea (Num. xi. 31). The next stopping place was Hazeroth (Num. xi. 35), the last station before they entered the wilderness of Paran (Num. xii. 16).

Robinson located Hazeroth at Ain Hudhera.[1] But if the original goal of the Israelites was Serabit, they would be moving in a northerly or north-easterly direction. In the opening lines of Deuteronomy occur the words Hazeroth and Dizahab (Deut. i. 1), for which the Septuagint substitutes Aulon, rich in gold (Αὐλὼν or Αὐλὸν καὶ καταχρύσεα).[2] The word Aulon signifies ravine, which suggests that Hazeroth must be sought somewhere along the escarpment of the Badiet Tîh, or "plain of wandering." The map of Sinai in a north-easterly direction shows Wadi Hafera, which has some likeness to Hazeroth. The Bir Shaweis and the Bir Themed are perennial wells which the people would strike if they moved in a north-north-easterly direction.

The next stopping place was " in the wilderness of Paran " (Num. xii. 16).

According to the Bible, in the first month (*i.e.* eleven months after leaving the Holy Mount), the Israelites abode in Kadesh, where Miriam died and was buried (Num. xx. 1). Moses once more struck water from the rock, the water as before was Meribah (Num. xx. 13), hence the name of the

---

[1] Robinson, E.: *Biblical Researches in Palestine*, ed. 1867, vol. i. p. 157.
[2] Comp. Hastings: *Dict.*, art. "Dizahab."

place Meribath-Kadesh (Ezek. xlviii. 28). The name Kadesh itself suggests a sanctuary, and Moses here again had communings with Yahveh (Num. xx. 7).

Kadesh appears as Cades in the life of Hilarion († 307), which was written by Jerome. The saint went there to see a disciple passing by Elusa (modern Khalasa).[1] There is Ain Kadeis or Gadeis marked on the modern map. Robinson, however, sought Kadesh of the Israelites near Mount Hor, at the present Ain el Waiba.[2]

Kadesh lay " in the uttermost borders of Edom," and the Israelites would now have marched through Edom, " keeping along the king's highway." Perhaps the road along the Mediterranean is meant. " But Edom refused " (Num. xx. 21). They were therefore obliged to seek an entry into Canaan by compassing the land of Edom, which meant turning in an easterly direction towards Mount Hor, and then in a southerly direction to the Gulf of Akaba, the so-called " Red Sea " (Num. xiv. 25). An intercalated passage in Deuteronomy states that " the children of Israel took their journey from Beeroth of the children of Jaakan to Mosera ; there Aaron died " (Deut. x. 6). The wells must therefore be sought close to Mount Hor, and may be the so-called Wells of Moses, which are named as such by the mediæval pilgrims. The modern map mentions Wadi Musa, which joins the Arabah coming from Petra. The Book of Numbers located the death of Aaron in " Mount Hor, by the " (border, not) "coast of the land of Edom " (Num. xx. 23). Here the Lord once more spoke to Moses, which suggests the existence of a sanctuary.

Eusebius (c. 320) wrote, " Mount Hor, in which Aaron died, a hill near the city Petra." [3] Mount Hor is the modern Gebel Haroun or Mount of Aaron, a few miles north-west of the classical Petra. The district at the time was apparently in the possession of the Kenites, since the prophet Balaam, called upon by King Balak of the Moabites, to curse the Israelites, foretold the fall of the Amalekites, and, looking towards the Kenites, declared " Strong is thy dwelling place, and thou puttest thy nest in a rock " (Num. xxiv. 21). This rock, a term which the Septuagint rendered as Petra, was

[1] *Vita*, c. 25 in Migne : *Patr. Lat.*, xxiii. p. 39.
[2] Robinson : ii. 175.
[3] Eusebius : *Onomastikon*, ed. Lagarde, 1887, p. 291.

probably the Ha-sela (Arabic *sila,* a mountain cleft) of the Bible, a name changed to Joktheel after its capture by Amaziah (*c.* B.C. 800, 2 Kings xiv. 7).

At Kadesh the Israelites had been told to " get you into the wilderness by the way of the Red Sea " (Num. xiv. 25), *i.e.* they moved south from Mount Hor. The intercalated passage further named " Gadgodah and Jotbath, a land of brooks and water " (Deut. x. 7 ; LXX, Etebatha). The modern map mentions Et Taba in the depression between the Red Sea and the Dead Sea, where Romans perpetuated the existence of a sanctuary in the name Ad Dianam, later Ghadiana. This movement brought the Israelites into conflict with the Amalekites and the Canaanites, with whom they fought and were discomfited even unto Hormah (Num. xiv. 45 ; LXX, Herman), perhaps the present El Hameima.

According to Arab tradition, Joshua fought against Samida ben Hagbar ben Malek, the Amalekite king of Syria in the land of Aila and killed him. Also Moses, after the death of Aaron, entered the land of the people El Eiss, called El Serah, and advanced to the desert Bab. There was then near Aila an important city called Asabaum or Aszyoun.[1]

This Aszyoun was " Eziongeber beside Eloth (*i.e.* Aila) on the shore of the Red Sea in the land of Edom " (1 Kings ix. 26). It was the port on the Gulf of Akaba which was used by King Solomon. By way of this the Israelites passed into the plains of Moab. "And when we passed by from our brethren the children of Esau which dwelt in Seir, through the way of the plain from Elath, and from Eziongeber, we turned and passed by the way of the wilderness of Moab " (Deut. ii. 8).

A list of stations with further names stands in Numbers (xxx. 12, 13, 17-30), which affords no guide and confuses the issues. It is now looked upon as a post-exilic collection of caravan routes which the scribe who compiled the Book of Numbers incorporated into his account, perhaps because the number of stations named in it was forty, corresponding to the forty years' wandering. Along some routes it mentions the stations that appear in the narrative in Exodus and Deuteronomy, but even here with deviations.

Having passed by the depression near the Red Sea, the

---

[1] Makrizi : *Desc.,* ii. 24, p. 530, " De la ville d'Eilah."

Israelites were in districts that were occupied by the allied Moabites and Midianites. They entered into friendly relations with the Midianites ; later they waged a cruel war against them.

The frontiers of Midian were always vague. According to the Bible Moses met Jethro in the "land of Midian," which suggests that the peninsula of Sinai was included in Midian at the time. Midian is called Madian in the Septuagint and by the Arab writers. Antoninus Martyr (c. A.D. 530) held that the city Pharan, situated between the convent and Egypt, was in "the land of Midian" with its inhabitants descended from Jethro (c. 40).

Makrizi († 1441) described Madian as of wide extent including many cities, chief among which were El Khalasa and El Sanuto. "On the side of the sea of Kalzouna (*i.e.* Suez) and El Tor the cities of Madian are Faran, El Ragah (*i.e.* Raithou), Kolzoum, Aila and Madian. In the town of Madian there are still to-day wonderful ruins and gigantic columns." [1]

In modern parlance the term Midian is applied to the eastern shore of the Gulf of Arabia, between Akaba and Muweileh, which has made some writers believe that Moses went into this part of Arabia, and further led to the identification of Jethro of Scripture with Shoeib, a prophet of the land of Midian.

Sir Richard Burton in 1877 visited the ruins of the city of Midian, the position of which agreed with that of Madiama mentioned by Ptolemy.[2] The valleys which here cut into the high plain of Nedched contained the remains of silver, copper and gold mines, and near the city were great loculi cut into the rock which were known as the Mughair (caves of) Shoeib.

Shoeib was one of the prophets of the Arab past. In the Koran we read, "And we sent to Madian, their brother Shoeib. He said, O my people, worship God, no other God have you than He : give not short weight and measure : I see indeed that you revel in good things, but I fear with you the punishment of the all encompassing day. . . . And when our decree came to pass, we delivered Shoeib and his companions in faith, and a violent tempest overtook the wicked, and in the morning they were found prostrate in

[1] Makrizi: *Desc.*, ii. 25, p. 540.
[2] Burton, Sir R. : *The Golden Mines of Midian,* 1878.

their houses as if they had never dwelt in them. Was not Madian swept off even as Themoud was swept off?" (xi. 89). According to other passages, an earthquake put an end to the dwellers in Al Ayka, the forest of Madian, who treated their apostles as liars (vii. 90, xxix. 30).

The name of Shoeib now attaches to the valley in Sinai in which lies the great convent, and tradition identified Shoeib of the forest of Midian with Jethro, the priest of Midian of the Bible. Their identification is said by Sir Richard Burton to go back to the Arab writer El Farga of about A.D. 800.

It was endorsed by Eutychius, patriarch of Alexandria (935–940), who stated that Moses fled to the Hadjaz and dwelt in the city of Madyan, where Jethro (whom the Arabs call Shoeib) was priest of the temple.[1] But Masudi († 951), while accepting that the daughter of Shoeib married Moses, pointed out that this Shoeib, chief of the Midianites, was a very different person from Shoeib the prophet, who was mentioned in the Koran. "There are centuries between these two Shoeibs." [2]

The identification of Jethro with the prophet Shoeib may be due, in the first instance, to the claims which these prophets made on their people. Moses, who was in contact with Jethro, received the standards of weight and capacity in the Mount, the strict adherence to which was henceforth a matter of religious observance to the people. Shoeib, according to the Koran, impressed upon the people of the forest the need to give measure and weight in fairness, and the disregard to his command was the cause of their destruction (Koran, lxxi. 88, xxvi. 178).

[1] Eutychius: *Annales* in Migne: *Patr. Græc.*, cxi. 930.
[2] Masudi: *Prairies*, c. 47, vol. iii. p. 305.

CHAPTER IX

THE NABATEANS

THE last Pharaoh whose activity was recorded in Serabit was Ramessu VI (B.C. 1161–1156), after whose reign information about the peninsula ceased for several centuries. The road along the north was trodden by the Egyptians when the country was in friendly relation with King Solomon (B.C. 974–35) and the kings of Judæa. It was trodden also by the Assyrian armies which invaded Egypt under Esarhaddon (B.C. 670), and under Ashurbanipal (B.C. 668–626). Although we hear nothing of the sanctuary at Serabit its importance must have continued. For in the list of temples which made gifts to Nitocris on the occasion of her adoption by the Pharaoh Psamtek I (XXVI 1), about the year B.C. 654, a gift was made of a hundred *deben* of bread by the temples of Sais, of Buto, and by "the house of Hathor of Mafkat " *i.e.* Serabit, and by Per-Seped, *i.e.* the sanctuary of Sopd in the city of Goshen.[1]

In the third century before Christ, Egypt passed under the rule of the Ptolemies. Ptolemy Philadelphus (B.C. 250–247), a man of wide outlook, built Arsinoë (north-east of the later Suez) to serve as a port in place of the ancient Heroöpolis, which was silting up. He further sent out an expedition to explore the coasts of the Red Sea under the charge of Ariston. Diodorus Siculus (*c.* B.C. 20), quoting Agatharcides (B.C. 110), and the geographer Strabo (*c.* A.D. 24), quoting Artemidorus (B.C. 100), give an account of the information that is preserved regarding Sinai. After describing the western

---

[1] Breasted : *Rec.*, iv. 956.

shore of the Red Sea with its countries and its inhabitants who were Ichthyophagoi (fish-eaters), and Troglodytes (cave-dwellers) or nomads, and the dangers which threatened shipping from storms and sand-banks, Diodorus, in his account, passed to the other side of the Gulf. Here Ariston erected an altar at Neptunium or Posidium. " From thence to the mouth of the Gulf, is a place along the sea-coast of great esteem among the inhabitants for the profit it yields them ; it is called the Garden of Palm-trees (Phoenikon), because they abound there, and are so very fruitful that they yield sufficient both for pleasure and necessity. But the whole country next adjoining is destitute of rivers and brooks, and lying to the south is even burned up by the heat of the sun ; and therefore this fruitful tract that lies amongst dry and barren regions (remote from tillage and improvement), and yet affords such plenty of food and provision, is justly, by the barbarians, dedicated to the gods. For there are in it many fountains and running streams as cold as snow, by which means the region from one side to the other is always green and flourishing, and very sweet and pleasant to the view. In this place there is an ancient altar of hard stone, with an inscription in old and illegible characters ; where a man and a woman, that execute here the priest's office during their lives, have the charge of the grove and altar. They are persons of quality and great men that abide here, and for fear of the beasts, have their beds (they rest upon) in the trees."[1] In the corresponding account Strabo mentioned no altar, but the man and woman who guarded the trees.[2]

The Phoenikon or palm grove of these writers, was sometimes located at Raithou ; perhaps the one at Ayun Musa is meant.

Diodorus then mentioned the Island of the Sea-calves on the coast of Arabia, and the promontory (i.e. Sinai) that shoots out towards this island, describing this as " over against Petra in Arabia and Palestine to which the Gerrhaens and Mineans bring incense." He then mentioned the Maraneans and Garindaeans (names which recall Mara and Wadi Gharandel, the Carandar of Pliny), who dwell along the coast,

[1] Diodorus Sic. : iii. 3, transl. 1814, I. p. 183.
[2] Strabo, xvi. 4, 18 ; 776.

and related how the Maraneans were absent on their quin-
quennial festival, sacrificing fattened camels to the gods of
the grove and fetching spring water, when the Garindaeans
killed those who were left behind and then murdered those
who returned and seized their country.

According to Diodorus (still quoting Ariston) there were
few harbours along the shore in the direction of the Aleanite
promontory where dwelt the Arabians called Nabateans,
who held not only the coast but large districts inland. The
Nabateans have a special interest for Sinai, since the numerous
rough rock-inscriptions along the wadis of the south, which
long puzzled the learned, are now generally attributed to them.

Josephus located Nabatea between Syria and Arabia
extending from the Euphrates to the Red Sea, and connected
the name Nabatean with Nebajoth, whose name stands first
in the confederacy of the Ishmaelite tribes (Gen. xxv. 13).[1]
On the other hand Strabo, like Diodorus Siculus, located them
in north-western Arabia, extending as far south as Leukokome on the Gulf of Arabia.[2]

The existence of Nabateans in districts that lay far apart
is explained by the recently discovered Annals of Assyria.
In the long list of peoples " Arameans all of them," who were
raided by Sennacherib (c. B.C. 705), mention is made of the
Nabatu, of whom large numbers were carried off into Assyria.[2]
Again, when Ashurbanipal (B.C. 668–626) set out to conquer
Arabia, King Vaiteh of Arabia sought refuge with Nathan,
king of Nabat, " whose place is remote." The Nabateans
were again raided, and numbers of them were transplanted.
" The road to Damascus I caused their feet to tread." [3]
The remote homes of the Nabateans was attested by Makrizi
(† 1441), who classed them with the Magi, the Indians and
the Chinese. These denied the Flood because it had never
penetrated to them, and traced their origin, not to Noah, but
to Kajumath.[4]

The efforts of the transplanted Nabateans to remain in
touch with their home sanctuaries, may have opened their
eyes to the possibilities of trade. In the fourth century

---

[1] Josephus : *Antiq.*, i. 12, 4.
[2] Birch : *Rec. Past.*, N. S., v. 120 ; vi. 85.
[3] Birch : *Rec. Past.*, i. 26, 93, etc.
[4] Makrizi : *History of the Copts*, transl. Wüstenfeld, 1845, p. 1.

before Christ, they attracted the attention of the western world
by seizing Petra, the Ha-Sela of antiquity, which lay halfway
between the head of the Gulf of Akaba and the Dead Sea at
the point where the old gold and incense route from Arabia
to Damascus was crossed by the overland route from India
to Egypt. This appropriation gave the Nabateans the control
of the Eastern trade. In order to check their progress
Antigonus Cyclops, king of Syria and Palestine since B.C. 312,
sent Athenæus and an army against them. The army
reached Petra at the time when the Nabateans were absent
on a pilgrimage. They easily overcame the aged, the women
and children, and seized an enormous booty in spicery and
silver. But the returning Nabateans overtook and well nigh
destroyed the invading force. Another army was sent
under Demetrius to seize Petra, and chastise the Nabateans.
But these drew the enemy along desert tracks, and the invaders
achieved nothing.[1]

Henceforth the Nabateans acted as a recognised nation,
whose kings from about B.C. 200 held their own by the side of
the kings of Judæa. Of these kings Aretas I (*Arabic* Harith),
the contemporary of Antiochus Epiphanes (B.C. 173–164),
received the fugitive Hasmoneans (2 Macc. v. 8) ; Malchos I
dwelt at Petra and struck a coinage ; Aretas III was master
of Damascus and king of Cœle-Syria. Their control over the
trade-routes extended in many directions. Along the
Mediterranean on the north coast of Sinai they secured a
foothold far beyond the limit of Cœle-Syria almost as far as
the Tanitic mouth of the Nile. For excavations made at Qasr
Ghait or Ouait between Kantara and Katia led to the discovery
of a Nabatean sanctuary with a Nabatean inscription.[2]

As the Romans advanced their frontier, they were brought
into contact with the kings of Nabat. Malchos II in the year
B.C. 47, supported the Romans under Cæsar, and entered into
an agreement with them. As a result, a Roman tax-collector
resided at Leukokome, the southernmost point of Nabat.
After the conquest of Egypt in B.C. 30, the Romans, their
imagination fired by the thought of the untold wealth of
Arabia, entered into an agreement with the Nabateans, and

[1] Diod. Sic.: xix. 6, transl. 1814, I. p. 398.
[2] Clédat, J.: *Fouilles* in *Memoires*, xii. 1913, p. 145–168, Institut
français d'Archéologie orientale.

sent eighty boats, with ten thousand men, including five hundred Jews and a thousand Nabateans. These sailed from Arsinoë around Sinai in B.C. 25 to invade and conquer Arabia. It was in vain that Syllæus, the Roman tax-gatherer at Leukokome, urged that the Arabians were rich in merchandise only. The expedition landed, camels were chartered and the Romans entered the country. But here they found a land bare of food and water, and no one to contend with. The expedition was a miserable failure, but Syllæus who tried to prevent it, was accused of treachery and condemned to death.[1]

The Nabateans had originally been content with pastoral pursuits. For a time they became pirates and had little skiffs, with which they despoiled all other merchants who trafficked in their seas. Their obvious intention was to protect the trade along their overland route which assumed great proportions as we learn from the remarks of Strabo.

One reason of their success in this direction was their extensive use of the camel as a means of transport. There are many references in the Assyrian annals to the large number of camels which were bred in Arabia. Ashurbanipal (B.C. 668–626) says that after his conquest of Arabia, "camels like sheep I distributed and caused to overflow to the people of Assyria dwelling in my country. A camel for half a shekel, in half shekels of silver, they were valued for at the gate."[2] The Nabateans employed camels in such numbers that Strabo spoke of their convoys of camels (καμηλέμποροι), which moved between Petra and Leukokome in the land of Nabat, with so many people and camels that they resembled armies. The camels moved to and fro at certain periods of the year, being timed by the arrival at Leukokome of the boats from the East. In between they were driven to pasture in the fruitful wadis which lay near the caravan routes. It was to the men herding these camels that the wadis of southern Sinai owed their inscriptions.

These inscriptions consist, for the most part, of a few words, including a name or a greeting, which are roughly incised on rock or boulder at about the height of a man above the valley floor. Some are accompanied by signs or by the rough drawing of animals or men, sometimes there are drawings and signs

[1] Strabo: xvi. 4, 22; 780.   [2] Birch: *Rec. Past*, i. 98.

without writing. The animals are chiefly camels, gazelles or cattle. There are some horsemen and some nondescript animals. Among the signs that are used are the Egyptian *ankh*, the Greek *alpha* and *omega*, and the Christian cross, showing that a great variety of persons passed there. The words are written without regularity, the animals and men are drawn with poor skill. They are, for the most part, unattractive scrawls, the interest of which lies in the information which they indirectly convey.

The inscriptions in the wadis of southern Sinai were first noted by the lady Etheria who visited the peninsula about the year 450. A century later they attracted the, attention of Cosmas, whose second name, Indicopleustes, marked the extent of his travels. Cosmas was in Sinai about the year 545, and in his *Christian Topography* wrote of the inscriptions, which he attributed to Israelite industry.

" And when they had received the Law from God in writing and had learnt letters for the first time, God made use of the desert as a quiet school and permitted them for forty years to carve out letters on stone. Wherefore, in that wilderness of Mount Sinai one can see, at all their halting places, all the stones that have been broken off from the mountains, inscribed with Hebrew letters, as I myself can testify, having travelled in those places. Certain Jews too, who had read these inscriptions, informed me of their purpose which was as follows : the departure of so and so of such and such a tribe, in such and such a year, in such and such a month,—just as with ourselves, there are travellers who scribble their names in the inns in which they lodge.—And the Israelites, who had newly acquired the art of writing, continually practised it, and filled a great multitude of stones with writing, so that all those places are full of Hebrew inscriptions, which, as I think, have been preserved to this day for the sake of unbelievers. Anyone who wishes, can go to these places, and see for himself, or at least can enquire of others, about the matter, when he will learn that it is the truth which we have spoken.—When the Hebrews therefore had been at the first instructed by God, and had received a knowledge of letters through those tables of stone, and had learned them for forty years in the wilderness, they communicated them to the Phœnicians at that time when first Cadmus was king of the Tyrians, from whom the

Greeks received them, and then in turn the other nations of the world." [1]

After the time of Cosmas we hear no more of the inscriptions, till the seventeenth century when they attracted the attention of Pietro della Valle about the year 1618.[2] In the eighteenth century copies were brought home of some of them which attracted further attention. In 1762 Niebuhr went to Sinai with the intention of visiting the Gebel Mukattab, or mountain of writing. He was taken, instead, by his sheykh to the inscribed ruins of Serabit. Some of the rough Sinaitic inscriptions appeared in the *Transactions of the Royal Society of Literature* in 1832 ; others were incorporated by Lepsius in his work on Sinai. They were first claimed for the Nabateans by Lévy in 1860.[3] Prof. Palmer of the Ordnance Survey collected over 3000 between 1868–70, and endorsed the view that they were the work of traders and carriers. Prof. Euting recently published over 300 in facsimile and collected similar inscriptions along the wadis west of Petra between Damascus and Palmyra, and elsewhere.[4] It is said to be habitual in Arabia to scrawl tribal marks on walls and rocks in order to show the rights of the tribe, a name and a greeting being frequently added as a notice to kinsmen and friends passing that way. These casual marks and inscriptions have recently gained a new interest, for the light which they throw on the development of the Arabic script.

Most of the inscriptions along the wadis of Sinai are in Aramaic or other Semitic script, a few are in Greek, a few are in Kufic. The larger number are pagan, and their character is indicated by such as the following, " Remember Zailu, son of Wailu, son of Bitasu " (no. 11).[5] " Think of Sambu, son of Nasaigu " (*Ibid.*, no. 120). Many names are those of the Bible, including Jacob (no. 510) and Moses (no. 337). How the sight of these names must have rejoiced the heart of Cosmas ! Others include names that are current in Arabia at the present day.

---

[1] Cosmas Ind.: *Christian Topography*, transl. McCrindle, 1897, p. 159.
[2] Cf. Weill : *La Presqu'île*, p. 288.
[3] Tischendorf: *Voyage en terre sainte*, 1868, p. 33.
[4] Euting, J.: *Nabataeische Inschriften aus Arabien*, 1885.
[5] Euting, J.: *Sinaitische Inschriften*, 1891.

In Greek script stand the words " Be mindful ($\mu\nu\eta\sigma\theta\hat{\eta}$) of Chalios the son of Zaidu " (no. 253). One inscription consists of an Egyptian *ankh* with the *alpha* and *omega* on either side, and the Greek words *Kyrie eleison*, with the figure of an animal that may be intended for a camel (no. 380). Again, in Greek stand the words " An evil race ! I, Lupus, a soldier, wrote this with my hand " (no. 613). Another inscription consists of a cross with the words " Amen, one God, our Saviour " (no. 581).

A definite date is conveyed by the following : " Blessed be Wailu, son of Sad Allahi, this is the 85th year of the eparchy" (no. 463). And again, " Think of Aallahi, son of Iali, in the year 106, which is that of the three emperors " (no. 451). In the year A.D. 105 Trajan attacked the Nabateans in Petra, which he conquered, and he established the Roman head-quarters at Bosra, from which the so-called era of Bosra was dated. The first of the inscriptions which mentioned the 85th year, therefore indicated A.D. 189 ; the second inscription, which mentioned the 106th year, indicated A.D. 211, the year in which the three emperors Septimus Severus, Caracalla and Geta succeeded one another.

Some authorities also make the Nabateans responsible for the circular huts built of stone, the so-called Nawamis, groups of which are found in the Wadi Wutah, the Wadi Sigilliyeh, and elsewhere. About the year 450 Etheria saw some on her way to the Mount of the Law, and looked upon them as houses built by the Israelites. The huts served at different times as store-houses, places of burial, and hermitages ; their origin is quite uncertain. Besides these huts, rectangulai huts were noticed in the Wadi Aleyat, the Wadi Nasb, and elsewhere. These also cannot, at present, be claimed for any age.

The introduction of the camel to the wadis of Sinai dealt one more blow at the vegetation of the peninsula. For the camel is to all purposes a huge goat, and, like the goat, is a most destructive animal. His introduction was necessarily followed by the loss of verdure which resulted in loosening of the soil and spread of the desert. In Egypt the intro-duction of the camel during Roman times depleted the flora and altered the fauna. Gazelles and antelopes sought pasture elsewhere, and the crocodile that lay in wait for them when they came to water, altogether disappeared. In Sinai the effects were equally marked. Gazelles, still numerous in early Christian times, are found now in the remoter wadis only, and the depletion of the soil which began with the destruction of trees for purposes of smelting and charcoal-burning, was carried one stage further by the havoc wrought among the lower growth by the camel.

The conquest of Petra by Trajan in the year 105 set a term to the existence of the kings of Nabat. The greater part of their domain was now incorporated in the Roman province of Arabia, which' was firmly and wisely administered by the prefect Aulus Cornelius Palma, who left Nabatean religious cults untouched. The annexation of Damascus followed, through which the control of the trade of the East altogether passed under the Romans.

The frontier line between Egypt and Asia during the period of Roman rule began at Raphia, modern Rafa, and ran in a westerly direction, then turning sharply south towards Arsinoë near the present Suez. The coastal province was called Augustamnica Prima according to Ammianus Marcellinus. It included a number of cities which, by virtue of being situated in a province belonging to Egypt, were later included in the patriarchate of Alexandria.

The first of these cities on the road from Syria was El Arish, situated near the Wadi el Arish, the river or "stream of Egypt" of the Bible (Isa. xxvii. 12). El Arish was accounted a very ancient city by the Arabs. Its land was cultivated soon after the Deluge and was called the Gate to Paradise. Abraham passed here. Makrizi († 1441) relates a tradition regarding the building of reed huts there, which recalls an incident preserved by Diodorus Siculus (c. B.C. 20), the origin of which may be sought in the wish to explain the later name of the city which was Rhinocorura or Rhinocolura. According to Diodorus, King Actisanes of Egypt, possibly Hor-em-heb (XVIII 14), having conquered Egypt, collected all who were suspected of thieving, and after their judicial conviction, caused their noses to be cut off, and sent them to colonise a city built for them at the extremity of the desert. Here, being destitute of means of subsistence, they resorted to the device of splitting reeds, which they wove into nets and stretched out along the sea shore to catch quails. The incident of the noses (quasi ῥῖνος κόλουροι = curti, al. ρ. κείρασθαι), determined the name of the place.[1] Its Egyptian name was probably Zaru (Fig. 18).

The city gained in importance during Roman times. Strabo called it a city of Phœnicia, close to Egypt, and an emporium of Indian and Arabic merchandise, which was discharged at Leukokome and conveyed via Petra to Rhinocorura, where it was dispersed.[2] The city is now partly enclosed by walls of considerable thickness, and lies half a mile from the coast on the edge of the desert. According to the travellers, Irby and Mangles, it contains some notable Roman remains. From this period probably date the marble columns, later appropriated to the churches which were eventually transported to Cairo.

West of Rhinocorura lay Ostracine, the site of which is nowadays surrounded by marshland which is flooded at certain times of the year. The city was formerly fed by a canal that brought water from the Tanitic branch of the Nile. The strategic importance of Ostracine attracted the attention of the emperor Vespasian. For the road coming from Syria divided at Ostracine. One branch led north of the Serbonian bog, *via* Casium, Gerra and Pelusium to Alexandria ; another passing south of the bog, was the old military road to Memphis with stations at Katia and Kantara. A third road led from Ostracine to Arsinoë (near the present Suez), which Pliny described as " mountainous and destitute of water " (asperum montibus et inops aquarum).

Ostracine has recently been excavated by Clédat. It consisted of two parts, an inland part with a fortress and a church which have been excavated, and a maritime port, Ostracine Majumas, where Roman remains were found, including mosaics and sculpture, now transferred to the museum at Ishmailia. The buildings were not constructed of brick, but of stone, which points to a certain wealth. Here also there were the remains of a church. The name Ostracine signifies shell, a meaning reproduced in the Arabic El Flousiyeh the name of the village that now occupies the site of the inland part of the town.

West of Ostracine lay the Serbonian bog which stood out in men's minds as the scene of the disaster which befell the

---

[1] Diod. Sic.: I. 5, transl. 1814, I 64.   [2] Strabo: xvi. 4, 23 ; 780.
[3] Irby and Mangles : *Travels in Egpyt*, etc., ed. 1844, p. 54.

invading Persian forces in the year B.C. 350. On the northern side of the bog, beyond the break in the narrow strip of land confining it, lay Casium, which had a hill with a temple dedicated to Zeus Casius or Jupiter Ammon. On the flank of this hill a tumulus marked the place where the beheaded body of Pompey the Great was buried. Pompey was murdered when he landed on the coast after his defeat at Pharsalia ; and Hadrian, at a later date, erected a monument to his memory of which remains were found near Pelusium.

West of Casium lay Gerra, from Greek *gerrhon*, a shield, a name which corresponds in meaning with Shur, Hebrew for wall, in the Bible. " Shur that is before Egypt as thou goest toward Assyria " (Gen. xxv. 18). Brugsch identified it as the Egyptian Aneb.[1]

Gerra was known also as the camp of Chabrias, the Athenian general, who entered the service of the Pharaoh Nectanebo (XXX 1, B.C. 378–61), and later commanded the forces of his successor Zeher (XXX 2), in opposing the Persian invasion of Egypt. The cities along the Mediterranean coast were at the distance of a Roman day's march, about 14 miles, from each other. Titus on his march from Egypt for the conquest of Jerusalem, pitched his camp in succession near the temple of the Casian Jupiter, at Ostracine, at Rhinocorura and at Raphia, as recorded by Josephus (*Wars*, IV. 11, 5). On the *Table Peutinger*, the Roman road map of the second century, land and water are roughly marked with the stations along the roads of communication. On this Table along the shore of the Mediterranean we note *Gerra* (?) miles to *Casium*, 26 miles to *Ostracine*, 24 miles to *Rhinocorura*, 28 miles to *Raphia*.

[1] Brugsch : *Dict. Geog.*, 1879, p. 52, 1105.

CHAPTER X

THE HERMITS IN SINAI

A NEW era in the history of Sinai began with the advent of the Christian hermit. The desert has ever been the home of liberty. The desire to follow the New Way, coupled with the need of escaping the Roman governor, drove many Christians into the wilderness, where, remote from the claims and the unrest of citizen life, they embraced life in a form which meant reducing physical needs to a minimum.

This life in itself was no new departure. Again and again in the course of history, a recoil from civilisation led men to seek enlightenment in remoteness, simplicity and solitude. Elijah the Tishbite, with rough mantle and flowing locks; John the Baptist, who lived on locusts and wild honey; the Essenes in Palestine, and the Therapeutæ near Alexandria, were one and all actuated by the belief that a higher life is possible here below, provided that the amenities and the comforts of this world count as nothing.

The hermits who came to dwell in Sinai, settled in the mountains of the south where many natural springs rendered possible the cultivation of vegetables and fruit, their staple articles of diet. Here they were outside the sphere of Roman influence. The extent of this influence can be gauged by the *Table Peutinger*.

On this Table two roads, the one coming from Syria, the other from Egypt, lead to *Pharan* in Sinai proper. The road from Egypt passed *Arsinoë, Clesma, Lacus Mar,* and a station, the name of which is obliterated, but which Weill reads as Medeia. From this it was 80 miles to Pharan. The road from Syria, starting from Jerusalem, passed *Oboda, Lyssa, Cypsana, Rasa, Ad Dianam* (later Ghadiana), i.e. *Aila*, from where it was 60 miles to *Pharan*. Pharan was no doubt the κωμή, *i.e.* village Pharan of Ptolemy, the later seat of the episcopate. This was, therefore, the southernmost point of Roman administration in the peninsula. It was beyond this, among the mountains of the south and on the coast near Tur, that the hermits settled by preference.

The inhabitants of the peninsula at this period were called Ishmaelites or Saracens. The origin of the word Saracen has been much discussed. Ptolemy, the geographer, located Sarakene on the borders of Egypt, and the Sarakeni east of the Gulf of Akaba.[1] According to Eucherius († c. 449), the Arabs and the Agarenes in his time were called Saracens.[2] But the historian Sozomenus († 443) held that the Ishmaelites deliberately called themselves Saracens in allusion to Sarah, because they resented the association with Hagar.[3] Sprenger connected the word with *saraka*, Arabic for robber ; the present view is that it signifies easterner.

The Saracens are mentioned in a letter which Dionysius, bishop of Alexandria, wrote about the year 250, in which he mentioned that the Christians fled to the desert to escape persecution. " Many were seized in the Arabian mountains by the heathen Saracens and carried off into captivity." [4] By the Arabian mountain he probably meant the hills between the Nile valley and the Red Sea, but he may be referring to Sinai.

An early hermit of Sinai was St. Onophrius, whom Nectarius, in his *Epitome of Holy History*, numbered among the founders of ascetic life.[5] Onophrius dwelt in a grotto in the Wadi Leyan, south of the Gebel Musa, which was visited during the Middle Ages by pilgrims and is still pointed out to travellers.[6]

Paphnutius († c. 390), a monk of Egypt, came across Onophrius on his wanderings and wrote a life of him. Onophrius told him that he had been in the desert seventy years. Originally he dwelt in the Thebaid with about a hundred monks, but hearing of Elijah and John the Baptist, he decided

[1] Sprenger : *Alte. Geog.*, nr. 326, p. 199.
[2] Eucherius : *Epist.*, ed. Geyer, *Itiner. Hier.*, 1908, p. 122.
[3] Sozomenus : *Hist.*, vi. 38.
[4] Dionysius : *Ep. ad Fabium.* Migne : *Patr. Græc.*, x. 1306.
[5] Nectarius : *Epitome of Holy History*, 1805, p. 75.
[6] Baedeker : *Lower Egypt,* 1895, p. 270.

that it was more meritorious to dwell alone in the desert, so he wandered away, led by an angel, and met a hermit who urged him to go five days further where he reached "Calidiomea" (perhaps a corruption of *calybem*, a hut), near which stood a palm tree where he remained. He suffered from hunger and thirst, from cold and heat, and lived on dates, his clothes gradually dropping from him. He took Paphnutius into his hut, and they were conversing together when a sudden pallor overspread his countenance, and he intimated that Paphnutius would bury him. He died there and then, and Paphnutius tore a piece off his own cloak, in which he wrapped him and laid him in a crevice in the rock.[1]

Onophrius was perhaps the unnamed hermit who was visited by a monk of Raithou, "where stood seventy palm trees in the place which Moses reached with the people when he came out of Egypt." This monk described how, on his wanderings, he came to a cell in which he found a dead monk whose body dropped to dust when he touched it. In another place he came upon a hermit who had lived in an ascetic community at Heroöpolis, but he associated with a professed nun, and yielded to temptation, whereupon he fled into the distant desert where, as time went on, his hair grew and his clothes dropped from him.[2]

Of similar appearance was the hermit whom Postumianus was bent on seeing when he went from Italy into Sinai some time before 400. In the *Dialogues* of Severus the words are put into his lips : " I saw the Red Sea and I climbed the height of Mount Sinai (jugum Sina Montis), the summit of which almost touches heaven and cannot be reached by human effort. A hermit was said to live somewhere in its recesses, and I sought long and much to see him, but was unable to do so. He had been removed from human fellowship for nearly fifty years and wore no clothes, but was covered with bristles growing on his body, but of divine gift he knew not of his nakedness." [3]

Another hermit who was drawn to Sinai was Silvanus, a native of Palestine, "to whom on account of his great

---

[1] Paphnutius : *Vita St. Onophrii*, Migne: *Patr. Græc.*, lxxiii. 211–22.
[2] *De Vita Patrum*, vi. 11, Migne: *Patr. Lat.*, lxxiii. 1009.
[3] Severus : *Dialogue*, i. 17, Migne : *Patr. Lat.*, xx. 199.

virtue, an angel was wont to minister. He lived in Sinai and afterwards founded, at Gerari (? Gerra), in the wadi, a very extensive and noted cœnobium for many good men, over which the excellent Zacharias, afterwards presided." [1] Like other hermits, Silvanus shared his cell with a youthful disciple, and cultivated a garden that was surrounded by a wall and served by a water conduit. Various anecdotes told of him bear witness to his good sense and humility.

" A certain brother once came to Sinai where he found the brethren hard at work and he said to them, Labour not for the meat that perishes. Silvanus, who overheard the remark, directed his disciple Zacharias to give him a book and lead him to an empty cell. When the ninth hour came, the brother looked towards the entrance expecting to be called to a meal, but no one came, so he went to Silvanus and said, Father, do not the brethren eat to-day ? Silvanus replied, Oh yes, they have eaten. Then why was I not called ? Because, said Silvanus, thou art a spiritual man who needs no such food. We others, being carnal, must eat, and therefore we work. Thou hast in truth chosen the better part, and art able to study all day requiring nothing. On hearing this, the brother saw that he was at fault, and said, Father, forgive me. Silvanus replied, Surely Martha is necessary to Mary, it was due to her that Mary was able to pray. Silvanus himself worked with his hands, chiefly at basket-making, so as to earn his living and not depend on alms."

The baskets, we gather from other remarks, were used to pack dates for export. Like other hermits, Silvanus had visions. One day he sat for a long time without speaking and then burst into tears. It was, he said, because he saw men of his own kind going to hell, while many secular persons went to heaven. Among the sayings atributed to him was this one, " Woe unto him who has more renown than merit." [2]

Other early hermits were Galaçtion and his wife Episteme, whose experiences were noted in the *Menology* of Basileus,[3] and were worked up into a longer account by Simeon

[1] Sozomenus: *Hist.*, vi. 32.
[2] Le Nain de Tillemont: *Memoires pour servir à l'histoire eccles*, x. p. 448–451.
[3] Nov. 5. Migne; *Patr. Græc.*, cxvii. 143.

Metaphrastes. They were from Emesa and took ten days to reach the height called Pouplios (? *Rubus*, the Bush), near Mount Sinai (τὸ Σινᾶ ὄρος), where they found ten hermits who were joined by Galaction. Episteme dwelt at some distance with four virgins. But the Roman governor (Ursus) sent for Galaction. Episteme, apprised by a dream, came forward to die for him. Both endured the penalty of death, and Eutolmios, at one time their slave, recovered and brought back their bodies.[1]

The settlement where Episteme dwelt was afterwards allotted to the slaves who were brought into Sinai and appointed to serve the convent by the emperor Justinian († 563). The settlement lay on a slope north-east of the convent facing the valley, and was pointed out to Bishop Pococke in the year 1734.[2] The existence here of a settlement of women, and the value which was set on the bodies of the hermits, are worth noting in connection with the finding of the body of St. Katherine of Alexandria, to which we shall return later.

Other saints who were connected with Sinai were the well-known Cosmas and Damianus, Arab doctors who taught Christianity. There are no traditions regarding their coming into Sinai, but their names were attached to a hermitage, now dilapidated, which stood at Tholas, in the Wadi Tla'ah, and was dedicated to them.

It was customary at the time for the hermits to wander from place to place. Among the famous hermits who visited Sinai was Julian Sabbas († 363), who left his cell near Osrhoene (Edessa), and, with a few devoted followers, sought the remoteness of Sinai where he remained some time. On reaching the desired height (τὸ ποθούμενον ὄρος), he built a church and set up an altar on the stone on which Moses, prince of prophets, rested. Theodoret (*c.* 450), who related this, stated that the altar remained in his day.[3] Antoninus Martyr (*c.* 530) noted the existence of an oratory above Pharan, with its altar on the stones which supported Moses when he prayed.[4] The plan and ruins of an oratory are figured in the Ordnance Survey (pl. X), which probably mark this spot.

---

[1] *Vita S. Galactionis*, Migne : *Patr. Græc.*, cxvi. 94.
[2] Pococke, Bishop : *A Description of the East*, 1743, i. 147.
[3] Theodoret : *Religiosa Historia*, Migne : *Patr. Græc.*, lxxxii. 1315.
[4] Antoninus Martyr : *Itinerarium*, c. 40, ed. Greyer, p. 186.

Its erection helped to locate the struggle of Moses and the Amalekites in this valley, which, according to other views, took place further south.

The hermits at this period occupied caverns and huts, an older man, called *abbas*, *i.e.* father, usually dwelling with a younger disciple. But as time wore on the cells were more and more grouped around a centre where the hermits assembled once a week for religious service. These centres or churches sometimes consisted of a square tower built of stone, its entrance raised above the ground, and in these the hermits sought refuge in times of danger. One such tower or church stood near Raithou, and formed part of the later convent of St. John ; another, the Arbaïn, now in ruins, stood in the Wadi Layan, near the grotto of Onophrius ; a third was near the Bush, and was included in the present convent. Tradition claimed that the tower near the Bush, was built by Helena, the mother of the emperor Constantine, and was dedicated to the Theotokos in order to commemorate the spot where the Lord appeared to Moses in the Burning Bush.[1] The tower was pointed out to Burckhardt, and was described by him as of older construction than the convent.[2] The pilgrimage of Helena to the East in the year 326 is well authenticated, but there is no contemporary reference to her entering Sinai. If there were, it would be the earliest association of the site of the convent with the coming of Moses.

We first hear of bishops established in cities of Sinai in connection with religious discussions and difficulties. At the beginning of the fourth century Arius raised doubts regarding the fundamental truth of the Divine Sonship, and a synod of three hundred and ninety bishops met at Nicæa in the year 325 to discuss the question. Among those who set their signature to the declaration of faith which rejected the claims of Arius was Peter, bishop of Ahila, *i.e.* Aila, a city which, by virtue of its situation was included in the province of Palestine.[3]

As a sequel to these discussions a Council was held in the church of St. Thekla at Seleucia in September of the year 359 by order of the emperor Constantius, at which there were

[1] Nectarius : *Epit.*, p. 95.
[2] Burckhardt : p. 544.
[3] Lequien : *Oriens Christianus*, 1740, iii. 759.

present a hundred and sixty bishops, about two-thirds of
whom were semi-Arians. Theoctistes, bishop of Ostracine, was
among them.[1] He was therefore deposed by Athanasius,
patriarch of Alexandria († 371), who appointed, in his stead,
Serapion.[2] But the representatives of the neighbouring see
of Rhinocorura firmly held by Athanasius, and Sozomenus
(† 443), after praising the hermits of Nitria, wrote of Rhinocorura, " celebrated at this period for its holy men, who were
not from abroad, but natives of the place. Among the most
eminent philosophers were Melas, who then administered the
church in the country; Dionysius, who presided over a
monastery to the north of the city; and Solon, the brother
and successor of Melas in the bishopric." When, owing to
a decision of Valens (c. A.D. 364), there was a reaction in
favour of Arius, officers appeared at Rhinocorura who were
charged with orders to eject those opposed to Arianism. Melas,
who did the lowliest work, offered a meal to the officers, waiting
on them himself, and declared his willingness to go into exile.
His brother Solon gave up commerce in order to embrace
the monastic life. " The church of Rhinocorura having been
thus from the beginning under the guidance of exemplary
bishops, never afterwards swerved from their precepts and
produced good men. The clergy of this church dwell in one
house, sit at the same table, and have everything in common."[3]
Among these bishops was Polybius, a disciple of Epiphanius,
bishop of Salamis in Cyprus († 403), who wrote a supplement
to the *Life of Epiphanius*.

The religious difficulties, combined with the general unrest
which followed the conjoint rule of the imperial brothers,
Valentinian and Valens (364-367), are reflected in the account
told by the Egyptian monk Ammonius of what happened at the
time when he was on a visit to Sinai with the hermits at the
Bush. The account which he wrote in Coptic is preserved
in Greek, in Syriac, and in Latin.[4] It is a composition of
considerable merit, to which the condensed account, which
follows, can do but scant justice.

[1] Epiphanius: *Hær.*, 73, 26.   Migne: *Patr. Græc.*, xlii. 454.
[2] Lequien: *Or. Chr.*, ii. 545.
[3] Sozomenus: *Hist.*, vi. 31.
[4] Nectarius: *Epit.*, p. 73–93; Smith-Lewis, Agnes: *The Forty
Martyrs of Sinai* in *Horæ Semit.*, no. 9, 1912.

" It occurred to me," wrote Ammonius, " as I sat in my little cell near Alexandria at the place called Canopus, that I could go a journey and thus escape the persecutions (by the Arians) of the faithful, who included our holy bishop Peter (II, 372–380), who was obliged to go into hiding, first at one place and then at another, and was thereby hindered from ministering to his flock. I was, moreover, fired by the desire to see the memorable places, including the Holy Sepulchre, the place of the Resurrection, and others that were associated with our Lord Jesus Christ. After worshipping at these places, I decided to seek the holy mountain called Sinai, going the desert journey together with others who were bent on the same purpose, and I journeyed thither (from Jerusalem) with the help of God in eighteen days. And when I had prayed I remained with the holy fathers in order to visit their several cells to the profit of my soul."

A description follows of the occupations of the hermits, their solitary life on week-days, and their gatherings in church on Sundays. " Their aspect was that of angels, for they were pallid and, so to say, incorporeal, owing to their abstaining from wine, oil, bread, and other food that tends to luxury, living on dates only, just enough to keep themselves alive."

." A few days later," Ammonius continued, " Saracens, whose sheykh (or king) had died, fell upon the fathers in their cells and slew them, so that I, together with the superior Doulas and others sought refuge in the tower, while the barbarians slew all the hermits who were in Thrambe (Syriac, Gethrabbi),[1] Choreb (Horeb), Kedar (Codar), and other places. They would have dealt the same with us, but a great fire appeared on the mountain which scared them so they fled, leaving behind their women, children and camels. We who saw this from the tower, gave thanks to God, and then sallied forth to the other settlements. We found 38 hermits who were dead. Twelve belonged to Thrambe, including Isaiah and Sabbas who were badly hurt. Isaiah died while Sabbas lamented that he was not in the company of the saints. But he died four days later (on the last day of the year)."

They were lamenting his death when an Ishmaelite brought

---

[1] Weill located this in the Wadi Eth Themed, the upper part of the Wadi Hebran. 1908, p. 198.

the news that the fathers who dwelt at Elim (Raithou) had been raided also. Raithou is described as " a level plain, situated at a distance of about twelve miles, with mountains to the east like a wall, which those only could cross who were familiar with the country. To the west was the Red Sea, which extended to the ocean." The words correctly describe the district about Tur.

The settlement here was attacked by the Blemmyes, a nomad race of Nubia, of whom we now hear in Sinai for the first time. Psoes, a fugitive hermit, who arrived in the wake of the Ishmaelite, gave Ammonius particulars regarding the hermits at Raithou, and their message. He had lived 20 years at Raithou himself, he said ; others had lived there 40, 50, and 60 years. There was Abba Moses of Pharan, who had the power of exorcising demons, and who had cured Obedianus, a sheykh of the Ishmaelites, which led to many conversions. There was also Sabbas, of whom Psoes was a disciple, but the way of living of Sabbas was so hard that Psoes left him. Again, there was Joseph from Aila, who built himself a cell with his own hands at a distance of two miles from the springs.

Forty-three hermits dwelt near Raithou, to which place the news was brought that the Blemmyes had seized an Egyptian boat which was bound for Clysma, and were coming across the sea. The men of Raithou at once collected their camels, their women and children, while the hermits sought refuge in the church. The barbarians spent the night on the shore, and then bound the sailors to the boat which they left in charge of one of themselves, and came across the mountain to the springs where they were met by the men of Raithou. But the invaders were the more skilful archers, and killed 140 men, the rest fled. Then they seized the women and children, and rushed to the tower or church, expecting to find treasures, and went round it screaming and uttering threats in a barbarous language while the hermits inside prayed and lamented.

Paul of Petra, who was the superior of the settlement, uttered words which were full of dignity, and concluded with saying : " O athletes of God, do not regret this good conflict ; let not your souls be faint, and do nothing unworthy of your cowl, but be clothed with strength and joy and manliness, that you may endure with a pure heart, and may God receive you into His kingdom."

In the meantime the barbarians, encountering no resistance, heaped tree-trunks against the wall from outside, broke open the door of the church, and rushed in, sword in hand. They seized Jeremiah, who was sitting on the door-sill, and commanded him through one who acted as interpreter, to point out the superior. When he refused, they bound him hand and foot, and tearing off his clothes, used him for a target. " He was the first to gain the crown " (of martyrdom). Then the superior Paul came forward declaring his identity, and they bade him reveal his treasures. In his usual gentle voice he replied : " Forsooth, children, I own nothing but this old hair-cloth garment that I am wearing." And he held it out, displaying it. But the barbarians hurled stones at him, shouting : " Out with your treasures," and, after ill-using him, cleft his head in twain with a sword.—" Then I, miserable sinner," continued Psoes, " seeing the slaughter and the blood and the viscera on the ground, bethought me of a hiding place. A heap of palm branches lay in the left-hand corner of the church. Unnoticed by the barbarians, I ran to it, saying to myself, If they find me, they can but kill me, which they are sure to do, if I do not hide."

From his hiding place he saw the barbarians cut down the hermits who were in church. He saw them seize the youth Sergius, whom they would have dragged away with them, but he snatched a sword from a barbarian and hit him across the shoulder, whereupon he was cut down himself. The barbarians after killing the hermits, searched for treasures not knowing that the saints own nothing here on earth, their hope being of the world to come. Finally they rushed off intending to embark. But the man who was left in charge of the boat, being a Christian, had cut the rope, so that the boat ran ashore and foundered ; he himself escaped to the mountain. The barbarians, who were at a loss what to do, murdered the women and children, and then lit a fire and cut down and burnt nearly all the palm trees of the place.

In the meantime the Ishmaelites from Pharan, some six hundred in number and all of them expert archers, drew near at dawn and attacked the barbarians, who, seeing no chance of escape, met them bravely and perished, to a man. Of the men of Pharan eighty-four were killed, others were wounded. The hermits were all dead except Andrew, who was wounded and recovered, Domnus, who died of his wounds, and Psoes, who was left to tell the tale. The men of Pharan left the dead enemies to the beasts of the earth and the fowls of the air. They buried their own dead at the foot of the mountain above the springs, and made a great wailing. Then, led by the sheykh Obedianus, they brought costly garments, in which, with the help of Psoes and Andrew they buried the saints. Psoes himself then left Raithou, which was deserted, for the Bush, where he begged to be allowed to stay with Doulas, a request which was readily granted. The account concludes with saying that Ammonius wrote all this down after his return to Memphis, and the words are added in one MS., "I, presbyter John, found this account written in Coptic in the cell of a hermit near Naukratis, and, knowing Coptic, I translated it into Greek."

The attacks made on the hermits were part of a wider movement. History relates that Mavia (or Mania), the widow of the phylarch or king of the Saracens, collected her forces and led them in person against Palestine and Egypt. The Romans, because they had to do with a woman, expected to quell the disturbance without difficulty. But the advantage was on her side, and the expedition was celebrated in song among the Saracens. Mavia proffered peace to the Romans on condition that Moses, a converted Saracen, should be consecrated bishop of Pharan, and Moses went to Alexandria under a military escort. But here a new difficulty arose. The patriarch Peter II (372–380), the same to whom Ammonius referred, was still absent. The Arian prelate Lucius (c. A.D. 378) occupied his see, and Moses refused to be ordained by him. The story was told by Sozomenus († 443), and by Socrates († c. 478), both of whom lived soon after the event.
     "I account myself indeed unworthy of the sacred office, Moses said, but if the exigencies of the state require my bearing it, it shall not be by Lucius laying his hand on me, for it has been filled with blood. When Lucius told him that it was his duty to learn from him the principles of religion and not to utter reproachful language, Moses replied, Matters of faith are not now in question : but your infamous practices

against the brethren sufficiently prove that your doctrines are not Christian. For a Christian is not a striker, reviles not, does not fight, for it becomes not a servant of God to fight. But your deeds cry out against you by those who have been sent into exile, who have been delivered up to the flames. These things which our own eyes have beheld are far more convincing than what we receive from the report of another. As Moses expressed these and like sentiments, his friends took him to the mountain, that he might receive ordination from the bishops who lived in exile there. Moses having been consecrated, the Saracen war was terminated, and so scrupulously did Mavia observe the peace thus entered into with the Romans that she gave her daughter in marriage to Victor the commander-in-chief of the Roman army. Such were the transactions in relation to the Saracens."[1]

The fame of Moses continued. In the *Itinerary of Willibald* (c. 750) we read that, after his return from Palestine, he was received by Pope Hadrian in Rome at a time when St. Boniface was asking for help on his mission to evangelise the Germans. The Pope, in his desire to persuade Willibald to undertake the task, referred to Moses the hermit, famous for innumerable miracles in the desert, " who was torn away from the solitary life he was leading at the request of Queen Mania to the Roman emperor, and placed as bishop over the nation of the Saracens, and in a short time he won to Christ that most fierce nation, and clothed them in the fleece of lambs." [2] The name of Moses was inscribed in the Roman Martyrology on Feb. 27. " In Egypt the feast of Moses, a venerable bishop, who at first lived a solitary life in the desert, and then, at the request of Mauvia, queen of the Saracens, being made bishop, converted that most ferocious nation in great part to the faith, and made glorious by his merits rested in peace." [3]

Moses was followed in the see of Pharan by Natyr, a disciple of Silvanus, who was a strict ascetic.

[1] Socrates: *Hist.*, iv. 36.
[2] *Itinerary*, transl. Pal. Pilg. Soc., vol. 3, p. 52, 1891.
[3] *Acta SS. Boll.*, Feb. 7, ii. p. 45.

CHAPTER XI

THE WRITINGS OF THE HERMITS

THE writings of the hermits from the fifth century onwards throw light on the aspirations and the attitude
of mind of these men of the desert, to whom the interests of
ordinary mankind were as nothing.

Foremost among these writings are those of Nilus, a man of
learning who, after occupying a high position at Constantinople, visited the hermits, with whom he remained. His
Narrationes contain valuable information on heathen sacrifice
at the time.[1]

About the year 420 Nilus decided to separate from his
wife in order to visit the " Bush at the foot of the holy mountain
on which God conferred with the people," taking his youthful
son with him. The barbarians, he tells us, dwelt from Arabia
to Egypt, from the Red Sea to the Jordan, ever ready to
draw the sword, hunting wild beasts, attacking travellers,
and making use of their camel-dromedaries for sacrifices which
they devoured with dog-like voracity. They had no regard
for God, but adored the Morning Star (Lucifer, ἄστρον
πρωϊνόν), to which they sacrificed the best product of the
chase, or boys of comely appearance, on an altar of rough
stones. Failing these, they took a fattened white camel
without blemish which they made to kneel. They encircled
it three times to the sound of chanting whereupon the sheykh
who acted as leader, made a thrust at the beast's neck, and all
of them hastily drank of the blood that gushed forth.

The whole band then fell upon the victim, and each person
hacked off and devoured a piece of the beast's flesh and skin.
It was the rule of the rite that the whole victim with body,

---

[1] Nilus: *Narrationes*, Migne: *Patr. Græc.*, lxxix. pp. 590–693.

bones, blood and entrails, was done away with before the rays of the sun appeared above the horizon (p. 613).

In contrast to this life was that of the hermits who dwelt in huts and rock shelters within call of one another, removed from the claims of the tax-gatherer, and emulating Moses and Elijah in their fasting and humility, some cultivating corn for bread, while others lived on vegetables and green meat, coming together once a week on a Sunday. Nilus was among them, having come down from the holy mountain with his son on a visit to the hermits who dwelt near the Bush. They happened to be in church, when a barbarian horde swept down on them like a whirlwind, seized the food which they had stored in their cells against the winter, and then called to the hermits to come out of church, to strip and to stand according to age. They cut down the priest Theodulos, and slew the fathers Paulus and John, and then seized the young men, bidding the older ones be gone. Many rushed up the mountain, "which they generally avoid since God stood upon it and conferred with the people" (p. 631). Nilus stood irresolute, when his son Theodulos, whom the barbarians had seized, signed to him to be gone. "O why," he exclaimed, "did not the ground open and swallow them like the sons of Korah? Why had the miracles of Sinai ceased, and no thunder rolled, no lightning flashed to scare them in their wickedness?"

When the barbarians had gone, Nilus helped to bury the dead, and was presently joined by one of the youths who had been carried off but escaped. He described how the barbarians erected an altar, collected wood as a preparation for sacrificing to Lucifer. This he was told by a fellow captive who understood their language. The youths lay bound ready for sacrifice, but he escaped by wriggling away on the ground like a snake. His account filled Nilus with apprehension as to the fate of his son, but in his misery he was upheld by the courage of a woman of Pharan, whose son had actually been murdered.

As there had been other outrages, it was decided in the council (βουλή) at Pharan to lodge a complaint with the phylarch or king of the barbarians (p. 663). His relation to the Roman empire was apparently that he must keep the peace and safeguard those who passed through his territory, in return for which he received a grant (annonæ). On much the same basis, the sheykhs of Sinai under British rule, are

responsible for keeping the peace, in return for which they
receive a grant in money which they must call for in person
at Suez.

Envoys were therefore despatched to the phylarch. They
carried bows and arrows, and a stone for striking fire, which
would enable them to live by killing and roasting game,
" for there is wood in abundance that serves as firewood,
since no one fells trees in the desert " (p. 663). During their
absence Nilus and others went the round of the neighbouring
settlements, where the hermits had been attacked. At
Bethrambe (or Thrambe) they buried Proclus ; at Salael [1]
they buried Hypatius ; Macarius and Marcus they found dead
in the desert ; Benjamin had been slain at Elim ; Eusebius
was still alive at Tholas ; in Adze they found Elias dead (p. 663).

The envoys on their return brought word that King
Ammanus was anxious to maintain his relations with the
empire, and was prepared to make good the losses which had
been incurred. He bade those who had claims to appear
before him. Nilus and others accordingly sallied forth. On
the eighth day Nilus, who was looking for water, actually
caught sight of the encamped Saracens ; on the twelfth day
of journeying they reached the end of their journey, which
may have been Petra). Here Nilus heard that his son was
alive and had been sold into slavery at Elusa. On the way
thither, he met a man who had actually seen him, and on
going into the church at Elusa, he found his son Theodulos,
who had been made doorkeeper of the church by the bishop
of the place. Theodulos told his father how he and others lay
bound on the ground all night near the altar with a sword,
a bason, a phial and incense beside them. But the barbarians
drank heavily at night and overslept themselves, and the sun
stood above the horizon when they awoke, so the occasion
for the sacrifice was forfeited. They therefore moved on to
Souka (perhaps a village, perhaps market, Arabic *suk*), from
where they sold Theodulos into slavery. Nilus and his son
now decided to settle permanently among the hermits looking
forward to a pleasant life. After being ordained by the
bishop of Elusa they returned to Sinai where they apparently
ended their days. Their memory there continues to be kept
to this day. Their bodies were raised together with those

[1] Weill located Salael in the present Wadi Sigilliyeh, p. 195.

of others in the reign of the emperor Justinus Junior (565–578), and were translated to the Church of the Holy Apostles at Constantinople.[1]

In the course of the fifth century the dispute regarding the dual nature of Christ entered a further stage when Nestorius, who had been under the influence of Theodore of Mopsuestia, and was promoted to the see of Constantinople, raised objection to the term God-bearer, Θεοτόκος, as applied to the Virgin. By doing so he raised a storm of dissent, the veneration of the Virgin being widespread and deep-seated, partly owing to having been engrafted on an earlier mother-cult.

Pope Celestinus (422–432) called upon Nestorius to recant, but he refused, and a Church Council therefore met at Ephesus in 431 to discuss the matter. Among the two hundred bishops who declared against Nestorius were Hermogenes of Rhinocorura, Abraham of Ostracine, and Lampetius of Casium.[2] The outcome of the dispute was that Nestorius, in the year 435, went into perpetual banishment. Hermogenes of Rhinocorura was praised as a man of moderation and humility, by Isidorus († 449), a monk and prolific letter-writer of Pelusium.[3]

After the Council at Ephesus, Hermogenes went on a mission to Rome with Lampetius of Casium, and was succeeded in his bishopric by Zeno, who was succeeded by Alphius.[4] It was, perhaps, this Alphius who sided with Lampetius (possibly the bishop of Casium) in the difficulty regarding the vagrant ascetics called Massaliani or Euchites, men and women, who gave themselves to prayer and lived by begging, refusing to work. They were censured at the synod of Ephesus,[5] and their condemnation henceforth acted as a deterrent to the wanderings of hermits generally. In consequence of his course of action Alphius was obliged to resign his see. He was succeeded by Ptolemæus of Rhinocorura, who acted in concert with Timothy, patriarch of Alexandria.

A further difficulty was created when the Church Council

---

[1] *Perigraphe of Holy Mount Sinai* (first issued by the archimandrite Jeremiah in 1768), ed. 1817, p. 173.
[2] Labbé: *Concilia*, ed. Mansi, v. 615–17.
[3] Isidorus: *Epistol. liber*, v. 358, 448, etc., in Migne: *Patr. Græc.*, lxxviii.
[4] Lequien: *Or. Christ.*, ii. 543.
[5] Labbé: *Conc.*, iv. 1477.

met at Chalcedon under the auspices of the empress Pulcheria and her husband Marcian, and in 451 laid down articles as to the nature of Christ which remain to this day the standard of the Catholic faith. Of the bishops of the sees in Sinai only Beryllus, bishop of Aila, set his signature to the declaration.[1] And when Juvenal, bishop of Jerusalem (451–458), returned to his see and declared his intention of abiding by the decision, the fanatical monks seized the city, turned him out and set the Egyptian monk Theodosius in his place. It was in vain that Juvenal sought to settle the matter by leniency. Theodosius ruled in Jerusalem during twenty months. When he was finally expelled he fled to Sinai. The emperor Marcian hereupon addressed a letter to Bishop Macarius and the monks of Sinai, warning them against Theodosius, who " went from place to place spreading heresy, and who is now in Mount Sinai (ἐν τῷ Σινᾷ ὄρει) where there are monasteries which are dear to you and which have our respect, in which he is working against the true belief." [2] The emperor also wrote to Juvenal saying that he had written about Theodosius and his adherents to " the most worthy bishop Macarius, to the archimandrite and to the monks," warning them of his false arguments, and asking them to eject him and hand him over with his satellites to the prefect of the province.[3] It is unknown what became of it.

Other writings of the hermits give an insight into the speculative zeal and boundless credulity of these devotees to a simple life, to whom everything surprising appeared in the light of a miracle. Collections of *Sayings of the Fathers* (Verba Seniorum), and incidents in their lives, were a favourite branch of literature at the time. Anastasius (*c.* 561–614), a monk of Sinai, John Climacus († 609), who dwelt at Tholas, and then at the convent, and John Moschus († 619), who habitually dwelt in Jerusalem, but went about visiting, were among those who collected anecdotes and sayings regarding Sinai.

Pillar saints at this time were attracting attention near Antioch. There was an older Simeon who died in 460, and a younger Simeon who died in 596. A monk of Raithou went

---

[1] Labbé : *Conc.*, vi. 567.
[2] *Ibid.*, vii. 483.
[3] Lequien : *Or. Christ.*, iii. 751.

to Simeon hoping to be relieved of a demon. But Simeon
bade him return to Raithou, and there seek the assistance
of Father Andrew, who had the power of expelling demons.
Andrew spoke to Moschus of his power to do so, which he
attributed to Simeon Stylites.[1] Again, Mena, also of Raithou,
deserted his post and sought the pillar saint, who, aware of his
failing, bade him return, as Abbas Sergius told Moschus
(no. 118). There was also Eusebius who was accosted by
a man in monkish garb, who asked to be admitted into the
community. Eusebius bade him utter the word Trinity,
and he vanished (no. 119). Those who dwelt in remote
districts often died unattended. Some fishermen were borne
by contrary winds to Pteleos where they found in a cell the
bodies of two hermits, which they carried to Raithou for
burial (no. 120). Again, two hermits dwelt on an island in
the Red Sea, from which they went on shore for water. They
lost their boat, and were found dead on the island, one of
them having set down in writing that his comrade lived for
twenty-eight days without drinking, when he died, while he
himself had lasted thirty-seven days at the time of his writing
(no. 121). There was growing, at this time, a feeling that the
devotees to a simple life should remain stationary. John
Cilix, abbot of Raithou, who wrote comments on some of
the chapters of John Climacus' *Ladder of Paradise,* praised a
monk who continued at Raithou for seventy years, living on
green meat and dates. He had been there himself for seventy-
six years, and he admonished the brethren in words recorded
by Moschus, " not to foul the place which the fathers had
cleared of demons," and always to remain in residence (no. 115).
    The collection of anecdotes of Anastasius, a monk of
Sinai, mentions several hermit settlements which have been
located in wadis near the convent, where ruins of huts and
garden walls remain to this day. According to a tradition
preserved at the convent, the monks in the peninsula at one
time were between six and seven thousand in number.[2]
    Among these settlements was Malocha, perhaps situated
in the Wadi Malga, north of Ras Safsaf. This was at one
time the home of Epiphanius, who was so devoted to ascetic

---

[1] Joannes Moschus : *Pratum Spirituale*, no. 117, in Migne : *Patr.
Græc.*, lxxxvii. pars. 3.
[2] Burckhardt : p. 546.

practices that he had the power of seeing demons (no. 21).[1]
Malocha at another time harboured Stephen, whose plantation
was ravaged by animals, here called χορογρύλλοι, *i.e.* porkers,
possibly they were hyænas. But Stephen reared a leopard
(probably a panther) from a cub whom he set to guard his
plantation (no. 13). This Stephen originally occupied a cell
near the cave of Elijah, which he left for Sidde, "situated
about seventy miles from the tower," perhaps in Wadi
Sidreh, a lower reach of the Wadi Umm Agraf. He then
returned to his cell where he found his two disciples and
died from exhaustion.[2] His body was conveyed to the
convent, where it was set up at the entrance to the crypt.
The *Perigraphe* of 1817 stated that " he is still at the convent,
not confined by coffin or sarcophagus, but standing upright
with crossed hands and bowed head." [3] And there the
shrivelled figure wearing hermit clothing remains standing to
the present day.

At Sidde we also hear of a hermit who was walking one
day in the desert and saw a Saracen approaching, whereupon
he "transformed himself into a palm tree." It was only
another hermit, and so he returned to his natural appearance.

Many stories were told of John the Sabaite who dwelt for
a time at Malocha. He was walking one day across the
desert with the imperial ruler (*archiater*) Demetrios, when they
came upon the footmarks of a dragon. Demetrios proposed
that they should fly, but John said they would pray, whereupon
the " dragon," was carried aloft and was thrown back to the
ground shattered to pieces (*Anast.*, no. 14). Another story
told of John the Sabaite shows how the imaginary world was
to these men the greater reality. He was dwelling in " the
most distant desert," when a fellow monk came to see him, who,
in reply to his question how other monks fared, replied, They
are well, thanks to your prayers. He then asked after a
monk who had a bad reputation, and heard that there was no
change in his behaviour. Afterwards he fell asleep and had
a vision of the crucified Christ, and himself kneeling. But
Christ called to His angels and thrust him forth, since he had

---

[1] Anastasius : *Récits inédits*, F. Nau, 1902.
[2] Joh. Climacus : *Scali Paradisa*, no. 7 in Migne : *Patr. Græc.*,
lxxxviii. 814.
[3] *Perigraphe*, p. 164.

passed judgment on a fellow monk, thus anticipating divine judgment. As he was thrust forth, his cowl caught in the gate and he lost it. He awoke, but the thought of his cowl lost in his dream, showed him that God had withdrawn from him, and he wandered in the desert seven years, eating no bread, sleeping in the open and speaking to no one, until he had another dream in which the Lord restored his cowl to him (*Anast.*, no. 17).

John the Sabaite also dwelt at Arselao (a place not identified), where he was approached by a female porker (or hyæna) who laid her blind young at his feet. He mixed his spittle with earth and applied it to the eyes of the creature which became seeing. On the following day the mother-beast reappeared dragging an enormous cabbage which she laid at the feet of the old man. But he smiled, charging her with stealing it from another man's garden, and bade her take it back, a command which she forthwith obeyed (*Anast.*, no. 15).

Arselao was the home also for a time of a certain George, who was fetched to the convent to pray for oil, as the store had given out, and " the road to Palestine was held by the barbarians." His prayers brought oil to the cask, like Elijah's to the widow's cruse, and like that of the cruse, it never failed. The cask was placed under the protection of the Virgin (*Anast.*, no. 9). The need of oil led the monks to cultivate the olive in their gardens, which they did with considerable success, olives being among their produce which attracted the attention of the Arab writers.

At Tholas, which was mentioned in the earlier accounts, John Climacus dwelt for forty years, at the conclusion of which he became head of the convent. The Wadi Tla'ah is one of the few valleys which has preserved its character. Prof. Palmer described it in glowing terms in the Ordnance Survey.

Another hermitage was at Gonda, situated fifteen miles from the Holy Bush (*Anast.*, no. 31). John the Sabaite was living here with Stephen of Cappadocia, when Father Martyrios arrived with a youthful disciple, who was John Climacus. John the Sabaite, having the gift of foresight, recognised the future superior of the convent in him (*Anast.*, no. 6).

This Stephen of Cappadocia told John Moschus that he was once in the church at Raithou when two men entered, who were without clothes. No one saw them but himself.

He followed them out and begged to be allowed to accompany them. But they bade him stay where he was, and he saw them walk away across the Red Sea (*Moschus*, no. 122).

There was also the monk Sisoeis, who dwelt in the hermitage of St. Anthony between the Red Sea and Egypt, where he was visited by a monk of Pharan who told him that it was ten months since he had seen a human being. To which Sisoeis replied that it was eleven months since he had seen one himself.

The hermit life in Sinai was at its height when the lady Etheria visited the peninsula, intent on identifying the sites of which she had read in the Bible. Her eagerness seems to have stirred the imagination of the monks, and led to decisions as to localities which were accepted as authentic for centuries to come. The account of Etheria calls for a few words of comment.

The MS. of her journey was discovered in the library of Arezzo by Gamurrini in 1883. It was incomplete and its author was not named. Gamurrini provisionally claimed it for St. Silvia of Aquitaine, and dated the journey between 378 and 383. But the abbé Férotin [1] has since pointed out that Valerius (*c.* 650), abbot of a monastery near Astorga in Spain, wrote a letter " In praise of the blessed Etheria," in which he described how this nun " with a bold heart undertook a journey across the world." He mentioned details of her journey which establish beyond a doubt that the writer of the Arezzo account was meant.[2] A German writer, Karl Meister, on the internal evidence of the account, hereupon dated the journey between 534 and 539. But he overlooked the fact that Etheria, in connection with her visit to Seleucia, mentioned by name her dear friend, the *diaconissa* Marthana, who is named also as one of the distinguished women of the place by Basileus, bishop of Seleucia who died in the year 456.[3] There were convents in the south of France before the close of the fifth century, as we know from the rules drafted by Cæsarius, bishop of Arles (501–573) ; the date of Etheria may be about 460.

---

[1] Férotin : *La veritable auteur de la Pereginatio Silviæ,* 1903.
[2] Valerius : *De B. Etheria* in Migne : *Patr. Lat.,* lxxxvii. 422.
[3] Basileus : *De Vita et Mir. S. Teclæ.* Migne : *Patr. Græc.,* lxxxv. 618.

The MS. account discovered at Arezzo was incomplete. But the account, in its complete form, was apparently in the hands of Peter the Deacon when he compiled his little book *On the Holy Places*, about the year 1157, for Guidobaldo, abbot of Monte Cassino. In this book Peter cited passages found in the account that was discovered at Arezzo together with others which seem to be taken from the part of the work which is wanting. In the account which follows, the initial passages are quoted from the book of Peter on the assumption that they were taken from the account of Etheria.

Etheria and her party entered and left Sinai from Egypt.

" Before you reach the holy Mount Syna, stands the fort Clesma on the Red Sea which the Israelites passed dryshod. The marks (*vestigia*) of the chariot of the Pharaoh are visible in the ground to this day. But the wheels are farther apart than those of the chariots (*currus*) of our days as they are seen in the Roman empire, for between wheel and wheel is a space of twenty-four feet or more, and the wheelruts (*orbitæ*) are two feet wide. These marks of the Pharaoh's chariot lead down to the shore where he entered the sea when he wanted to seize the Israelites. On the spot where the Pharaoh's wheel-ruts are visible, two signs are set up, one on the right, and one on the left, like little columns (*columella*).[1]

Orosius (c. 400) in his *History of the Universe*, also mentioned the marks of the chariot wheels of the Pharaoh, which were still visible.[2] Cosmas Indicopleustes about the year 550 referred to them as " a sign to unbelievers."[3] The consensus of opinion of these writers suggests the existence of some feature that attracted attention. The word *Clysma* itself signified beach or jetty. Perhaps the ruts were the marks made by the keels of the boats that were hauled in, in which case the little columns were perhaps the bollards on which the ropes were worked.

" Beyond the place of crossing lay the desert Shur and Mara with its two wells that were sweetened by Moses (probably the Ayun Musa). Three days' journey lay Arandara, the place called Helim, where the river, in places, disappeared

---

[1] Petrus Diaconus: *Liber de locis sanctis*, p. 115 in Geyer: *Itinera Hieros.*, 1898.
[2] Orosius: *Hist.*, i. 10, Migne: *Patr. Lat.*, xxxi. p. 717.
[3] Cosmas Ind.: v. p. 193.

I

in the ground and where there was much herbage and many palm trees. From the crossing of the Red Sea near Sur there was no pleasanter place." The description and the name Arandara point to the present Wadi Gharandel.

Etheria was bent on seeing all the sites, including the place where it rained manna, the cells with Hebrew writing, the desert of Pharan "where there were neither fields nor vineyards but water and palm trees," the place Faran, where Amalek opposed the Israelites, the place where the Israelites called for water, and the place where Jethro met Moses, his son-in-law, "the spot where Moses prayed while Joshua fought Amalek, is a high, steep mountain above Pharan, and where Moses prayed there is now a church" (Petrus, ed. Geyer, p. 118). This was probably the church mentioned above which was founded by Julian Sabbas.

From Pharan Etheria's party moved to a place where the mountains opened themselves out, and found a great valley beyond which appeared " Syna, the holy Mount of God," which is united with the place where are the Graves of Lust (*i.e.* Kibroth Hata-avah). The guards said that it was customary to offer prayers. " So then we did." From here to the Mount of God it was perhaps four miles altogether, the length of the valley being sixteen miles (c. 31) The plain was presumably the present plain of Er Raha.

According to Etheria the Israelites waited in this plain when Moses went up into the Mount of God—there was also the place where the calf was made—it was the valley at the head of which was the place where holy Moses was when he fed the flocks of his father-in-law when God spoke to him from the Burning Bush. But as their route was first to ascend the Mount of God at the side from which they were approaching because the ascent was easier, and then to descend to the head of the valley where the Bush was, thence retracing their steps so as to see the places mentioned in Scripture, they spent the night at a certain monastery where kindly monks dwelt and where they were all well received. There was a church there and a priest (this place has not been identified). It was the night preceding the Sabbath, and early on the following morning they made the ascent of the mountains one by one with the priests and the monks that lived there. " And you must go straight down each mountain until you arrive at the foot of the central one, which is strictly called Sinai. And so, Christ our God commanding us, and encouraged by the prayers of the holy men who accompanied us, although the labour was great, for I had to ascend on foot because the ascent could not be made in a chair (*sella*), yet I did not feel it." At the fourth hour they reached the peak of Sinai where the Law was given, the place where the majesty of God descended on the day when the mountain smoked, and then they found a church, small because the summit of the mount where it stood was small, but with a large measure of grace. They were joined by the priest of the monastery who served the church, for no one permanently lived on the mountain where was the cave and the church where holy Moses was (c. 33). Passages were read of the book of Moses, the party communicated and received a present of first fruits (*pomis*) from the monks, and Etheria asked questions about the various sites, including the cave where Moses was when he ascended the mountain a second time to receive the tables and "other sites, both those which we asked to see, and those about which they themselves knew. But this I would have you know, ladies, venerable sisters, that the mountains which we had at first ascended without difficulty, were as hillocks compared with the central one on which we were standing. And yet they were so enormous that I thought I had never seen higher, did not this central one overtop them by so much. Egypt and Palestine, the Red Sea and the Parthenian (*i.e.* Mediterranean) Sea, which leads to Alexandria, also the boundless territories of the Saracens, we saw below us, hard though it is to believe ; all which things these holy men pointed out to us " (c. 34). As a matter of fact, the Red Sea is not visible from the Gebel Musa, but from the Gebel Katrin. Etheria's mention of a church on the height, however, shows it was the Gebel Musa she ascended.

From the Mount of God they descended to the mountain joined to it called Horeb, where there was a church and where they saw the cave where Elijah hid and the stone altar (*sic*) which he built. This description and the later account of Antoninus Martyr (cf. below) show that at this period Horeb was accounted a different height from the Mount of the Law. After seeing a great rock with a flat surface on which stood Aaron and the seventy elders when Moses received the Law—

" and in the middle there is a sort of altar made of stones "—
the party began the descent at about the eighth hour and at
the tenth hour they reached the Bush ; " it is alive to this
day and puts forth shoots." Here there were many cells,
a church, and a garden with the Bush, and the party partook
of a light meal in the garden and remained the night (c. 35).
On the next day they explored and saw the following : the
place of the camp of the Israelites,—the place where the
calf was made, " a great stone is fixed in that place to this
day,"—the spot from which Moses watched the Israelites
dancing,—the rock on which the tables were broken,—the
dwelling places of the Israelites " of which the foundations
made in circular form remain to this day,"—the place where
the Israelites ran from gate to gate,—also the place where the
calf was burnt, and the stream out of which the Israelites
drank,—the place where the seventy received the spirit of
Moses (Num. xi. 25),—the place where the Israelites lusted
(Num. xi. 34),—the place where the camp took fire (Num.
xi. 2), and the place where it rained manna and quails. The
reader is aware that according to the Biblical account, these
latter sites were far removed from the spot where the Law was
given. " Thus having seen all the places which the sons of
Israel visited both going and returning," Etheria and her
party started back to Pharan, distant thirty-five miles. They
then stayed at a station (*mansio*) in the desert of Pharan ; then
near the coast, and then at Clysma (near the present Suez),
where they rested, " for we had stoutly made our way through
the soil of the desert." Etheria had previously passed
through Goshen on her way from Egypt into Sinai ; but she
now decided to follow up the places visited by the Israelites.
So she journeyed to Migdol " with its fort and an officer
commanding the soldiery in accordance with Roman discipline,"
and passed Epauleum (LXX for Pihahiroth) on the further
side of the water ; and another fort " Balsefon" ; also "Othon "
(LXX for Etham), Succoth and Pithom. "The present Pithom
is now a fort," she wrote, and reached Hero, ancient Heroöpolis.
Here the party entered the borders of Egypt leaving behind
the territories of the Saracens (c. 39), and moved on to the
city of Rameses, described as a " come " (*i.e.* κώμη) situated
near the present Tell er Rotab. Finally they reached " the
city of Arabia," and met its bishop. Probably the ancient

Per-Sopd, later Phacusa, the capital of the nome, is meant.   A
bishop of Phacusa is mentioned.[1]   From here the road went
" from the Thebaid to Pelusium by way of Tathnis," probably
the Greek Daphne, the Tahpanhes of Jeremiah, following the
course of an arm of the Nile to Pelusium.   Etheria had been
before on her way to Alexandria.   She now journeyed along
the   coast   "passing   several   stations,"   and   then   entered
Palestine (c. 40).

The detailed account by Etheria and her location of the
various holy sites in Sinai was the first of its kind, and
apparently remained the only one for centuries to come.   Before
her pilgrimage we only hear of a church built above the valley
of Pharan which commemorated the struggle between Moses
and the Amalekites, while the Bush, Horeb, and Elim were
names of settlements which had been chosen by the monks
in remembrance of Moses and Elijah whom they accepted as
their patrons.   On the same basis a monastery or laura near
Jerusalem, mentioned as the abode of John Moschus, was called
Pharan.   The names which were given to settlements in Sinai
may have caused these places to be looked upon as those that
were actually visited by Moses and Elijah.

The " Bush " was mentioned without further comment by
Ammonius (c. 372) as a settlement.   It was described as the
" Bush at the foot of the mountain where God conferred with
the people " by Nilus (c. 449).   About the same time Etheria
(c. 450) spoke of " a church in the place where the Bush is,
which Bush is alive to this day," while Procopius, the secretary
of Justinian, remarked (c. 550) in a more cautious strain,
" here it was that Moses was said to have received the Laws
from God and   proclaimed them."   It   was   Etheria who
claimed to have seen during a single day all the places visited
by the Israelites including, in the plain below, Taberah, the
place of Burning (Num. xi. 2) and Kibroth Hata-avah (Num.
xi. 34), where the Israelites stayed long after they left the
holy mountain.

The monkish settlement Horeb or Choreb was mentioned
also by Ammonius (c. 372), and, judging from his description,
it was quite separate from that of the Bush.   As a height,
Horeb was also held separate from the Mountain of the Law
both by Etheria and by Antoninus.   But Etheria, and others

---

[1] " Moses in Phacusis."   Lequien : *Or. Hist.*, ii. 546.

after her, looked upon Horeb not only as the site to which Elijah fled after crossing the desert, but as identical with the place where he set up the great altar at which he confounded the prophets of Baal.

Elim, again, was mentioned as a monkish settlement by Ammonius (c. 372), and his description leaves no doubt that Raithou near the present Tur on the coast, two days' journey from the Bush, is meant.   This settlement retained its name, Elim, till recent times.   Some of the mediæval pilgrims looked upon it as the actual Elim of the Bible.   Thus the Ritter von Harff, who visited it in 1497, held that the Israelites here left the Red Sea, and asserted that bones that lay on the shore were those of the pursuing Egyptians.   But Etheria and Cosmas (c. 550) with a better appreciation of possibilities, located the passage of the Israelites near Clysma (near the present Suez), and sought Elim of the Bible, not at Raithou, but at Arandara, the present Wadi Gharandel.

CHAPTER XII

THE BUILDING OF THE CONVENT

FROM the reign of the emperor Justinian (527–563) dates the fortification of the hermit settlement known as the Bush, which was thereby transformed into a convent, and as such, braved the vicissitudes of many centuries. The fortification was apparently part of a wider scheme by which the emperor used the peninsula of Sinai as a bulwark against the invasion from the east. Movements among the Eastern people were threatening the frontier line of the Roman empire at the time, and its internal organisation was by no means secure.

The care which was bestowed on the convent itself may have been due to the favour which the monophysite form of belief found for a time with Justinian, and more especially with his wife, the empress Theodora († 548). It was owing to her influence that Anthimus I was raised to the see of Constantinople, but a synod convened in the year 536 deposed him. At this synod there were present Paulus II, bishop of Aila,[1] and Theonas, who described himself as "presbyter of Holy Mount Syna, and legate of the church of Pharan and the hermitage of Raithou."[2] Theonas apparently acted as legate owing to the age and infirmity of Photius, bishop of Pharan. His appointment shows the close connection that existed at the time between the three chief hermit settlements in Sinai proper. The presence of Theonas at Constantinople no doubt furthered, if it did not originate, the idea of fortifying the convents of Sinai.

The building activity of Justinian began about the year 535. Procopius, his secretary, wrote an account of his

---

[1] Lequien : *Or. Christ.*, iii. 759.
[2] Labbé : *Conc.*, viii. pp. 884, 889.

relations with Sinai and described the life of the monks as " a careful study of death." They therefore sought the solitude that was dear to them. The emperor, he says, built a church for them which was dedicated to the Theotokos, so that they might spend their life in continual prayer in the service of God, not on the summit of the mountain, but below it, for on the summit thunder and other heavenly phenomena were heard at night, which made it impossible to spend the night there. Here it was that Moses is said to have received the Laws of God and proclaimed them. At the foot of the mountain Justinian built a military station, so that the Saracens might not unawares attack Palestine.[1]

A later age produced a decree of Justinian dated to 551, which declared the independence of the foundation. The decree is no doubt a forgery, but the independent standing of the convent was generally accepted. The terms of the alliance which secured the safety of the settlement were first set forth by Said ibn Batrick, otherwise Eutychius, patriarch of Alexandria (933–40), to whom we owe a full account of the building of the convent.

" The monks of Sinai," he wrote, " hearing of the piety of Justinian, and the delight that he took in building churches and monasteries, went to him and described how the Ishmaelite Arabs harmed them by plundering their food stores, invading and emptying their cells, and entering their churches where they devoured the eucharist. When the emperor enquired into their wishes, they said : We beg for a monastery in which we shall be safe. For at that time there was no convent building in which the monks could congregate. They dwelt scattered in the mountains and along the valleys near the Bush from which the Lord spoke to Moses, having only a large tower above the Bush which is standing to this day, and a church dedicated to the Virgin, where they sought protection when those approached whom they dreaded. The emperor despatched with them a legate with full authority to the prefect of Egypt, asking that he should be supplied with building materials, with men and provisions in Egypt. He was charged to build a monastery at Kelzem (Clysma), and a monastery at Raya (Raithou), and one on Mount Sinai, this to be so fortified that no better could be found."

[1] Procopius : De Ædific., v. 8, transl. Pal. Pilg. Soc., ii. 1897, 147.

After building the church of St. Athanasius at Clysma, and the monastery at Raithou, the legate came into Sinai, where he found the Bush in a narrow valley with the tower near it,

Fig. 16.—View of the Convent.   (Petrie: *Researches in Sinai.*)

also bubbling springs and the monks scattered along the valleys.   He intended building the monastery on the summit of the mountain, leaving the Bush and the tower below, but he altered his plan because of the lack of water on the mountain, and built the monastery near the Bush enclosing the tower, and a church on the summit of the mountain where Moses accepted the Law. The name of the superior was Doulas. But the change of plan so annoyed the emperor that it cost the legate his life.

In order to safeguard the building, Roman slaves were brought from the Black Sea (traditionally from Wallachia), a hundred in number, and transferred to Sinai with their wives and children, together with a hundred men with their wives and children from Egypt. Dwellings were erected for them in Mount Sinai so that they might safeguard the monastery and the monks ; they received their supplies from Egypt. Their settlement was known as the Deir Abid (*i.e.* monastery of slaves), and their descendants continued there till the spread of the Moslim faith. Moreover the Benu Saleh were appointed to act as *ghafirs* or protectors to the monks, that is, they were responsible for those moving to and fro across the desert, in return for which they received largess in the form of food.[1] The same terms were mentioned by Makrizi († 1441) in his *History of the Copts*,[2] and by the *Perigraphe* in its Arabic translation of the year 1710.[3] According to this the Benu Saleh, the Saïdi and the Halig (Aleyat) were attached to the service of the convent which, in return, supplied them with food.

The importance which the agreement attached to the Benu Saleh, was in keeping with the ancient establishment of this tribe in the peninsula, and their association with rites of religious importance in close vicinity to Gebel Musa and on Gebel Musa itself. The tomb of Nebi Saleh lies in the Wadi Sheykh at a distance of a few miles from the convent. It is the scene of an annual tribal festival which concludes with a pilgrimage half-way up the Gebel Musa, where a sheep is sacrificed over a natural hole in the rock. This is looked upon as a footprint of the holy camel, no doubt originally of the Naga, which was the creation of Nebi Saleh.

Early references and the nature of the festival leave no doubt as to its antiquity.

---

[1] Eutychius : *Annales*, 1071.
[2] Makrizi : *History of the Copts*, p. 116.
[3] Cheikho : *Les archévèques du Sinai*, in *Melanges de la faculté orientale de St. Joseph*, ii. 1907, p. 408, ff.

Thus, the writer Antoninus Martyr, who, about the year 530, entered Sinai from Gaza, journeyed by way of Elath (Elusa), " at the beginning of the desert that goes to Sinai," and mentioned a festival that was about to take place. The people who entered the greater desert were in number twelve thousand (c. 36). On the eighth day after leaving Gaza, he reached the place where Moses brought forth water from the rock, and came to Horeb, which, in his estimation, was distinct from Sinai.

" Mount Syna," he wrote, " is stony, and there is little earth, and in its neighbourhood are many cells of men who serve God, the same in Horeb. And in this part of the mountain the Saracens have an idol of marble white as snow. A priest (*sacerdos*) of theirs dwells there, who wears a dalmatica and a linen cloak (*pallium*). And when the time of their festival comes previous to the appearance of the moon (*præcurrente lunæ*), before it appears on the festive day, the marble begins to change its colour, and when they begin to adore it, the marble is black as pitch. The time of the festival being over, it returns to its former colour. At this I wondered greatly." [1]

The rites that are accounted holy in this neighbourhood are associated with different prophets. Prof. E. H. Palmer († 1882) remarked that the Bedawyn " often fail to discriminate between Nebi Saleh, Moses and Mohammad. Thus, the footprint of the camel which was venerated at the conclusion of the festival of Nebi Saleh, has been incorporated in a tradition regarding Mohammad, who after death was carried aloft by a camel of so prodigous a size that it stood with one foot in Damascus, one in Cairo, one in Mecca, and one in Sinai. [2]

The monk Antoninus Martyr made a short stay at the convent, and wrote that " the days of the festival of the Ishmaelites were drawing to a close, and the order went forth that no one should remain in the desert through which we had come, so some returned to the Holy City (*i.e.* Jerusalem) through Egypt, others through Arabia " (c. 39).

---

[1] Antoninus Martyr, c. 38. According to another text printed by Geyer : " Quando etiam venit tempus festivitatis ipsorum recurrente luna, antequam egrediatur luna, ad diem festum ipsorum incipit colorem mutare marmor illa " (ed. 1898, p. 184, 213).

[2] *Ord. Survey*, i. 67.

The work of feeding the Arabs who came to the convent was no mean undertaking. Anastasius, the monk, wrote that the Armenians more especially came there,—" it was their custom as it was the custom of every one." There were six hundred of them on one occasion, and a man among them who waited on them and then disappeared. In the estimation of Anastasius this was " Moses himself, who came to receive his visitors " (no. 7). The number of pilgrims at this time (c. 600) was less, he remarked, than thirty years before, when as many as eight hundred came and ascended the holy mountain, where they saw a vision of God and a miracle, the summit of the mountain appearing enveloped in fire (no. 38). The appearance of fire on the mountain had previously been mentioned by Ammonius about the year 372. It may have formed part of a system of signalling adopted by the Bedawyn.

This confusion between the different prophets is reflected in a statement in the *Perigraphe* in the Arabic translation of 1710, which described Saleh as a Christian who had his tomb not far from the monastery.[1] This tradition should be compared with one current in the Middle Ages that Mohammad the Prophet was the disciple of a Christian monk.

The tomb of Saleh in the Wadi Sheykh was noticed by Bishop Pococke in 1726 (i. 141), and Burckhardt, in 1816, mentioned the celebration held here which took place in the last week in May (p. 489). This festival was described in detail by Tischendorf who saw it in 1846,[2] and by Prof. E. H. Palmer, who witnessed it in June of 1870.[3]

The festival took place at the time when the dates ripened, and lasted three days. Tribes from all parts of the peninsula, including women and children, assembled in the Wadi Sheykh near the insignificant-looking tomb which consisted of a domed chamber cemented over, with an empty coffin standing inside. Pieces of cloth, ostrich eggs, tassels and other parts of camel equipment were brought as offerings and suspended from the roof. The first step in the festivity consisted in renovating and whitewashing the tomb. In a large tent erected outside forty to fifty men assembled and sat in a

---

[1] Cheikho: p. 411.
[2] Tischendorf: *Voyage*, 1868, p. 55.
[3] *Ord. Survey*, i. 209.

circle, while the first of all the sheykhs barefoot and wearing the white garment (*Imam*) and a white turban over his red fez, sat near the fire.   A procession headed by the women encircled the tomb.   The young men then brought out fifty to sixty lambs which were cut on the forehead, and blood was drawn before they were slaughtered, skinned and cut up.   While the food was boiling a camel race took place, four to six camels racing at a time.   Four to six persons then sat around each lambskin which was spread on the ground, and on it their share of boiled lambs' flesh was poured out, which they ate using their fingers.   Besides the flesh there were meal-cakes (*bilaw*), and water to drink.   A dance followed in which men and women took part, and which was timed to singing and clapping of hands.   Besides this, two women danced figures outside the group.   Men and women remained conversing in couples till late at night.   The celebration struck Tischendorf as dignified.   At its conclusion some of the Bedawyn repaired to the summit of the Gebel Musa, where there stood a small and highly revered mosque (mentioned as early as 1335), which they entered, wearing the *Imam* or white garment.   Over the natural hole, called the footprint of the prophet's she-camel, they sacrificed a sheep.

A further festivity took place in former days near the summit of the Gebel Musa which we hear of in the sixteenth century only and not again.   Early writers agree that no hermit or monk ever spent a night on the summit of the mountain. Nilus (c. 400) remarked that the height was generally avoided " since God conferred there with the people," while Etheria and Antoninus Martyr simply noted that no hermit spent the night there.   This fact Procopius (c. 550) connected with " heavenly phenomena."   At a later date the hermit Simeon, for a time, dwelt " on the summit of Mount Sinai, where the Law was given, a place deserted because of the restless Arabs."

This avoidance of the mountain-top at night by the Christians finds its explanation in the account of Gregor, prior of the Carthusian house of Gaming, who came into Sinai with Martin Baumgarten and others in the year 1507. The party decided to spend the night on the Mount of the Law, where the building that was close to the summit was the scene of a Saracen festivity of so noisy a character, that the

Christian pilgrims hardly slept all night. It included " a bestial service in the belief that those who were here conceived were endowed with a holy and prophetic spirit " (proles enim hic concepta, sancto et prophetico spiritu plena ab eis æstimatur).[1] The spot chosen seems to have been a cave between the chapel of Moses and the small mosque. Similar unions led, from the same belief according to Tobler, to the desecration at one time of the holy cave at Bethlehem.[2] This cave, according to a statement of Jerome, was connected with the cult of Adonis in ancient times. Perhaps the hold which the Saracens had on the Gebel Musa in early days was another reason why the convent builder chose the lower site.

No further mention is made of the church of St. Athanasius which the emperor Justinian had constructed at Clysma. The monastery which he built or fortified at Raithou frequently served as a refuge to the monks of the convent in times of stress. Its church was dedicated to St. John the Baptist, and continued till the period of Turkish domination when it was destroyed.

The convent of the Bush alone continued. It had an independent standing, perhaps owing to its being originally merged with the bishopric of Pharan. The head of the house was chosen from its inmates, and he called himself bishop. Later he assumed the title of archbishop. Owing, however, to his peculiar standing he was referred to as archbishop at a time when he called himself bishop only, as we shall see later.

The convent at first served as the nucleus of the numerous hermitages in southern Sinai. Later, as these disappeared, it continued in proud isolation. In addition to the house at Raithou, it acquired property and built priories in many outlying districts, and rose to a position of importance that was in every way exceptional.

The convent retains to this day its original appearance. It is enclosed by walls built of well-dressed blocks of grey granite forming an irregular quadrangle, 280 feet at its greatest length, and 250 ft. at its greatest breadth. The walls enclosed the old tower, a church, and the convent buildings, with the

---

[1] Gregor von Gaming : *Ephemeris peregrinationis,* in Pez : *Thesaurus Anecdot.,* ii. part 3, p. 408.
[2] Tobler : *Golgotha,* ed. 1849, p. 139.

cells for the monks, a guest-house, bakeries, stables, and a library. Adjoining these buildings was the garden, which extended on one side, along the valley about 200 feet, with several springs of good water, and plantations of fruit trees, including olive, pomegranate, almond and peach, pear and apple trees. The produce of these remained famous throughout the Middle Ages.

The church was a basilica in the Byzantine style. It was lighted by five windows on either side, and the entablature of the nave rested on round arches which were supported by six pairs of granite columns with leafy capitals. The roof was of cypress wood covered with lead, and contained three contemporary inscriptions. One of these commemorated " our holy king, Justinian the Great ; " another was devoted to the memory of Theodora, who died in 548 ; the third called a blessing on the builder, Stephanos and his family. " Lord God, who didst appear on this spot, save and bless thy slave Stephanos, the builder of this monastery, from Aila, and Nonna (his wife), and give rest to the souls of their children, George, Sergius, and Theodora." [1]

The church was dedicated to the Virgin, as we learn from Eutychius, whose statement was confirmed by Magister Thietmar in 1217, and by the Papal Bull of 1226. In the Middle Ages it was sometimes spoken of as the church of St. Katherine, and later still as the church of the Transfiguration. The latter name was due to a great mosaic representation on the apse which is shown by its style to belong to the seventh or eighth century. The mosaic was first drawn and described by Laborde and Linant. [2] On this mosaic the youthful Christ was represented soaring towards heaven, with Elijah on one side pointing to Him, while Moses on the other side stands with hand upraised. John is seen kneeling, James also is represented kneeling, Peter is prostrate. Each figure is named. This scene is framed by thirty medallions, which represent the Twelve Apostles, Paul, the superior of the convent, who is not named, and sixteen prophets. Above, to the right, Moses is seen kneeling before the Bush ; to the left, he is represented holding the Tables. Below, are two angels with extended

---

[1] Nectarius : *Epit.*, p. 159. Another reading is "Stephanos, son of Martyrios, builder and architect, from Aila."

[2] Laborde et Linant : *Voyage de l'Arabie P.tríe*, 1830.

wings and two further portraits of which the one shows a bearded man with flowing locks, the other a woman with close-fitting head-dress. They are sometimes pointed out as Constantine and Helena, sometimes as Justinian and Theodora, but their identity remains unknown. Below, stand the words in Greek, " In the name of the Father, the Son, and the Holy Ghost, the whole of this work was executed for the salvation of those who contributed towards it by Longinus, most holy priest and superior (τοῦ ὁσιωτάτου πρεσβυτέρου καὶ ἡγουμένου)." [1] The floor was covered with a mosaic which was torn up by the Arab treasure seekers in the fifteenth century, but restored by Bishop Anastasius (1583–1592).

Two crypts inside the convent walls served to house the bones of the dead. Their corpses were first laid for two or three years on an iron grating in a cellar ; the skull was then transferred to one crypt and the bones to the other. The bones were sorted and added to the piles of corresponding bones, so that the femurs, the tibias, etc., lie piled together. The archbishops' corpses were, however preserved intact, and, wearing their robes, [2] were placed in mummy coffins. The use of the iron grating and the crypts dates back to the earliest days of the convent, for among the stories collected by Anastasius, one described how two corpses were laid side by side on the grating, but the one, disliking the proximity of the other, repeatedly moved, throwing it out of place, until it was officially adjured not to do so.

The convent included a hostel for the aged and for pilgrims, built by a certain Isaurus (*quodam Isauro*). It attracted the attention of Pope Gregory the Great (592–604), who, hearing of it, forwarded to John Climacus, who was superior at the time, woollen coverings and bedding for fifteen beds, together with money wherewith to purchase feather-beds. At the same time he wrote to Father Palladius, to whom he forwarded a cowl or tunic. The Pope had previously written to John Climacus, complimenting him on having reached a harbour of safety while others were tossing on a sea of religious difficulties. [3] He seems to have made a permanent grant to

---

[1] Nectarius : *Epit.*, p. 159.
[2] Robinson, E. : *Researches*, vol. i. 99.
[3] Gregorius : *Epist. Liber* in Migne : *Patr. Lat.*, lxxvii. xi. 1, p. 1118 ; xi. 2, p. 1119 ; ii. 23, p. 562.

the convent. A pilgrim of 1341 mentioned that the day of St. Gregory was kept at the convent, since he had bestowed on it alms out of the treasury of the Church, by which the number of convent inmates was raised to four hundred.

The interest which Pope Gregory took in the convent was probably connected with a pilgrimage made by the Roman patrician lady Rusticiana. In the year 592 she took her daughter, who was ill, to Sinai in the hope of effecting a cure. The husband of the daughter was also of the party. They started from Constantinople and returned sooner than was expected. This we learn from a letter which Rusticiana wrote to Pope Gregory.[1]

In Sinai the monk Anastasius recorded the visit of a patrician lady who came with her daughter and wished to consult Father Orontius, "who was so filled with divine fire that he could hold his hand in the flame, and burn incense on the palm of his hand." On one occasion, however, he lost a finger by burning. But Orontius refused to see the ladies, he sent them some grapes instead. When the demon who was in the daughter, saw the grapes, he cried out : Father Orontius, why do you come here ? And he departed out of her (no. 18). It was doubtless the same hermit, in this case called Orontos, who once came into church with his cowl all awry. When his attention was drawn to it, he said that all things being awry in the church, his cowl was in keeping with them. If they would set things straight there, he would see to his cowl.

A great feature of the convent of Sinai was its library, where the monks amassed books and manuscripts, and added to the world's literature by copying and writing. The place was a polyglot centre. Antoninus Martyr found three Fathers there who spoke Latin, Greek, Syriac, Egyptian (Coptic), and Bessam (Persian), and many interpreters in each language (c. 37). The hermit Simeon, who came into Europe about the year 1025, spoke Egyptian, Syriac, Arabic, Greek and Roman (*i.e.* Latin).

The contents of the library, in spite of losses incurred at different times, are still considerable. Among its most notable treasures was the *Codex Sinaiticus*, dated to about the year 400, which helped to revise the text of most of the

---

[1] Gregorius: *Epist.*, v. 49, p. 719.

K

Greek Old Testament, of the New Testament, and of some important early Christian works, including the *Shepherd of Hermas*. Attention was attracted to this *Codex* by Tischendorf, who came to the convent in 1844 to inspect the MSS., and having identified some of its pages, returned in 1853, in 1854, and in 1859, when he finally acquired it for Petrograd, a facsimile copy being deposited at the convent. A few leaves are at Leipzig. Another notable treasure was a Syriac *Codex* of the Gospels of a very early date, which was discovered as a palimpsest and photographed by the sisters, Mrs. Smith-Lewis and Mrs. Gibson, in 1893. Again, there was the *Evangeliarium Theodosianum*, a collection of passages from the New Testament written in gold lettering on parchment, which was seen and described by Burckhardt in 1816, and is dated to about the year 1000.

The Greek MSS. that are in the library were recently examined and catalogued by Prof. Gardthausen of Oxford. The list contains 1230 entries of MSS. that are all of a religious character. Prof. Gardthausen noted the names of over two hundred scribes, and other details which show that some of the MSS. came from Crete, Cairo, and Cyprus.[1] The Syriac and Palestinian-Syriac MSS. were catalogued by the ladies Smith-Lewis and Gibson. They are over three hundred in number. The Christian Arabic MSS. catalogued by the same ladies, amounted to six hundred and eighty entries.[2]

The importance which was secured to the convent reacted on the standing of the bishopric of Pharan, the representative of which seems to have removed to the convent. When Peter, patriarch of Jerusalem, (524–544) summoned his bishops to a synod in 538, Photius, bishop of Pharan, who was close upon seventy years of age, was "unable to leave Mount Sinai," which suggests that he lived there. Stephen of Cappadocia, mentioned above, Dulcetius and Zosimus were deputed to represent him. We again hear of Zosimus as one of three monks of Sinai, whom Apollinaris, the orthodox or Melkite patriarch of Alexandria (550–568), summoned to Alexandria. Of these he consecrated Theodor bishop of Leontopolis, an unnamed monk, bishop of Heliopolis, and Zosimus bishop of Babylon (Cairo). But Zosimus had no

---

[1] Gardthausen, Victor : *Catalog. Cod. Græc. Sin.*, 1886.
[2] Smith-Lewis, Agnes : *Sinaitic Studies*, nr. 1, nr. 3.

taste for the episcopate, and soon returned to his cell in Sinai.[1]

Likewise do we hear that Gregorius, who had presided over the monks in Sinai, was chosen to succeed Anastasius, bishop of the see of Antioch who was evicted in the year 569. According to information provided by Evagrius (593), he had there been besieged by the Kenite Arabs.[2] The country generally seems to have been at the mercy of the Arabs, which resulted in the abandonent of the hermitages, while it added to the prestige of the convent.

About this time the convent became the home of a young monk who was always silent. He was the only surviving son of the emperor Maurice, and was saved by his nurse when all the other sons were put to death by Phocas (602–608).[3] When he died his body disappeared. " Perhaps it was carried by God to the realms of the living," was the verdict of the monk Anastasius (no. 29).

The last bishop of Pharan we hear of was Theodor, who proposed the so-called monothelite modification of the monophysite doctrine, hoping thereby to secure re-union with the Church. In its interest he went to Constantinople, where he was honourably entertained by the patriarch Sergius (610–638), who impressed Pope Honorius (625–638) in Theodor's favour. Objection was, however, raised to the new doctrine by the monk Sophronius, who later became patriarch of Jerusalem (634–638), and disapproval of it was expressed by the Lateran Synod of 649,[4] and by the Sixth General Council of Constantinople in 681.

In the Wadi Feiran lie the ruins of a convent and a church of some importance which were described by the *Ordnance Survey* (i. 210), and are without doubt the remains of the episcopal seat of Pharan.

---

[1] Moschus : *Pratum*, no. 123–4, 127.
[2] Evagrius : *Hist. Eccles.* Migne : *Patr. Græc.*, lxxxvi. 2, p. 2803.
[3] Eutychius : *Annales*, p. 1082.
[4] Labbé : *Conc.*, x. 1071.

CHAPTER XIII

MOHAMMAD AND ST. KATHERINE

THE collapse of the Roman power in the East prepared the way for the Moslim conquest of Sinai and Egypt. During the lifetime of Mohammad changes were effected along peaceful lines. The efforts of the Prophet were directed, in the first place, against standing abuses and obsolete customs in Arabia itself. But the strong desire for expansion westwards among the Arabs drew his attention outside the limits of Arabia proper, and we hear of his entering into relation with neighbouring centres. Thus it is said that Tahhieh Ibn Robah of the port of Aila, waited on the Prophet when he was staying at Tarbuk, and that he received from him a woollen garment in return for paying a poll-tax. Ibn Ishak cited by Makrizi († 1441) stated that thus *firmân* was dated to the ninth year of the Hegira, *i.e.* 530–531, and assured protection to Tahhieh, the people of Aila, the bishop and all on land and water. " And the city did not cease to prosper." [1]

The garment which Makrizi called a cloak of the Prophet, was subsequently purchased by the Caliph of the Benu el Abbas. Aila continued to flourish, and Mukaddisi (*c.* 985) described " Wailah " as " a populous and beautiful city among many palm trees with fish in plenty, and the great port of Palestine and emporium of the Hedjaz," but the true Aila lies near by it and is now in ruins.[2]

A later age claimed that the convent of Sinai also secured a *firmân* under the hand of the Prophet. It was alleged that Mohammad, on one of his journeys with Ali, alighted under the wall of the convent, and that Ali penned the *firmân*, to which Mohammad, who could not write, set the mark of his

---

[1] Makrizi: *Desc.*, ii. 25, trad. 1900, *De la ville d'Eilah*, p. 532.
[2] *Description of Syria*, transl. Pal. Pilg. Soc., 1892, vol. 3, p. 64.

blackened hand. The monks told Burckhardt that the Ottoman Sultan Selim, after the conquest of Egypt (A.D. 1517), appropriated it and carried it off to Constantinople, but that a copy of it remained with the monks. This he was shown, but declared it to be a forgery.[1] Bishop Pococke also saw another copy of it in Cairo, which he copied, and of which he published a translation in the appendix to his book. It claims to have been written in the second year of the Hegira, and granted protection to the Nazarenes, declaring that the places where the monks dwelt should be protected ; also that they were exempt from paying the poll-tax, and should receive tithes, and that the Christians generally should not be called upon to pay a poll-tax exceeding ten drachmæ.[2]

The followers of the Prophet, after overrunning Syria, attacked Egypt. They seized Damietta which was governed by Abu Thour, a Christian Arab, and were opposed by an army of 20,000 men. But Abu Thour was seized, and the invaders spread into Egypt. The descendants of Abbas, the uncle of the Prophet, now reigned over large possessions, of which Egypt was part, from the year 750 to 868. After a break the old line of rulers returned from 905 to 969.

Under the Moslim system of administration the whole of Sinai was included in the province Hedjaz, which comprised Tur, Faran, Raya (i.e. Raithou), Kolzoum (i.e. Clysma), Aila, Midian, and its territory, El Oweid, El Hamr (or El Hour), Beda and Shaghb.[3] The Christians were declared a tolerated sect, but they were sorely oppressed under Abd-el-Melek ibn Merwan (705–708), and by Qurrah Sherig (709–714).

During the reign of Abd-el-Melek (705–708) an attack was directed against the convent of Sinai, where many of the slave population, who had been settled there by Justinian, were slain, others fled, others became Moslim,—" whose descendants to this day remain in the monastery and are called Benu Saleh, being reckoned their descendants,—from them sprang the Lachmienses." The monks themselves destroyed the houses of the slaves, lest anyone should dwell there and they are in ruins at the present day (c. 930).[4]

It is related in an appendix to the stories of Anastasius

[1] Burckhardt : p. 546.   [2] Pococke : i. p. 258.
[3] Makrizi : *Descrip.*, 1895, i. 25, p. 209.
[4] Eutychius : *Annales*, p. 1072.

how the Christian Saracens, who dwelt near the tower of Pharan and the Holy Bush, sought refuge in the holy mountain, but could not resist the numerous invaders, and therefore decided to accept the faith of the Prophet. One man was about to fly, when his wife begged him to kill her and the children rather than leave them at the mercy of the barbarians. He did so, and then fled to Horeb, where, like Elijah, he dwelt with wild beasts till he felt the approach of death. Then he repaired to the Holy Bush, where he lay in the guest-house, and where "some of the monks, still among the living," saw him and heard him describe the shining figures which he saw approaching as he lay on the point of death. ".They were, I believe, the angelic bands of the martyrs who came forth to greet him " (no. 45).

In Egypt itself, the Christians continued to be oppressed. A government survey, undertaken by the minister of finance, Obeidallah Ben Hab-Hab, resulted in a poll-tax being levied on them in addition to the usual land-tax. Again, Osanna ben Said el Tanuchi confiscated the property of the Christians, branded each monk with a sign on the hand, and he who had no sign forfeited his hand. Hence the Copts of Egypt to this day are marked with a cross on the hand. Moreover, every Christian who had no legitimation papers was mulcted ten dinars. In 737, in 750, and again in 831 or 852 the Copts of Egypt were in revolt.[1]

In spite of the Arab conquest, Sinai, like Jerusalem and Rome, continued to stand out as a goal of Christian pilgrimage. According to the account of a monk of Redon in Brittany, a certain Fromont and his brother, men of high standing, went there. They had murdered their uncle, an ecclesiastic, and repented, and went before King Lothair (855–859). His bishops decreed that the brothers should be chained and bound together and should do penance by going to Rome, Jerusalem and Sinai. In Rome they were received by Pope Benedict III (858–888), who gave them his blessing, and they took boat for Jerusalem, where they spent several years. From there they went into the Thebaid, where they fasted with the monks, and they finally reached Sinai, where they spent three years. Still wearing the chains that bound them together, they returned by way of Rome to Rennes, where the

---

[1] Renaudot, E. S.: *Hist. Patriarch. Alex.*, 1713, p. 841.

one brother died. Fromont then went to Redon, and once more started for Rome. But he returned to Redon where, his penance being at an end, his chain was taken from him, and where he died.[1] Bishop Pococke was shown a cell some way up the Gebel Musa where two brothers dwelt who were chained together.[2] The brothers from Rennes are pro-bably meant.

Another account which seems to date from the first half of the ninth century described the Houses of God, and thus described Sinai. " In holy Mount Sina there are four churches, one where the Lord spoke to Moses on the summit of the mountain ; one dedicated to St. Elijah ; another dedicated to St. Elisæus ; and a fourth in the monastery of St. Mary. The abbot is Elias, who has under him thirty monks. The steps that lead up and down the mountain are 7700 in number." [3]

A list of the " archbishops " of Sinai was compiled at the convent in the seventeenth century, which begins with Marcus, whose date is given as 869.[4] But the official report of the Fourth Synod held at Constantinople, in 869–870, contains the signature of Constantine, bishop of Syna.[5] Another bishop was Jorius, who died and was enshrined in Bethune in Belgium in the year 1033. A hymn there written in his honour described him as " bishop of Sinai." [6] He was probably travelling for the purpose of collecting alms for his convent.

From the historian Rodolfus Glaber (c. 900–1044) we hear that the dukes of Normandy, more especially Duke William (927–942) and his successors, were liberal in their gifts to churches and convents, and that monks from Mount Sinai came every year to Rouen, from where they departed loaded with gifts (exenia) in gold and silver.[7] It was in connection with these grants that the fame of St. Katherine of Alexandria spread to Europe in the course of the eleventh century.

The cult of St. Katherine, virgin saint and martyr, is

---

[1] De Frotomundo, in Mabillon : Acta Ord. St. Benedicti., vol. ii, 219.
[2] Pococke : i. 146.
[3] Commemoratorium, a MS. of the 9th or 10th century, edit. Tobler :
Descriptiones Terræ Sanctæ, 1874, p. 139.
[4] Perigraphe, p. 152.
[5] Labbé : Conc., vol. xvi. p. 194.
[6] Lequien : Or. Chris., iii. 754.
[7] Glaber : Hist. Lib. Quinque, in Collection pour servir à l'histoire,
1886.

among the curious developments of legendary history, for
her name appears for the first time about three hundred years
after her reputed existence. She is first named in the *Life of
Paulus Junior* († 956), who was called a Latro from Mons
Latrus, where he dwelt. The account of his life was written
by a contemporary.[1] It describes how three hundred monks
from Sinai and Raithou sought refuge in Mount Latrus in
Karia from the persecutions of the Saracens (c. 8).

The monks continued in close connection with Sinai.
Gabriel sang the Psalms of David as he had done at the Bush,
and when a pilgrimage was undertaken to pray for rain,
Gabriel obtained the desired result (c. 18). The fame of the
monks of Sinai as rain-makers was noted by Robinson and by
Prof. Palmer.[2] Paulus himself was devoted to various saints,
among whom was the martyr Aekatherina ; the thought of
her filled him with joy, and gave him a special power. One
day the monks were sitting down to a meal in the open air when
a rain cloud came up. Paulus bade them remain seated, and
not a drop of rain fell until they had finished their meal, when
it poured.

Direct information on St. Katherine, in this case called
Aekatherina, stands in the *Menology of Basileus* which is
dated between 957–1027. It stated that the saint dwelt
at Alexandria, and was the daughter of a wealthy king.
She was dignified in appearance and learned in Greek letters,
philosophy, and language. After witnessing a festival of the
Greeks, she approached the emperor Maximianus (A.D. 307)
and blamed him for ignoring the living God and adoring lifeless
idols. The emperor summoned fifty learned men to meet
her in argument, threatening them with death if they failed
to confound her. But the learned men were convinced by
the lady and accepted baptism, whereupon they were put to
death. Aekatherina was beheaded.[3]

A detailed account of the martyrdom was written by
Simeon Metaphrastes († c. 956), with discussions between the
learned men and the lady, and with further incidents including
the conversion of the general, Porphyrios ; the interest which
the Augusta took in Katherine ; the fashioning of spiked

[1] Vita Pauli Jun., in *Analecta Boll.*, xi. 1892, p. 1–74, 136–182.
[2] Robinson : i. p. 132 ; *Ord. Surv.*, i. 60.
[3] Nov. 25. Migne : *Patr. Græc.*, cxvii. 179.

wheels for torturing the saint, which broke of their own accord ; the flow of milk instead of blood when she was beheaded, a proof of her virginity; and the taking up of the body of the saint after death by angels who carried her to Mount Sinai.[1]

On turning to the writers who lived about the time alleged, we find that Emperor Maximianus, as recorded by Eusebius (c. 320), actually visited Alexandria, where he seized high-born women for adulterous purposes. Among them was a most distinguished and illustrious lady who overcame his intemperate and passionate soul. "Honourable on account of wealth and parentage, she esteemed all things inferior to chastity, and the emperor, who could not bring himself to put her to death, punished her with exile and confiscated her property." [2] Eusebius did not mention the lady's name, but the details of his story fit the legend and may underlie it.

The name Aekatherina (i.e. the pure one) was rendered in Latin as Katherina or Catherina. Her association with Sinai added the cult of a Christian saint to that of Saleh, Moses and Mohammad. It was chiefly the veneration of St. Katherine which brought pilgrims to Sinai during the Middle Ages. According to Giustiniani certain knights, as early as 1063, banded together in a semi-religious order to guarantee safe conduct to these pilgrims in Sinai, in the same way as the Knights of the Holy Sepulchre protected the pilgrims to Jerusalem.[3] The date mentioned seems rather early and may need revision.

A great impetus was given to the cult of St. Katherine in Europe by the visit to Rouen of the hermit Simeon about the year 1026. His journey was described in an account by Eberwein, abbot of St. Martin's at Trèves, who knew him,[4] and in the *Translation of the Relics of St. Katherine to Rouen*, which was written soon after the event.[5]

From these accounts we learn that Simeon was from Constantinople, and went to Bethlehem and then to Sinai, where

---

[1] *Martyrium St. Catherinæ* in Migne : *Patr. Græc.*, cxvi. 275–302.
[2] *Hist. Eccles.*, viii. 34.
[3] Giustiniani, Bern.: *Hist. cronol. dei ordini militari*, ed. 1672, i, p. 188.
[4] *Vita St. Symeon* is in *Acta SS.* Boll. June 1, pp. 89–95.
[5] *Translatio et Miracula St. Kath.* in *Analecta Bolland.*, 1902, vol. 22, pp. 423–39.

he served for several years in the convent before he became a hermit near the Red Sea. But here he was so much disturbed by the sailors and others who came for the oil (? petroleum), that flowed from the rock near his cell, that he removed first to the summit of Mount Sinai, where the Law was given, a place deserted because of the restless Arabs, and then to the convent itself. It was the time of the great famine in Egypt, (probably that of 1017), but in the convent there was plenty of food for the brethren and for the Arabs who crowded there with their wives and children.

From the *Chronicle* of Hugo of Flavigny (*c.* 1096) we learn that it was customary for the monks at the convent to take turns in ascending the mountain on the sabbath, in order to celebrate mass at the shrine of St. Katherine and collect the oil that flowed from the bones.[1] This shows that the body of the saint at this time lay enshrined on a mountain which was probably the Gebel Musa itself. For an ancient prayer contains the words " Lord, who didst give the Law to Moses on the summit of Mount Sinai, and who, on the same spot, didst deposit, through thy holy angels, the body of the blessed Katherine, virgin and martyr." [2] At a later date we hear of bodies of saints lying enshrined in the small church that stood on the summit of the Gebel Musa. The fact that oil flowed from the bones is told of many saints. Contrary to the usually accepted belief, the scientific explanation is probably as follows. The body lay in a coffin of cedar wood or other wood that is naturally charged with oil. If the heat generated in the coffin is great, it would cause the oil to ooze and collect on the bones or any other cold substance, forming into drops.

The monk Simeon was serving his turn at the shrine, and drawing off the oil that had collected into a glass phial, when three small (finger) bones of the saint came loose and were carried down with it. Simeon took charge of them as a priceless treasure. As an envoy was needed to go to Normandy to collect the usual alms, he started, carrying the relics with him. He travelled by way of Egypt, but the Italian galley in which he sailed was seized by pirates. He escaped by jumping overboard and eventually reached Antioch, where he fell in with a band of pilgrims, with whom he journeyed to Normandy

[1] *Chronicon*, ii. 26 in Migne: *Patr. Lat.*, cliv. 25 .
[2] Canisius, H.: *Thesaurus Mon. Eccles.*, iv. 1725, p. 345.

by way of Belgrad and Rome. In the meantime, Duke
Richard III, duke of Normandy (993–1026), had died, but
an abbey was in course of construction near Rouen, and Simeon
deposited the relics with the abbot Isambert before he left
for Verdun and for Trèves. The relics worked wonders.
Isambert suffered from toothache and was divinely directed
to the oil which brought him relief. Other miraculous cures
followed. And the Abbey of the Trinity near Rouen gained

[*Photo: Exclusive News Agency.*

Fig. 17.—Chapel on Gebel Musa.

such renown that it came to be known as the Abbey of St.
Katherine.[1]

A wave of enthusiasm for St. Katherine now swept across
Europe. Her name was inscribed on the local Norman
Kalendar,[2] her story was written and re-written in Latin
and in the vernacular, in prose and in verse. A Latin version

[1] *Translatio*, p. 423, footnote.
[2] Hardwick: *Historical Enquiry*, etc., 1849.

was the work of Amandus, a pupil of Isambert of Trèves, and a semi-Saxon version was written during the reign of Henry II. An early French version of about 1200 was perhaps the work of a nun. There were a host of others, many of which are in MS. and await tabulation.[1] All accounts conclude with the translation of the body to Sinai; the earlier ones dwell on the oil, a cure for all ills. And the story was not only read. In 1119 Geoffroy of Gorham came from Paris to Dunstable and wrote a *Ludus de Katerina*, which was performed by his scholars, on which occasion the clothes that had been borrowed, took fire and were burnt.

Churches and chapels were now built and placed under the protection of the saint. In 1148 Queen Matilda founded the hospital and church of St. Katherine near the Tower which continued till 1825, when it was destroyed to make room for the docks. In 1229 King Louis of France built a church of St. Katherine in Paris, which had been vowed by his knights at the Battle of Bouvines. First the University of Paris, and then the University of Padua, accepted St. Katherine as its patron saint, and in the year 1307 the Doge Pietro Gradenigo founded the *Festa dei Dotti* in Venice, in honour of her. The numerous incidents in her story supplied pictorial art with a new cycle of subjects. The scene of the martyrdom and translation to Sinai were first represented on small pictures of a great panel painted by Margaritone d'Arezzo (1216–93), which is now in the National Gallery.

In Sinai itself the importance of St. Katherine was more tardily recognised. We look in vain for mention of her in the account of the *Anonymous Pilgrim* of the eleventh century, and in the booklet *On the Holy Places*, which Fretellus, archdeacon of Antioch, wrote for the Count of Toulouse about the year 1130. It is not till the year 1216, when Magister Thietmar visited Sinai that we hear of the exhibition to a pilgrim of the relics which had now been translated from the height of the mountain to the convent church.

[1] Knust: *Geschichte der Legenden der heil. Katharina von Alex.*, 1890.

CHAPTER XIV

SINAI DURING THE CRUSADES

VARIOUS circumstances combined to raise the convent of Sinai to great prosperity during the early Middle Ages. On the one side it received regular contributions in money from Europe ; on the other it attracted the attention of the pilgrims owing to the increasing fame of St. Katherine. Further it secured the direct protection of the Moslim rulers of Egypt owing to a development in trade.

When the Arabs conquered Egypt, the desire arose for a direct communication by water to Arabia, and the fresh-water canal which connected the Nile with the Red Sea was cleared. Corn was now shipped on the Nile for Djar, the port of Medina, where goods coming from India and China were disembarked and re-shipped for Egypt. But owing to a dispute between the ruler of Egypt and his uncle at Medina, in the year 775, the port of Djar was closed to the Egyptians. The ships bearing Eastern goods for Egypt for a time landed at Roman Clysma, near Suez, which secured a new lease of life as Arabic Kolzoum. But Kolzoum like Arsinoë, silted up, while Suez as a port was not yet in being. On the west coast of the peninsula of Sinai lay Raithou, near which a landing stage offered the advantages of a natural harbour. Ships therefore landed near Raithou, called Raya by the Arabs, where the goods were transferred to camel-back for conveyance to Cairo and Alexandria.

The monks of the convent of Sinai were in direct connection with the monks at Raithou, who owned large palm groves, and doubtless controlled the landing stage. For the place which here grew up came to be known as Tur, an Arabic word signifying height, which was first applied to the convent of Sinai. Mukaddisi (c. 985) mentioned Tur Sina and noted that the Christians had a convent there, and some well-cultivated fields, and olive trees of great excellence.[1] The Christians called it Porta Santa Katerina or simply Santa Katerina (1383). The use of Tur as a port brought the Sultan of Egypt into relation with the monks, and acted as a safeguard to the convent.

In 1010 the Saracens bore down on the Church of the Holy Sepulchre at Jerusalem and destroyed it. They then moved on to Sinai with the intention of destroying the convent also, but they were warned off by seeing the mountain aglow with fire. The chronicler, Ademar, stated that when the report of the proposed attack reached the Sultan, he and his Saracens repented.[2] An attack on the port of Aila may have caused a further deviation of trade to Tur. Makrizi († 1441) recorded that Aila was pillaged by Abd Allah ben Edirs ben Dgofair, governor of El Korah, with the help of the Benu el Garrah.[3] This put a stop to the transit of goods via Aila to Damascus, and the Eastern goods for Syria as well as those for Egypt were now disembarked at Tur. This change is reflected in the fact that Tur, sometime between 1020 and 1050 took the place of Kolzoum as a customs station, although it remained for some time so poor a place that the appointment there was considered equal to a disgrace.

The rule of the Moslim until now had brought endless burdens and oppression to the Christians in Egypt. The churches had been robbed, the convents had been mulcted and their inmates had been disgraced by the emir who acted for the Sultan. But a change now took place. Bononius, a Benedictine monk from Bologne, came to Cairo in 1025, having obtained an interview with the Sultan to request that the Christian prisoners should be set at liberty. Bononius also visited Sinai and Jerusalem.[4] In 1045 the patriarch who had hitherto dwelt at Alexandria, removed to Cairo, and we now hear, in the sparse annals of the convent, of direct relations between the monks and the Sultan.

In the year 1069 John the Athenian, bishop of Sinai, was killed during his stay in Egypt under circumstances that are

[1] Mukaddisi : 3, 65.
[2] Ademarus : *Chronicle*, 3, 47, ed. 1897, p. 170.
[3] Makrizi : *Descrip.*, ii. 24.
[4] *Vita* in *Acta SS.* Boll., Aug. 30, p. 627.

not recorded. He was canonised at the convent. In the
year 1103 the bishop Zacharias was mentioned in a *firmân*
(εἰς ἕνα ὁρισμόν) of Emir Elmoumne, a term explained as
imperator fidelium ; perhaps it was Amir Abu Mansur (1101–
1130). The next bishop, George, was also recognised by the
Sultan in 1133. His successor at the convent named Gabriel,
who was mentioned in 1146, was learned in Arabic, and wrote
sermons as is shown by an Arabic book in the convent. He
was in touch with the Sultan " Kaim Impnes Rhaila," who was

Fig. 18.—El Arish. (*Times History of the War.*)

perhaps Zafir Abu el Mansur Ismael (1149–1151). The next
prelate was John, whose date is fixed at 1164 by an Arabic
letter which he addressed to the monks at Raithou. The
next bishop was Simeon.[1]

Of the religious life of the cities along the Mediterranean
coast little is known at this period. The last bishop of Ostracine known by name was Abraham, of the year 431. At
Rhinocorura called El Arish by the Moslim, later bishops
were Ptolemæus and Gregorius. Lequien made the mistake
of identifying Rhinocorura with Farma, and mentioned the

[1] Nectarius : *Epitome,* p. 211 ; *Perigraphe,* p. 153.

Jacobite prelates of Farma as prelates of Rhinocorura. Farma, famous for its palm groves, was near the ruins of the ancient Pelusium. El Arish continued an important city under Moslim rule, but its architectural features were not respected. Abu Saleh, the Armenian, who wrote an account of the churches and monasteries of Egypt about the year 1071, mentioned El Arish or Rhinocorura. "In this region there are two large churches which have stood from ancient times and are now in ruins, but their walls remain up to our time ; and the wall of the city which ran along the side of the Salt Sea, is still existing. It is said that of all the marble and columns which are to be found at Misr (*i.e.* Cairo) the greater part and the largest specimens came from El Arish." [1] (Fig. 18.)

The connection of the monks and the Sultan attracted the attention of Arab writers to the convent. Edrizi (*c.* 1153), Ibn Zobeir (*c.* 1183), mentioned its existence in general terms. Benjamin of Tudela, the Jewish rabbi who acted for a time as vizier to Adid († 1171), the last of the Fatimite rulers, held that it was occupied by Syrian monks, who were subject to the Sultan. He also remarked that at the foot of the mountain lay Tur Sina, a large town, the inhabitants of which spoke the language of the Targum (*i.e.* Syriac). It was close to a small mountain and five days' journey from Egypt. [2]

The trade via Tur naturally brought the monks into contact with the Further East. Fretellus of Antioch (*c.* 1130) declared that the monks of Sinai, "from the confines of Ethiopia to the utmost bounds of the Persians, were venerated in every tongue, possessing their property freely and quietly among themselves. They had cells throughout Egypt and Persia, around the Red Sea and Arabia, from which all they required flowed most liberally." [3] In addition to this, grants were made to them by the Crusaders in the lands which they conquered.

The Pope, from the first, had favoured the Crusades as a means of extending the influence of Latin Christianity. When Jerusalem was conquered in 1099, the Greek patriarch

---

[1] Abu Saleh : *Churches, etc.*, trans. Butler, 1895, p. 167.
[2] Benjamin of Tudela : *Itinerary*, trans. Adler, 1907, p. 77.
[3] Fretellus : *Jerusalem*, etc., Pal. Pilg. Soc., 1892, vol. 5, p. 16.

happened to be absent. He was passed over and a Latin patriarch was appointed in his stead. The authority of this prelate was extended with the advance of the Crusaders. Godfrey was proclaimed king of Jerusalem in 1099. He was succeeded by Baldwin, who, in 1115, made an expedition to "Mount Oreb, commonly called Orel," *i.e.* Mount Hor near Petra, the present Gebel Haroun. "Starting from here, Baldwin overcame the desert places and vast solitudes by conveying a quantity of food on mules, and reached Aila, which he found deserted, and of which he took possession. Here he heard of the monks, who dwelt in Sinai, and served God, and he desired to go to them across the mountain in order to pray. But he was prevented by a message from the monks who feared that their Moslim master might be annoyed by the king's visit, so he gave up the idea." [1] He turned back, and on his way to Syria he conquered Petra, near which he erected the fortress of Monreale. He then moved along the shores of the Mediterranean as far as Farma, where he died in 1117. According to Makrizi he burnt down the mosque and perished in its flames. Roger of Sicily in 1155 completed the work of destruction by a descent on Farma, which he set on fire and pillaged.

When Baldwin, disappointed of his visit to Sinai, seized Petra, this became a Latin bishopric, and the Latin patriarch of Jerusalem eventually had under him four bishops, of Tyre, Cæsarea, Nazareth, and Petra. [2] The name of the Latin bishop of Petra is not preserved. [3] According to Jacques of Vitry († 1244) the bishop of Petra had one suffragan, *i.e.* "the bishop of Sinai, superior to the convent of St. Katherine the Virgin, and the monks of that convent." [4] In Sinai itself no record of a Latin prelate was preserved. But irregularities in the succession suggest that the Latin bishop of Sinai was Simeon, who advocated the cause of the monks with the Pope.

On the other side of the peninsula, the appropriation of Aila by the Crusaders called for interference. Saladdin, in

---

[1] Albert of Aix : *Hist.*, xii. 21 in Migne : *Patr. Lat.*, clxvi. p. 707.
[2] William of Tyre, *Hist.*, xxi. 3 in Migne : *Patr. Lat.*, cci. p. 781.
[3] Lequien : iii. 727, mentioned that "Dorotheos, bishop of Petra," was present at the Council of Bethlehem in 1672.
[4] Jacques of Vitry : *Histoire des Croisades*, transl. Guizot, iii. 197.

1170, had a fleet built, with which he sailed around the peninsula, and attacked and retook Aila. But the enterprising Renaud de Chatillon (the Alaïris of Makrizi) collected material for ships on the Dead Sea, conveyed them to the Gulf of Akaba on camel-back, and seized Aila from where he pillaged the coast, and made piratical descents on the shipping for over a year. The small island, Iotabe, later Emrag, the present Zigiret el Faraun, lies at a short distance from Aila. It has no harbour, but is almost entirely built over by a castle with squared towers in the mediæval style. The work was probably begun in Roman times, but was added to by Renaud de Chatillon. But in 1184 Melek el Adel (Abu Bakr, 1199–1218), the brother of Saladdin (1171–1193), came with a fleet to Aila and attacked and finally routed the Franks. Advancing across the country he re-conquered Petra, which henceforth remained under Moslim rule.

In the meantime the monks were profiting by the good graces of neighbouring prelates. In 1203 the archbishop of Crete, described as " a lover of St. Katherine, the Virgin," bestowed on the monks of Sinai property in Crete which represented an annual income of four hundred ducats,[1] whereupon Simeon, bishop of Sinai went into Crete, where he built a priory ($\mu\epsilon\tau\acute{o}\chi\iota o\nu$). In 1204 the Venetians acquired the whole island of Crete by purchase from Boniface, marquis of Montferrat, and Simeon went to Venice where losses incurred by the monks, were made good to him.[2] A letter is extant of the Doge Pietro Ziani of 1211, in which he confirmed the ruler of Mount Sinai in the possessions which he held in Crete. It describes the ruler as " archbishop," which seems to be the earliest use of this title. Crete remained in the power of the city of Venice till 1645, and letters are extant from successive doges which confirm the rights held by the monks in the island.[3]

From Venice Simeon probably went to Rome, where a general synod was convened by Pope Innocent III (1198–1216) in 1211. Its purpose was to discuss the state of the Holy Land, " where the son of the bondswoman (i.e. Hagar), the most detestable Agarenes, hold our Mother of all the

[1] Tafur, P.: (1435–39): *Andances et Viajes*, ed. 1874, p. 94.
[2] Muralt: *Essai de Chron. Byz.*, p. 312.
[3] Gregoriades: *Holy Mount Sina*, p. 98.

faithful in bondage." [1] A sermon in Arabic, written by
Simeon, " bishop of Sinai," is among the MSS. of the Vatican.[2]
In the *Regesta* of Pope Honorius III (1216–27) we come across
repeated mention of Simeon, bishop of Sinai.   A grant of 1217
gave the protection of St. Peter to the Monastery of the Virgin
at the foot of the mountain and to its possessions ; another
confirmed the bishop of Sinai and his chapter in those possessions which they held at the time of the great synod (of 1211)
or had acquired since ; others advised the bishop of Crete to
respect the monks and hold them exempt from paying tithes
on the property which they held in Crete.[3]   In the year 1226

[*Photo: Exclusive News Agency.*

Fig. 19.—Zigiret el Faraun.

Pope Honorius granted a bull to Simeon and the monks of
Sinai, " of the order of St. Basil."   It is difficult to procure
the text ; its wording was probably much the same as that
of a bull granted in confirmation of it by Pope Gregory IX
(1221–41), of which a copy was preserved at the convent.
This bull enumerated the possessions which the convent held
in those countries over which the Pope claimed authority
by virtue of the conquests made by the Crusaders.
    The bull [4] first named Roboe, Fucra, Luach, places that

    [1] Mann, H. K. : *Lives of the Popes*, vol. 2, p. 293.
    [2] Assemanni : *Bibl. Orientalis*, ii, p. 511.
    [3] Honorius, Pope : *Regesta*, 1888, i. 123 ; ii, 178, 391, 394, 396.
    [4] Chabot : *A propos du convent* in *Revue de l'Orient. Chrétien.*,
vol. v., 1900, p. 495.

have not been identified. Mention was then made of Rayton (*i.e.* Raithou), with its palm groves and property ; of houses and property near the city of Egypt (*i.e.* Cairo) ; land on the Red Sea ; property and palm groves in Faran ; rights (*obedientia* in the church of St. Michael in Alexandria, and liberty of transit by land and water ; vineyards and olive groves in the valley of Moses (*i.e.* near Petra) ; in Monreale, houses, a mill, vineyards and olive groves ; property in Croce (not identified) ; in Jerusalem, rights in the church of St. Michael, houses and a bakehouse ; in Jaffa, houses and land ; near Acre, houses and the church of St. Katherine ; in Laodichea (near the sources of the Orontes), the hospital of St. Demetrios and a house ; in Damascus, the church of St. George, houses and property ; at Odaverosa (not identified), houses, land and vineyards ; near Antioch, a house and a bakehouse ; near Constantinople, rights in the church of St. George of Mangana ; in Crete, extensive property, including several churches with land pertaining thereto, several mills, vineyards, etc. ; in the island of Cyprus, houses, vineyards, woods, rights of pasture and of trading.

Simeon, who secured the Papal recognition to these rights, was bishop of Sinai from 1203 to 1253, according to Gregoriades. But the list of bishops which was compiled at the convent by Nectarius named Euthymius in 1223 ; Macarius (I) in 1224 ; Germanus in 1228 ; Theodosius in 1239 ; and Macarius (II) in 1248, who was named also in an ancient Arabic MS.[1] In the year 1258 the ruler was again Simeon. Some writers hold that this was the same Simeon who went to Europe, and possibly he was the suffragan of the Catholic bishop of Petra. The statements regarding him are difficult to reconcile. According to Gregoriades, the monks of Sinai, owing to the liberality of the Crusaders, owned property also in Tripoli and Gaza, and the produce of these places and that of Damascus was so plentiful as almost to supply their entire needs.

In the year 1216 a truce was concluded between the Sultan of Egypt and the Christians, which restored freedom of movement to the pilgrims. Magister Thietmar,[2] who was in the Holy Land, availed himself of it " to carry out his fervent

[1] Nectarius: *Epit.*, p. 211 ; Cheikho: p. 418
[2] Thietmar, Magister: *Peregrinatio*, ed. Laurent, 1857.

wish to visit the body of the blessed St. Katherine which exuded the sacred oil " (c. 8). In order to do so with impunity he adopted the appearance of a Georgian monk (c. 28), and journeyed by way of Mount Abarim, where Moses died, Mount Neb, Mount Phasga (Pisgah) and Mount Phagor in the land of the Moabites and Midian. By way of Roba he reached Crach and Petra, in Gallic Monreal, in Saracenic Scobach, where there was a great fortress that belonged to the Sultan of Babylon, and where Christians and Saracens dwelt in the suburbs. Here a Gallic widow gave him advice and provided him with food, and the Boidiwinos (Bedawyn) undertook to take him to Mount Sinai along a road that was known to none but themselves and to bring him back dead or alive. Leaving Kadesh Barnea on the right, he crossed the desert of Pharan, and reached the Red Sea and a fort (Aila), where captive Franks, English and Latins lived on fishing (c. 17). Three days later he reached Mount Sinai, " which the Saracens called Tur Sin." He was much impressed by the church of the Virgin which was resplendent with marble, and roofed with lead, and contained many hanging lamps. The monks were Greeks and Syrians, and their food included fish which was brought from the Red Sea and many things from Babylon (Cairo). The original Bush of Moses being no longer in existence, a golden bush (*aureus rubus*), hung with golden images of the Lord and of Moses, had taken its place. Small stones, engraved with a bush, were cut or dug up (*effodiantur*) which served against all infirmities. When the Sultan (probably Melek el Adel, 1199–1218) came there, he took off his shoes before entering the chapel (c. 20).

In the convent church stood the tomb of St. Katherine, a small chest of white marble. The bishop, hearing of the arrival of Thietmar and his wish to see the relics, approached the chest with prayer and incense, and had the cover removed. Thietmar saw the relics of St. Katherine and kissed her bared head. The limbs still hung together and were steeped in oil, which " exuded from the bones, not from the sarcophagus, like drops of sweat."

" When I inquired about her translation from the mountain to the church," wrote Thietmar, " I was told that a certain hermit who dwelt in another part of Mount Sinai from that on which the body of St. Katherine was laid by the angels,

frequently saw, by day and by night, a light of great brightness
in or near the place where the body lay. Wondering.what it
was, he went to the church at the foot of the mountain, and
described the sight that he saw and the place where he saw it.
The monks, after fasting, ascended the mountain, in a procession that was led by him. When they found the body,
they greatly wondered whose it was, whence it had come, and
how it was taken there. As they stood there wondering, an
aged hermit from Alexandria declared, like Habakkuk the
prophet who spoke to Daniel, that the body had been brought
to Sinai by the grace of God, and he assured those who doubted,
that it was the body of the blessed Katherine, and had been
carried there by angels. At his instigation, the bishop and
the monks translated the body to the church because the
place where it lay was quite inaccessible (c. 19).

Thietmar then asked to be taken to the height on Mount
Sinai, where Moses received the Law, and on his way thither
he saw the chapel where the Virgin met the monks who, on
account of the lack of food, and the verminous condition of
the convent, were about to leave, but she bade them turn
back (c. 22). He also saw the spot where the Virgin promised
the monks a plentiful supply of oil for their lamps ; likewise
the chapel of Elijah on Horeb ; the imprint on the rock of
the body of Moses ; and the place where the body of St.
Katherine was laid by the angels (c. 23). Before leaving the
convent he received some of the precious oil (c. 27). His home
and the place to which he went are unknown. An account of
the Moslim faith which he added to his narrative, reflects a
liberal spirit, and, taken together with his Latinity, indicates
a man of learning and understanding.

The call of Pope Innocent III, in 1211, stirred up anew the
spirit of the Crusaders, but efforts were now directed, in the
first place, against the Sultan in Egypt. Damietta, which lay
on the Tanitic mouth of the Nile, where the Moslim had
a fort, was the scene of many struggles. From January, 1218,
to November, 1219, it was occupied by the Franks. In the
meantime, the emperor Frederick invaded Palestine on his own
account, and in 1229 secured a truce by which the Christian
pilgrims were once more enabled to travel to Jerusalem. The
advantages which he received were forfeited, however, owing
to quarrels among the Christians themselves. The Sultan

marched on Gaza in 1244, and attacked Jerusalem, which was finally lost to the Christians.   It was in vain that the French king Louis IX, in 1249, occupied Damietta and pillaged Ostracine, which altogether disappeared.   But Louis was taken prisoner and the restoration of Damietta was part of his ransom.   Changes among the Moslim rulers hurried on events. The Mongols, pressing in from the East, overthrew the Caliph of Baghdad and destroyed the Syrian kingdom.   A descendant of the true Prophet was established on the throne of Egypt as a nominal ruler, while the general, Bibars († 1277), with the title of Sultan, extended his authority over the greater part of Arabia and Syria.   Bibars successfully led the campaign against the Crusaders.   Antioch fell in 1268, Tripoli in 1289, Acre in 1291.   By these losses the spirit of the Crusaders was broken.

Of the bishops of Sinai during this period, little is known. In succession to Simeon (I or II), John III ruled from 1265 to 1290, and was followed by Arsinius, who was a book lover. Several books in Greek which are now in the convent library were written at his instigation, and one of them was owned by him.[1]   The next bishop was Simeon (II or III), who ruled from 1306 to 1324, and was followed by Dorotheus (1324–1333), who secured a *firmân* from the Sultan,[2] and a bull from Pope John XXII, who was at Avignon at the time.   In this bull, dated 1328, the pope called upon Hugh, king of Cyprus, to respect the rights which former kings of Cyprus had granted to the monks of Sinai.   He also recognised their right of burial in the church of St. Simeon at Famagusta in Cyprus, and granted one year's indulgence to pilgrims who visited the shrine of St. Katherine in Mount Sinai.

It was presumably Bishop Dorotheus who received Duke Henry II of Brunswick in Sinai in 1330, who came bearing a letter from the Greek emperor to his " dear relatives," the Greek prelates.   According to the German record, the " archbishop of Sinai " received the duke in person, and bestowed on him, among other relics, a thorn from the crown of Christ, which he had himself received from the king of France to whom he was sent as envoy.   Duke Henry received also oil, and perhaps a bone, from the shrine of St. Katherine,

---

[1] Gardthausen: nos. 94, 657, 662, 670.
[2] Nectarius: *Epit.*, p. 212.

which, together with the thorn, he deposited in the church of the monastery of Walkenried after his return to Germany.[1]

The ruler in succession to Dorotheus was Germanus III, and he was followed by Marcus who is named in an Arabic MS., and went to Rome in 1376 to collect alms for his convent. It was probably owing to his influence that a bull had been granted to the monks by Pope Innocent VI in 1360.[2]

Later bishops included Job, whose name appears in an inscription in the convent church, and the following, who were named in a Arabic MS. without record of their date: Athanasius (I); Sabbas; Abraham; Gabriel (II); Michael; Silvanus; Cyrillus. Mention is also made of one Solomon, whose name is not otherwise recorded.

[1] Maderus: *Antiquitates Brunvicenses*, 1661, p. 267.
[2] Bulls in *Archives de l'Orient Latin*, 1881, i. 274, 283.

CHAPTER XV

THE PILGRIMS OF THE MIDDLE AGES

I

A KEEN interest in the Near East was aroused in Europe by the Crusades. At their conclusion travellers of every kind, more especially pilgrims and merchants, started for Palestine and Sinai, eager to visit the holy places, and to see some of the marvels of which the Crusaders had brought back accounts to their homes. The movement was for a time hindered by the difficulties which were raised by the Sultan, who suspected a further alliance between the "Franks" and the Tartars. But the princes of Europe interfered on behalf of the pilgrims, and Sultan Melik el Nasir, who ruled with some interruptions from 1293 to 1341, was a man of wider outlook, who entered into diplomatic relations with the Pope, the king of Aragon, and the king of France. He did his utmost to protect the pilgrims. Crowds of them now started for the Holy Land, a certain number extending their voyage to the shrine of St. Katherine in Sinai, a visit to which formed part of the so-called Long Pilgrimage.

The flow of pilgrims was naturally influenced by the social and political events of the day. Of those who took the Long Pilgrimage, six,[1] between the years 1331 and 1346,

[1] Antoninus of Cremona (*c.* 1331): *Itinerarium* in *Zeitschrift des deutsch. Palestin. Vereins*, vol. xiii. year 1890 ; Jacopo of Verona (*c.* 1335): *Liber Peregrinationis,* ed. 1895, in *Revue de l'Orient Latin,* iii. p. 163–302 ; Wilhelm de Baldensel (*c.* 1336): *Hodoeporicon,* ed. 1725, in Canisius: *Thesaurus,* vol. iv.; Ludolf of Sudheim or Rudolf de Suchen (*c.* 1336–41): *Reise,* ed. 1609, in Feyerabend: *Reissbuch,* 1610, p. 803, ff. ; Sir John Maundeville (*c.* 1340): *Travels,* ed. Halliwell, 1866 ; Rudolf von Fraymansperg (*c.* 1346), ed. 1725 in Canisius: *Thesaurus,* vol. iv. pp. 358-60.

wrote an acount of their journey, and made mention of
Sinai.   After this there was a break, no doubt attributable to
the Black Death which swept across Europe in 1348–49, and
to the war which Peter, king of Cyprus, waged on Egypt,
which led to the sack of Alexandria in 1365.   Towards the
close of the century pilgrims again became numerous, and six
further accounts between the years 1384 and 1397 describe
a visit to St. Katherine.[1] Again, during the first half of the
fifteenth century visitors to St. Katherine were relatively
few, whereas large parties of pilgrims sought the convent
between 1460 and 1497, several members of the same party
sometimes writing a description of their journey.

The pilgrims, for the most part, sailed from a port in Italy,
more especially from Genoa or Venice, in galleys, which were
timed to meet the caravans which brought the produce of
the East to Alexandria and Jaffa.   From Alexandria they went
to Babylon (Cairo), where they procured a *firmân* from the
Sultan which established their peaceful intentions in the eyes
of the Bedawyn (Baldensel, p. 343 ; Frescobaldo, 1384, p. 99,
etc.).   Or they went to Jaffa and Jerusalem where those who
wished to extend their pilgrimage to Sinai proceeded on
mule-back to Gaza, where camels were chartered for crossing
the desert.   Travel was facilitated at the time by the
permanent foothold which the Franciscans, following in the
wake of St. Francis himself (1226), had secured at Jerusalem
and at Gaza, and by the establishment, in various cities, of
consuls whose chief duty it was to befriend and protect the
pilgrims.   The cities of Florence, Venice, Genoa, and the
Catalans each had a consul in Alexandria in 1384 (Frescobaldo, p. 72).   Venice had a consul in Jaffa in 1413, and one
in Jerusalem in 1415.[2]   There was a house or hostel set
apart for the use of pilgrims in Cairo in 1384 (Sigoli, p. 16),
where food was given to poor pilgrims who were on their way
to St. Katherine (Martone, p. 596).

[1] Sigoli, Simone (1384): *Viaggio al Monte Sinai*, ed. Piroti, 1831 ;
Frescobaldo, Lionardo (1384): *Viaggio* , ed. 1818 ; (Gucci: *Viaggio* in
Gargiolli: *Viaggi in terra santa*, 1862 ;) Martone, Nic (1393): *Liber
Pereg. ad loca sancta* in *Revue de l'Orient Latin*, iii. 1895 ; Briggs (1392)
in *Archives de l'Orient Latin*, 1884; Anglure, Ogier d' (c. 1395): *Le
saint voyage*, ed. Bonardot et Legnon : *Soc. des anciens textes français*,
1878.
[2] Heyd, W. von : *Gesch. des Levanthandels*, 1879, vol. 2, 466.

Among the earlier accounts was that of the friar Antoninus of Cremona, who set out from Cairo to Sinai with seven Latin pilgrims in 1331, going on to Jerusalem by way of Gaza. The wish to visit the shrine of St. Katherine was aroused in him by paintings, representing her story, which were a gift to his city by a merchant of Piacenza (p. 170). Again, there was the Italian notary, Jacopo of Verona, who, after a stay in the Holy Land in 1335, proceeded to Gaza, which he left on August 28, arriving at the convent on September 10. Jacopo mentioned as stopping places between Gaza and the convent, Nocale (Kala'at en Nakhl) " in our language called Phurfur " (? bran), and Colebmaleo. At Nocale at the Fountain of the Sultan (*Puteus Soldani*) he met over twelve thousand pilgrims with six thousand camels, who were on their way back from Mecca, and who moved in bands according to the countries to which they belonged, an arrangement which greatly impressed Jacopo (p. 228). At the *Puteus Soldani* the Seigneur d'Anglure who was on his way from Gaza to the convent in October of 1395, met ten thousand Moslim pilgrims (p. 45).

Another pilgrim, Wilhelm de Baldensel, in the summer of 1336, rode on horseback from Cairo to the convent in ten days, much to the surprise of the monks. From here he went on to Jerusalem (p. 344). Again, Ludolf of Sudheim, during the thirteen years which he spent travelling in the East visited the convent some time between 1336 and 1341, and Sir John Maundeville was there some time in the course of his twenty-five years of travel. These pilgrims, like Thietmar, in 1216 found the relics of St. Katherine enshrined in a marble chest or sarcophagus which stood in the convent church, and were allowed to see them after they had been the usual round of the sights (Ludolf, p. 840).

The relics of St. Katherine consisted of the head and some of the limbs. Jacopo stated that, besides these, the monks had bones stored away in another chest or *arca* (p. 230). Maundeville writes he saw " the head of St. Katherine rolled in a bleeding cloth, and many other holy and venerable relics, which I looked at carefully and often with unworthy eyes " (p. 60). Wilhelm de Baldensel first noted a silver scoop or spoon which was used for taking up the drops of oil which exuded " not from the sarcophagus, but from the bones " (p. 344), and which was given in small glass phials to the pilgrims (Jacopo, p. 230). This use of a scoop shows that the oil flowed less plentifully than at the time when the chest that contained the bones stood on the height, where it was " drawn off " by Simeon.

The view was now held that the body of the saint was originally laid by the angels, " not on the Mount of the Law, but on the Mount of St. Katherine," as we learn from Antoninus. Here the impress made by the body on the stone was shown, which induced the pilgrims to make the ascent of the Gebel Katrin. The impress of the body was seen also by Rudolf von Fraymansperg, who visited Sinai in 1346 (p. 359), by Simone Sigoli in 1384 (p. 84), and by others. According to different accounts, the body lay exposed on the height two or three or four or five hundred years before it was brought to the convent.

Other legends are related by the pilgrims. Antoninus stated that about a hundred " ravens " were fed every day at the convent kitchen in memory of Elijah, who was fed by ravens (p. 167). Sir John Maundeville improved on this statement by relating that " all ravens, choughs and crows of the district flew once a year in pilgrimage to the convent bearing a branch of bay or olive " (p. 59). In connection with these legends, both the story of Elijah, and the " ravens " that flocked to the convent, it is well to bear in mind that the words for raven and Arab sound alike in Arabic.

Many hanging lamps were now kept burning in the convent church, the number of which Jacopo estimated as three hundred. Sir John held that they indicated the presence of as many monks, and he added that when the prelate of the abbey died, his lamp went out and lit again of its own accord, if his successor were worthy (p. 60).

On the Mount of the Law stood the small church which at one time contained the relics of St. Katherine, and which continued to contain bodies of saints as late as 1384. Near it was the cavern in which Moses stood when the Lord passed (Sigoli, p. 82 ; Maundeville, p. 62). Beyond it was the small mosque which the Saracens sought in pilgrimage, and which to Antoninus was " an idol of abomination " (p. 168).

The relative position of these buildings and sites is shown on the topographical sketch made by Jacopo, which is here reproduced (Fig. 20). On it we note the convent church with

Fig. 20.—Sketch of convent surroundings about 1335.

its tower, and we are told that inside the convent walls there
" stood likewise a mosque with a tower of its own, from which
the *cazes*, or priest of the Saracens, proclaimed the Mohammedan
faith, a proceeding to which the *kalogeri* or monks could raise
no objection, since they were under the dominion of the
Sultan who would have it so " (*c.* 1335, p. 321). This mosque
of the *maladetta fede* was noticed also by the party of
distinguished Italians who came to Sinai from Cairo in 1384.
These included Leonardo dei Niccoli Frescobaldo from Florence,
Simone Sigoli from Venice, and a certain Giorgio di Messer
Gucci di Dino, each of whom was attended by his serving
man.

The sketch of Jacopo further shows the path leading up
from the convent to the Mount of the Law " where the law
was given to Moses," with the chapel " where the Blessed
Mary appeared; " the church of St. Elijah; and the mosque of
the Saracens. There is also a garden with a fountain, and
a zigzag path leading up to a higher mountain where " lay the
body of the Blessed Katherine." From the summit of this
mountain Jacopo saw the Red Sea, and watched the ships that
carried pepper, ginger, cinnamon, and other spicery from
India. He also went the two days' journey to Tur, which
he called Elim, where he bathed in the Red Sea. Here he
saw the place where the Israelites came out of the water,
and remains of the Pharaoh, apparently bones, lying on the
sea shore. In the belief that this was Elim of the Bible, he
noticed that there were here, not seventy palm trees as stated,
but ten thousand date palms, the produce of which the
monks sold at a high price at Cairo (p. 237). From an Arabic
source we hear that special attention was given to Tur in the
year 1378, by Salah ed Din Ibn Gourram, grand vizier of
Egypt.[1]

The number of pilgrims from Europe who visited Sinai is
difficult to estimate. The guide who was engaged to conduct
the Italians from Cairo to the convent in 1384, had taken
pilgrims along this route seventy-six times (Sigoli, p. 15).
The knights who wished to be enrolled as Knights of the
Order of St. Katherine, hung up their arms in the convent
church (Tafur: " *dexe mis armis* "), and received a badge
which showed a broken wheel that was pierced by a sword.

[1] Weill: *Presqu'île*, p. 93.

Some pilgrims noted the names and scutcheons of earlier ones, which, together with coats of arms, were scratched on the wall spaces.

The zeal of the pilgrims was responsible for further developments in the story of St. Katherine. Ludolf of Sudheim in 1341 sought the spot outside Alexandria where the saint was beheaded (p. 827) ; the Italians of 1384 identified the prison in which she was confined, the columns on which were placed the spiked wheels that broke of their own accord, and her dwelling place " where now stands the palace of the lamelech," *i.e.* the emir of the Sultan (Sigoli, p. 90 ; Frescobaldo, p. 82). The columns which were of red porphyry were noticed also by Thomas of Swynburne, an Englishman and mayor of Bordeaux at the time, who paid a hurried visit to Egypt and Sinai in 1392, of whch his companion, Briggs, wrote a short account.

And more than this. The oldest account of Katherine claimed for her royal descent. The *Speculum* of Vincent of Beauvais (*c.* 1190–1264) gave her father's name as Costus. Another line of tradition called him Constantius and made him into a king of Cyprus, where the monks of Sinai had possessions in the year 1216. A chapel dedicated to St. Katherine situated near " Salamina " or Constantia in Cyprus, was visited by Ludolf in 1341 (p. 826). In the year 1394 Niccolo de Martone, the Italian notary from Carniola, whose desire " to reach the dominion of the blessed Virgin in Sinai " took him to the East, went from Famagusta in Cyprus to Constantia, which in his estimation was built by Constantius, the father of St. Katherine, Here he saw the palace and the chamber, " now in ruins," where St. Katherine dwelt, and near it her chapel, which many persons sought in pilgrimage (p. 632). From Famagusta he visited an island to which St. Katherine went at the suggestion of her mother, in order to consult a hermit regarding her marriage. His advice was that she should wed Christ, and in the night an angel appeared, who gave her a ring (p. 633). This is the first we hear of the mystic marriage of St. Katherine, which henceforth formed an incident in her legend and was further developed. The *History of St. Katherine*, which was written by the Augustinian monk Capgrave about the year 1430, described how a hermit named Adrian was sent to Alexandria by the Queen of Heaven. He took the maid into the desert where Christ appeared to her in a dream and gave her a ring.[1] This incident does not appear in the story of St. Katherine as told in the *Legenda Aurea* of Jacopo of Voragine, which was written about the year 1255. But the English version of the *Golden Legend*, which was printed by the Caxton Press about the year 1483, described the gift of an actual ring, further developing the story. For according to this account Costus, king of Cyprus and the father of the saint, was the son of Constantius, king of Armenia, whose second wife was Helena, the daughter of King Cole of Britain, and the mother of the emperor Constantine. Thus St. Katherine was linked up with the kings of Britain on the one side, and with the emperors of Rome on the other !

In the convent of Sinai no attention was given to these developments, and the *Life of St. Katherine* that was read in the convent confined itself to the facts related by Simeon Metaphrastes.

The convent reached the high-water mark of its prosperity during the fourteenth century. It drew a large income from its outlying possessions, it received gifts from the Sultan and from the pilgrims, it levied tribute on the goods that were unshipped at Tur. The basis of this arrangement is not directly stated, but the writer Piloti, about the year 1440, declared that the tax levied on the goods at Tur was 10 per cent. of their value,[2] and the Ritter von Harff, about the year 1497, held that the monks went shares with the Sultan in the profit made on the goods.[3]

The Italians who visited the convent in 1384 found two hundred monks in residence, of whom one hundred and fifty served the convent chapels, and fifty the chapels on the Mount of the Law. There were besides a very large number of Moslim, who dwelt inside the convent precincts (Frescobaldo, p. 121).

Food was cooked in the convent kitchen every day for four hundred persons, in huge cauldrons that came from Venice, and were conveyed across the desert on camel-back

---

[1] Ed. 1893, p. 247.
[2] Piloti: *Tractatus*, in *Monuments pour servir à l'histoire;* Brussels, vol. iv p. 357.
[3] Harff, A. von: *Pilgerfahrt*, ed. 1860, p. 133.

(Frescobaldo, p. 167). Largess was distributed daily to a thousand Arabs of the desert (*Ibid.*, p. 121). In the year 1393 the monks and their dependents were two hundred and eighty in number, and two loaves were given daily to each pilgrim and to every Arab and mariner, of whom large crowds applied for food at the convent (Martone, p. 608).

Some of the pilgrims supply information on the Saracens or Bedawyn, who all through showed an independent spirit. During the whole of the Mameluk dynasty (1250–1517), they were complete masters of Suez. Wilhelm de Baldensel, calling them Ridelbim, stated that they lived on their camels and goats, neither sowing nor reaping, and eating such bread as they procured in Syria and Egypt. They were brown, fleet-footed, and carried a shield and a spear, rode on camels, wrapped themselves in linen, and acknowledged the authority of the Sultan, who, however, gave them presents since they could easily expel him and occupy Syria and Egypt (p. 345). Antoninus in 1331 also remarked that the Arabs had no fear of the Sultan (p. 165), and Ludolf held that the Sultan lavished on them gifts and flattery, since they could easily subjugate his territory (p. 89).

The attitude of these Bedawyn in matters of religion was perplexing to the Europeans, who began with looking upon Mohammad the Prophet as the incarnation of all wickedness, and then realised that his followers had a standard of dignity and hospitality which were by no means despicable. Ludolf, in 1341, noted that the Saracens did homage to St. Katherine (p. 66), and Frescobaldo remarked that the Saracens held the mountains of Sinai in veneration. " And be it known," he continued, " that the Saracens reverence the Virgin Mary, St. John the Baptist, St. Katherine, and all the patriarchs of the Old Testament and hold that Christ was the great prophet previous to Mohammad ; also that Christ was not born of the flesh, but that the Divine Father, through the lips of an angel, sent the Divine Word, and that in many ways they approximate our faith " (pp. 91, 101).

An English poem of about the year 1425 is extant, which describes the chief sites of pilgrimage at the time. They included the shrine of St. James of Compostella in Spain, the city of Rome, Jerusalem, and Mount Sinai. The poem is about 1500 lines long, of which about thirty

M

deal with Mount Sinai, and are as follows (the spelling is modernised) :

> In that mount up high
> Is a minster of our Lady :
> The minster of the Bush, men call it,
> Wherein the body of St. Katherine was put.
> Also behind the high altar
> Is where Jesus did appear
> In that church to Moses,
> When he kept Jethro of Midian's sheep truly.
> In the midst of that hill is a place
> Where did penance the prophet Elijah ;
> On the height of that hill, by Clerk's saws,
> God gave to Moses both the Laws
> Written in tables, without miss.
> Plenary remission then it is.
> A garden there is at no distance
> Where Onorius (*i.e.* Onophrius) did his penance.
> Another hill also is there,
> To which angels did bear
> The blessed body of St. Katherine,
> She was a holy virgin.
> Under that hill trust thou me,
> There runneth the Red Sea.
> At each of these places, that I told,
> Is VII years, and VII " lentonez," [1] be thou bold.
> Thus from Sinai would I skip
> And tell of the pilgrimage of Egypt ; etc. [2]

---

[1] The meaning of this word may be Lenten pardons
[2] In Purchas : *His Pilgrims*, reprint, vii. 566.

CHAPTER XVI

THE PILGRIMS OF THE MIDDLE AGES

II

THE war of retaliation, which the Sultan waged against the king of Cyprus, interrupted the flow of pilgrims to the East in the first half of the fifteenth century. Moreover, the sultans, more especially Bursbai (1423–38), began to squeeze the Christian merchants. Their grievances raised the ire of Emmanuel Piloti, a native of Crete, who spent twenty-five years in Egypt and Syria, and acquired considerable insight into affairs generally. He was moved to compose a missive which he addressed to Pope Eugenius IV (1431–47). In this he spoke of the achievements of the Crusaders, insisting that Mohammad had called for toleration of the Christians, a call that was disregarded by Sultan Bursbai, who oppressed them grievously. The resources of the Sultan were enormous. He ruled from Mecca to India, and had full control of the spicery that was unshipped at " Torre, as the port of St. Katherine is now called." He levied 10 per cent. on the value of these goods, not once, but several times over, as they passed through his dominions. Why, asked Piloti, did not the head of all Christendom arise in defence of the Christians, sally forth like the Crusaders, conquer Cairo, and supplant the Sultanate ? In doing so, he would have the support of the Arabs of the desert.

The Church of Rome, however, was bent on propaganda along more peaceful lines. After the Crusades the Franciscans, starting from Jerusalem, penetrated into Tartary and China. The plan was now formed of securing a foothold in Sinai as a stepping-stone on the way to India. With this end in view

Pope Calixtus III (1455–58) addressed a letter to the Franciscans urging that they should secure further sites, including one on Mount Sinai ("concedimus ut nova loca etiam in Monte Sina capere possitis ").[1] The direct steps that were taken are not known, but in the course of the fifteenth century we hear of Franciscans, popularly known as Cassis, moving to and fro between Gaza where they had a house, and the convent, where at first a room and later a chapel was reserved for the celebration of a Roman Catholic service.

The desire to penetrate to India and beyond was very general. Thus, Pero Tafur, a Castilian nobleman, arrived at the convent in the year 1435 on his way to Tur, where he hoped to embark for India. But at Tur he met Niccolo da Conti, for many years a resident in India, who was on his way to Cairo, where he intended to lodge a complaint with the Sultan (Bursbai), because of the indignities to which he was exposed. His account made Pero Tafur give up the thought of his journey.

Tafur found only about fifty to sixty monks at the convent, which had fallen on evil days. The Turk was advancing. In the year 1453 he took possession of Constantinople. As he advanced on Sinai, he laid a heavy hand on the convent, from which he claimed an annual tribute of three hundred ducats. Jacob, the patriarch of Jerusalem († 1482), hereupon despatched a monk of Sinai to the princes of Europe, with a letter asking for help. This monk, besides the letter, carried with him some valuable relics, including a tooth of St. Katherine.[2] His appeal met with a ready response. King Louis XI of France (1463–83) made an annual grant to the convent of two thousand ducats,[3] which was still paid by King Charles VIII in 1497 (Harff, p. 122). Queen Isabella of Spain (1481–1504) gave five hundred ducats a year, a sum which was still paid by King Phillip in 1558.[4] The emperor Maximilian I (1493–1517) and the king of Hungary gave money (Fabri, ii. 623).

Unrest, however, now spread to the Bedawyn. A German

---

[1] Lammens: *Mélanges* in *Revue de l'Orient Chrétien*, vii., 1902, p. 503, ff.

[2] Lequien: *Or. Chr.*, iii. 515.

[3] Gregoriades: p. 95.

[4] *Ibid.*, pp. 101–107.

pilgrim named Leman in the year 1472 sailed from Beirut to Alexandria in the largest galley of the time, which carried two hundred and sixty Christians and nine hundred Moslim. He was bent on going to the convent, but was prevented from entering Sinai owing to the hostile attitude of the Bedawyn.[1] However, matters again improved, and the pilgrims and the accounts of voyages multiplied. The most notable accounts which describe a visit to the convent are enumerated below.[2]

Among these pilgrims the Flemish knight Anselm Adornes and his party were advised by the monk of Sinai who acted as their guide from Egypt, to adopt the appearance of monks in order to travel with safety. They reached the convent where there were about forty monks in residence, who told them that the Arabs frequently invaded the convent (p. 162). On one of their raids they entered the sanctuary and broke open the marble chest which contained the relics of St. Katherine but, instead of the expected treasures, they found a few bones (Gregor, p. 504).

Towards the close of the century the accounts of pilgrims show that these now came in large parties. In 1479 the Nürnberg patricians Hans Tucher and Sebald Rieter, went to Gaza where they entered into an agreement with a dragoman that was set down in writing to convey them to the convent or Cairo. This agreement is worded exactly in the same way as these agreements are worded at the present day. They travelled with seven Franciscan friars, and on their arrival at the convent Latin mass was celebrated (Tucher, p. 365). Again, in 1483 two parties of Germans, numbering twenty persons in all, visited Palestine and Syria. They included Bernhard von Breydenbach († 1493), of the Chapter

[1] Röhricht: *Deutsche Pilgerreisen*, 1880, p. 104.
[2] Adornes, Anselme (1470): *Voyage au Mt. Sinai*, 1893, in *Annales de la Société d'Emulation*, Ser. v. tom. 4 ; Tucher, Hans (1479): *Beschreibung der Reise* in Feyerabend: *Reissbuch*, 1609, p. 652–99 ; Rieter: *Reissbuch* 1884 ; Bernhard v. Breydenbach (1483): *Pilgerfahrt* in Feyerabend: *Reissbuch*, pp. 91–229. ed. with Rewich's woodcuts, 1486 ; Felix Fabri (1483): *Wanderings*, i., ii , transl. Pal. Pilg. Soc., vols. 7–10 ; Jan van Aerts (1484), cf. Neefs: *Revue Catholique*, vol. ix. 1873, p. 566 ; Joos van Ghistelle: *Tvoyage*, ed. 1572 ; Joannes de Hese (1489): *Reise* in appendix to Oppert: *Presbyter Johannes*, 1864 ; Ritter von Harff (1496–99): *Pilgerfahrt*, ed. 1860 ; Martin Baumgarten (1507): *Peregrinatio*, 1594 ; Gregor von Gaming (1507): *Ephemeris Peregrinationis*, in Pez: *Thesaurus*, 1721, ii.

of Mayence, who came east with the artist Rewich of Utrecht, whose drawings served to illustrate his patron's account of his journey. The other party included Felix Fabri, who acted as chaplain to the young Count Solms. Fabri became a friar in 1452 " out of love of St. Katherine, his spouse." On the arrival at the convent of their party mass was also celebrated in the chapel set apart for Latin use (Fabri, ii. 547).

Another pilgrim was Jan van Aerts of Malines, who sailed from Venice for the East in 1484, with a party of twenty Franciscan friars travelling with a Portuguese whom Jan referred to as the *grand facteur*. It was customary at the time for each visitor to deposit two ducats in the chest of St. Katherine. In addition to this, the grand facteur gave a thousand ducats to the monks. From the convent he and his party proceeded to Tur, where they took boat for India. But at the port of Medina they were forced to turn back owing to the enmity of the Arabs. The desire to penetrate to the far East was increasing. Mynher Joos van Ghistelles visited the convent in 1485, and went on to Tur, where he met the Venetian Bonajuto del Pan (Albani) and the Milanese Benedetto da Navara, who were on their way to Ormuz on the Persian Gulf, in order to visit the coral and pearl fisheries (Joos, p. 227). In 1487 the two Portuguese, Pedro da Cavillan and Alfonso da Paiva, came from Cairo to Tur, from where they sailed for Aden, Alfonso on his way to Ethiopia, the lesser India, in search of Prester John ; Pedro on his way to the coast of Malabar, in order to see the spice-growing districts and to collect information on Madagascar and Calicut, which he laid before his king.[1]   In 1489 Joannes de Hese passed through the convent and Tur on his way to India. The Ritter von Harff went from the convent with a letter of introduction to the monks at the convent of St. John in Tur, where he left for Mecca and Madagascar, returning to Egypt by way of the Mountains of the Moon and the course of the Nile. Von Harff illustrated the account of his journeys with many cuts, of which the one here reproduced shows the knight before St. Katherine (Fig. 21). These various writings supply information on the cost and routes of travel at the time. According to the English *Information for Pilgrims*

[1] Francesco Alvärez: *Voyage* in Ramusio: *Primo volume delle Navigazioni*, 1588, p. 236.

of about 1450, the cost of going from Venice to the Holy Land and back was 50 ducats.[1] One party of pilgrims of 1483 paid 42 ducats each on the understanding that they were allowed full time to see the Holy Places, and received two meals a day ; the other party paid 45 ducats each, their meals including wine. The party of twenty persons in 1484 paid a thousand ducats, *i.e.* 50 ducats for each person. Half the money was paid at Venice before starting, the other half on arrival at

Fig. 21.—Ritter von Harff before St. Katherine.

Jaffa. A certain Zülnhart fell ill at Venice after paying his 25 ducats, and as he was unable to sail, his money was forfeited.[2]

From Jaffa the pilgrims visited Jerusalem, where he had the option of returning home *via* Jaffa or going on to Sinai and Cairo. If he decided on this course he was allowed ten ducats on his return fare, and was provided by the Franciscans with an escort to Gaza. The charge for the round was twenty-three ducats, half of which was paid at Jerusalem,

[1] Ed. 1824, Roxburgh Club.　　　　　　[2] Röhricht : p. 311.

the other at Gaza.   An agreement was drawn up in writing
by the dragoman, the wording of which is much the same as
the one that is drawn up at the present day.   In the course
of the fifteenth century Noe Bianchi, a Franciscan, wrote a
guide book called *The Way from Venice to the Holy Sepulchre
and Mount Sinai*, which contained practical advice for
pilgrims.   It estimated the cost of going the round from Venice
to Jerusalem, Gaza, the convent, Cairo and back to Venice
at two hundred ducats, *i.e.* one hundred for general expenses,
fifty to serve in case of sickness, fifty for the sea-voyage.
The pilgrim was advised to carry a mattress (*strapontino*), a
barrel for water, a barrel for wine, and he was warned against
discussing matters of faith with infidels.

The chief danger which threatened the pilgrims was sickness.   Many died on the way.   The Italians in 1384, between
Cairo and the convent, met nine Frenchmen ;   eleven out of
their party of twenty had died on the way.   In 1483 there was
so much sickness in Gaza that many pilgrims gave up the
thought of going to the convent ;   and the young Count
Solms died on the way back (Fabri, ii. 446).   There were
other dangers.   Arnold von Harff in 1497 saw the effect of
a sandstorm which had cut off a caravan ;   the corpses of six
hundred camels and of fifty men, mauled and rotting, strewed
the roadside (p. 120).   The pilgrims were often in dread of
the Bedawyn, who swooped down on them clamouring for food,
and calling for the payment of dues for crossing their territory.
The shortage of food at the time was aggravated, no doubt, by
the curtailed largess at the convent.   The pilgrims of 1483
carried three times as much bread as they needed for themselves in order to meet all possible demands.

The routes followed by the pilgrims were the ordinary
caravan routes, subject to some variation.   Thus the pilgrims
of 1479, mindful of the raiding of a caravan by some Catalans
between Gaza and Tur, left Gaza by " a route that had not been
followed fortwenty years ; "   they went by " Rappa " (Rafa),
" Makati Nockra " (low-lying ground), where there were many
gazelles and entered the "Wadi el Arish " (Rieter, p. 91).   The
pilgrims of 1483, after leaving " Gaza," stopped at " Lebhem,"
where there was a mosque, crossed a sandy plain to "Chawatha,"
" called Cades by the Latins," where it rained, and where
there were large cisterns in ruins (Fabri, ii. 494), Ain Kadeis

of the present day. Here they entered the " Wadi Gayan "
" Gyon " of Joos, p. 147), the present Wadi el Jain, and stopped
in the "Wadi Wadalar," the scene of the Catalan outrage (Fabri,
ii. 502 ; Breydenbach, p. 187), with the " Wadi Magdabee " or
"Mahgaby " and the " Gebel Hallel," the present Gebel Hellal.
They then camped near " Magara," a name signifying holes,
where Fabri, setting out from the camp, ascended a hill on
which he found piles of stones and fluttering rags which he
thought were intended to work magic, so he tore them down
and set up a cross, but he well-nigh missed his way going
back to the tents.   The next stopping place was " Hachsene,"
an important watering station, where the party of the year
met many Arabs, and where the pilgrims stored water for three
days.   This was doubtless the present Bir Hassana, for they
were moving over white ground (noted as white chalk mounds
on the modern map) to " Minshene " (Fabri, ii. 515), modern
Minshera, where they entered the " Wadi el Arish," camping at
" El Harock " or " Barak " (Fabri, ii. 510), the " Wadi Torcko "
or " Borricko " of the travellers of 1479 (p. 697). Here they must
have been near Nakhl.   After passing the white mountain
"Chalep" or "Calpio" (perhaps the Colebmaleo of Jacopo), they
reached the white " Wadi Meshmar" (Mesmar of Joos), where
silver and gold had been worked in the mines as was shown by
the smelting.   The name corresponds to modern Gebel Megmar.
Following the " Hallicub," where the water was bad, they
crossed the wilderness "Elphogaya," and then entered the red
sandstone district of " Rackani" (or "Rochi" or "Roachyne"),
where they encamped in an exposed situation. On the following
day they descended along the steepest gorge Fabri had ever seen,
the modern Naghb el Racki.   At its foot they camped in *Rama-
thaym, i.e.* bushes, and saw a star at night which, they were
told, stood above the convent of St. Katherine.   Later stopping
places were " Scholie " or " Schoyle," " Abelharock," and
" Magara " (or " Mackera " or " Mackasea "), where the road
branched off to Tur.

The pilgrims of 1479 and 1483 noted the place where Moses
pastured his flocks near " Wackya," probably the present El
Watiyeh, which is still associated both with Nebi Saleh and
with Moses.[1]   On the twelfth day after leaving Gaza, the
pilgrims arrived at the convent.

[1] Baedeker : 1895, p. 276.

Here they were taken the usual round of the churches and
chapels, and ascended the Mountain of the Law, access to
which was now forbidden to the Jews. They repaired to the
convent of the Arbaïn from which they made the ascent of
Gebel Katrîn. They saw the stone in the shape of a Golden
Calf, about which Fabri had his doubts (ii. 594) ; the stone
on which the Tables were broken ; the convent of St. John
Climacus ; the convent of SS. Cosmas and Damianus, with its
well-kept garden ; the spot where Dathan and Abiram disappeared (ii. 590) ; the boulder with twelve channels of
water, one for each of the twelve tribes. Finally, they were
shown the relics of St. Katherine, lying in their chest, into
which they dropped two ducats each, and were allowed to
touch the relics with trinkets they had brought for this
purpose (ii. 600). The flow of sacred oil had ceased. There
was none available in 1483 ; in 1489 it was collected at the
rate of three drops a week (Joannes de Hese, p. 181). This
is the last we hear of it. Pilgrims received, instead, a piece of
cotton wool or of silk which was taken out of the chest of St.
Katherine, and steeped in the oil of the lamps. The cessation
of oil was attributed to the desecration of the shrine by the
Arabs.

From the convent some of the pilgrims went on to Cairo
by way of "El Phat," and the white hills of "Lacrara,"
where they joined the caravan road coming from Tur. Further
stations along the road were "Enaspo" (Wadi Nasb), "Ho-
renden" or "Dorenden" (Wadi Gharandel), "Werdachii"
(Werdan), and "Marath" or "Merach," perhaps the old
Mara, and the present Ayun Musa. These stopping-places
are the same as those chosen by pilgrims and travellers at
the present day.

CHAPTER XVII

THE LATER HISTORY OF THE CONVENT

THE size of the caravans that plied between Sinai and Egypt were a source of wonder to the mediæval pilgrim. This development of trade received a check in the sixteenth century, through the discovery of the sea-route to India by the Portuguese. Prince Henry of Portugal († 1460) brought the west coast of Africa within reach of his country. In the year 1487 Bartholomew Diaz sailed from Portugal to the Cape of Good Hope, which Vasco da Gama doubled ten years later, sailing on to Calicut. Every year a fleet now left Lisbon for India, where spicery was shipped direct for Portugal.

This trade detracted from the resources of the Sultan, and spelt ruin to the seaports of Italy. In 1503 the Sultan addressed a letter to the Pope in which he threatened destruction to the Holy Places, including the Holy Sepulchre and the convent of Sinai, if the Portuguese were not interfered with. But King Manuel of Portugal induced the Pope to ignore the letter, and, on his side, offered spicery free of duty to the Venetians, if they fetched it at Lisbon, instead of Alexandria. But the Venetians, averse to the change, persuaded the Sultan to set up a direct communication by boat between Suez and India, and a tower was accordingly built to fortify Suez. Tur was passed over; its days as a port on the way to India were drawing to a close, for the Portuguese were determined to monopolise the trade with India. They seized a boat coming from Egypt with the 24,000 ducats it contained. They fitted out a war fleet (1504) which enforced their superior claims in India, and attacked all other shipping. In 1509 they entered the Red Sea with their war fleet, and interfered with the pilgrims to Mecca. It was in vain that the Venetians,

whose annual turn-over at Alexandria fell from 600,000 to
100,000 ducats in 1511, pleaded with the Sultan to diminish
the tax on Eastern goods, so as to enable them to compete with
the Portuguese.   The Sultanate was at the mercy of short-
sighted and intriguing emirs, and was weakening.   The
conquering Ottoman Turk was steadily gaining ground.
There had been rejoicing at Cairo when Constantinople, in
1453, fell to the power of Islam, but the struggle for supremacy
soon afterwards began between the Egyptian and the Ottoman
Sultanate.   In 1516 the Ottoman Sultan Selim († 1520)
occupied Damascus, and in the following year he advanced
along the road of El Arish with wheeled transport.   After
defeating the Mameluks at Radunieh in 1517, he led his
disciplined janissaries into Cairo, where he appropriated the
sacred banner of Islam and the relics, which he removed to
Constantinople.

In the meantime the shipping languished even at Suez.
Odoardo Barbosa, who was sent to Egypt to report on matters
of navigation to the merchants of Italy in 1516, mentioned
Suez as the station for spicery, but added that the traffic had
almost ceased.[1] Certainly the Ottoman Sultan, roused to
the needs of the hour, made the attempt to facilitate the transit
of Eastern goods by cutting through the isthmus of Suez.
He also built a castle at Suez in order to defend himself against
the Portuguese.   But the centre of the Ottoman rule was no
longer Cairo, but Constantinople, to which the wealthy more
and more migrated.   Egypt was placed under a pasha, who was
appointed at Constantinople, and who was frequently changed
so as to anticipate any scheme on his part of making himself
into an independent ruler.   Cairo retained its university and
remained a centre of learning ; its halcyon days as a centre
of art and luxury were at an end.

The Suez canal was still in course of construction in 1529,
but was never finished,[2] and no term was set on the advance of
the Portuguese.   In 1541 Dom John (João) de Castro, who bore
the proud title of viceroy of India, sailed up the Red Sea with
a fleet, intending to attack Suez, but when he espied the
fort and the ships at anchor there, he turned back.   In
sailing up the Gulf of Suez, and again in sailing down, Dom John

[1] Barbosa : Letter in Ramusio : *Delle Nav.*, 1888, p. 291.
[2] Heyd : *Levanthandel*, ii. 540.

stopped at Tur, where he communed with a monk of Sinai, who told him that the convent was occupied by monks of the order of Montserrat (*sic*), and that the body of St. Katherine had been removed to Cairo. Another informant denied all knowledge of this fact. Dom John was a man of some pretensions, who identified Suez as Heroöpolis, and Tur as Aelana of classic times. His observations were laid down in a *Description of the Lands bordering on the Red Sea*, which Sir Walter Raleigh considered of such importance, that he had it translated into English.[1]

Throughout this period we hear little of pilgrims and of the convent. The spirit of the Reformation was abroad, and the thought of St. Katherine was losing its hold on the imagination of Europe. Gregor, prior of the Carthusian house at Gaming, who came to the convent in 1507 together with Martin Baumgarten, stated that the monks were miserable owing to the clamorous Arabs, who occupied the mosque and kept their festival on the Mount of the Law as already related. In the estimation of Gregor, the monks of Sinai professed the order of St. Basil, but, he declared, they would be glad to be taken under the protection of Rome (p. 498). About the year 1546 the learned Belon of Mans, who travelled in the interest of science and archæology, visited Sinai, which he mentioned in his *Observations de certaines singularités*, etc., a work that reflects the spirit of the new age. Belon remarked on the Franciscan settlement at Gaza, the arsenal at Suez, and the canal of thirty miles' length. In the convent he found about sixty monks.[2]

Of the bishops at this period we know very little. There was an interregnum of about thirty years before 1540, which may be connected with the rule of Sultan Selim. According to information preserved at the convent, he abstracted the original *firmân* which was supposed to have been given to the convent by Mohammad. Sultan Selim was responsible for the fortified stations along the route for pilgrims from Egypt to Mecca, of which one was built at Ajrud near Suez, the second at Nakhl, on the high desert, and the third at Akaba, which was situated east of the ancient Aila. These stations were reckoned about three days' journey from one

---

[1] Ed. Purchas: *His Pilgrims*, reprint 1905, vii. 236–310.
[2] Belon: *Observations de certaines singularités*, 1554, p. 126.

another, and the road continued in use till recent times.
But whatever the reason, the bishop of Sinai at this time
incurred the displeasure of the surrounding prelates. Marcus,
the Cyprian, who was appointed in 1540, perhaps owing to
some fault of his own (Nectarius called him κάκος),[1] was
deposed by a synod held in Egypt under the auspices of the
patriarchs of Alexandria, of Cairo, and of Jerusalem, and the
bishopric of Sinai was declared abrogated.[2]

But a new protector to the monks now arose in the Tsar
of Muscovy, who, when Constantinople fell to the Turks,
took it upon himself to protect the orthodox. In the year
1547 Gregorius, a monk of Sinai, visited Moscow, where he
complained of the tax which the Turk levied on the convent.
The Tsar at the time was Ivan the Terrible (1533–84), who
forthwith arranged that Gennadius, archdeacon of St. Sophia,
at Novgorod, together with the merchant Posniakow and
another should visit the patriarch of Alexandria and the
archbishop (sic) of Sinai, and present them with 1000 ducats
each. At the convent, after praying at the shrine of St.
Katherine, they spread over it a covering of gold brocade,
a gift of the Tsar. Posniakow, to whom we owe an account
of the embassy, looked upon the monks as connected with
St. Basil, and described the mosque inside the convent as
originally a church of St. Basil.[3]

The Muscovite further arranged that a caravan bearing
food should be annually despatched from Cairo to the convent,
at his expense, as we learn from the account of the German
pilgrim Wormbser, who went from Egypt to the convent in
the year 1561 (Reissbuch, 1609, p. 396 ff.). His companion, Count
Loewenstein, on his return to Alexandria, there asked for an
official attestation of having been the Long Pilgrimage, which
he included in the account of his journey (Ibid. p. 393). These
travellers in 1561 found between thirty and forty monks at
the convent, but were told that these sometimes left the place
altogether because of the clamorous Arabs (Loewenstein, p. 369).
It had recently stood empty four or five years (Ibid., p. 369).
Another party of Germans, who reached the convent in 1565,
actually found it empty and its gates walled up. They were

[1] Nectarius: Epit., p. 212.
[2] Perigraphe, p. 153.
[3] Voyage, ed. 1889 in Khitowo: Itinéraires russes en Orient, p. 288.

met outside by a monk who, apprized of their coming, hurried over from Tur to act as their guide. From the height of the Mount of the Law they looked down on the empty convent with its deserted garden (*Ibid.*, Helfferich, p. 726).

Owing to Muscovite influence a change was effected. A letter is extant drafted by Jeremiah II, patriarch of Constantinople (1572–78), which bears the signature of the patriarch of Antioch, the patriarch of Jerusalem, and others by which the bishopric of Sinai was restored.[1] The decision was based on the decree of Justinian which is dated to the year 551 and is preserved at the convent, but which is looked upon as a forgery. Anyhow, a prelate was reinstated in the person of Eugenius (1565–83), who, in the capacity of "bishop of Sinai and Raithou," wrote to Emperor Maximilian II (1564–76), declaring that the monks were called upon to pay 5000 ducats to the Turkish Sultan, which were they unable to raise. The outcome of the appeal is not recorded. They probably made an appeal also to King Henri III of France (1574–89).[2] In the year 1579 Eugenius of Sinai was in Jerusalem, where the patriarch Germanus abdicated because of old age.[3]

Direct intercourse with Russia continued. We hear of one Korobeïnikoff who was in Sinai in 1583, and again in 1593. It was, perhaps, with the help of the Muscovite that Bishop Anastasius I (1583–92) laid down the mosaic pavement in the convent church, which had been destroyed by Arab treasure-seekers. Anastasius was succeeded by Laurentius (1592–1617), but Melitos, patriarch of Alexandria, objected to his appointment, whereupon he appealed to Sophronios VI, patriarch of Jerusalem (1579–1606), who ratified his appointment.[4] Perhaps the gates of the convent were walled up in connection with these difficulties, and anyone wishing to enter was now hauled up by means of a rope and a pulley. Henri Castale who visited Sinai in 1600, was the first to describe the arrangement, which continued till the British occupation of Egypt. Castale, in the account of his journey, enlarged on

[1] *Perigraphe*, pp. 156–160.
[2] Lammens: *Mélanges*, p. 503.
[3] Lequien: *Or. Chr.*, iii. 517.
[4] Cf. Dobschütz: *Sammelhandschrift* in *Byz. Zeitschrift*, vol. 15, 1906, pp. 247-51.

the starving men and women in the desert.   He found one
starving monk in the convent.[1]

But things now improved under Bishop Joasaph, who
ruled from 1617 to 1658, and travellers gave a better
account of the convent.

The thought of the " inscriptions of the children of Irsael "
brought Neitzschitz into the desert about the year 1639.   He
was a Lutheran to whom " many of the stories were fables."
He was received by the " archbishop Joasaph " and found
twenty-three monks at the convent, who distributed food
daily to between fifty and a hundred Arabs.[2]   The thought
of the inscription was prominent also in the mind of Balthazar
de Monconys, who, in 1647, visited the convent.   Here he
remarked on the tunic of gold brocade embroidered with
pearls and on the splendid tiaras, presents of the Muscovite,
that were worn by Joasaph.[3]   Again, Thévenot came to the
convent in 1658, and saw a silver chest, a gift from the empress
Anna of Russia, in which the relics of St. Katherine were now
enshrined.   Thévenot related that on some days as many as
150 Arabs, on others as many as 400, clamouring for food,
assembled outside the convent.   He also related that the
Turks had destroyed the church which the monks owned at
Tur (perhaps that of St. John the Baptist), in order to make
room for a fort where an *aga* was stationed, who had the
command of cannon.[4]

A papal bull, apparently the last, was granted to the
convent by Pope Urban VIII (1623–37).   It confirmed the
monks in their various possessions, and has the additional
interest that it enumerated the popes who previously granted
bulls to the monks.   They were Honorius III (1216–27),
Gregory IX (1227–41), Paul II (1458–64), Innocent VIII
(1484–92), Julius II (1503–13), Leo IX (1513–19), and Paul III
(1534–50).

During the rule of Joasaph, Nectarius, a Cretan by birth and
a man of considerable ability, came to the convent, the interests
of which he furthered in various ways.   The Vaivode Basil
(1634–61), of Moldavia, was encouraging the establishment of

---

[1] *Le saint voyage*, 1619, p. 564.
[2] Neitzschitz : *Siebenjahr Wanderung*, ed. 1674, p. 544.
[3] Monconys : *Journal de Voyage*, ed. 1665, p. 164.
[4] Thévenot, Jean de : *Voyages*, 1689, vol. v. p. 532.

Greek schools in his dominion. Nectarius visited Athens, Bukarest, and Jassy, where the monks of Sinai now built priories and secured a lasting foothold. It was probably Nectarius who definitely secured the title and standing of an archbishop to the ruler of Sinai. The title had been applied to Simeon as early as 1211 by the doge of Venice in connection with the property which the convent held in Crete, but the rulers continued to style themselves bishop. However, the title once claimed was retrospectively applied. Nectarius, after his return to the convent, compiled an *Epitome of history from the earliest times*, with special chapters on the convent and a list of its rulers. They are all designated as archbishops. It was probably due to Nectarius, also, that many MSS. were brought from Crete and elsewhere and added to the convent library. At the convent itself literary activity was resumed, and we hear of a gift of paper to the monks that was conveyed there on camel-back.[1]

At the death of Joasaph, Nectarius was chosen as his successor. He was in Gaza on his way to Jerusalem to seek confirmation of his appointment at the hands of the patriarch Païsios, when he was met by delegates from Jerusalem, bearing the news that Païsios was dead, and that Nectarius was chosen patriarch. As Joasaph died in 1658, and the meeting happened in April 1660, the intercourse between the sees seems to have been attended with difficulty. The rule at the convent therefore devolved on Ananias (1658–68), who was followed by Joannicus (1668–1703).

According to Lacroix, the Muscovite fell out with the patriarch of Constantinople in 1671, and summoned to Moscow several prelates, among them "Antoninus, bishop of Sinai." He dared not refuse, and was kept in Moscow for over a year.[2] But no prelate of this name appears in the list of the bishops.

About this time the Papacy made renewed efforts at propaganda, with the help of the Franciscans. Pope Innocent XI (1675–89) entered into correspondence with the patriarch of Cairo with a view to winning over the Copts of Egypt to the Roman Catholic faith, and Francesco Maria of Salerno spent several years in Cairo where he established a school. He also visited Sinai, but the Copts found it impossible

[1] Monconys: *Journal*, p. 203.
[2] Lacroix: *Le Turchie Chrétienne*, 1695.

to accept the declaration of faith that was submitted to them, and nothing came of it.[1]

Joannicus, in 1672, was in Bethlehem where he subscribed to a declaration against Calvin, in which the Maronites, the Copts and the Armenian Christians joined.   In 1675 he went on an embassy to Turkey.   He also engaged in correspondence with Ignatius, archbishop of Ochrida in Serbia, on the *firmân* which had been granted to the monks of Sinai by the emperor Justinian.   A visit to Moldavia resulted in the gift of the property called Rimineke to the monks of Sinai by Vaivode Brancovan († 1719).   The traveller Poncet, who visited the convent about the year 1699, coming from Sherm, was received by Joannicus, who was in his ninety-third year and paralytic. Like other travellers Poncet was hauled into the convent by means of the seat attached to a rope.   He was treated to some of the liqueur called *arac*, which was made by the monks out of the fermented juice of the date.[2]

The prelate in succession to Joannicus was Cosmas I of Chalcedon, who became patriarch of Constantinople within a year of his election, but he soon abdicated and returned to the convent where he spent the rest of his days under Athanasius II of Bari (1706–18).   The next prelate was Joannicus II of Mytilene (1718–22), during the term of whose rule Jeremiah, patriarch of Constantinople, was deposed by the vizier and exiled to Sinai.   He was staying there at the time of Bishop Pococke's visit (i. 150).

It was probably Athanasius of Bari who received the Franciscan prefect Claude Sicard of the mission *De Propaganda Fide*, wearing an exquisite crown.   The Franciscan prefect wrote a short account of his visit which attracted the attention of Bishop Pococke and was translated into English by Bishop Clayton in 1753.   This translation was addressed to the Society of Antiquaries in London, and Bishop Clayton offered the sum of £500, spread over five years, to assist in an exploration of Mount Sinai.   But no definite step was taken in the matter, its chief result being to add to the Biblical explorers of the peninsula.

[1] Gubernatis (Dom. de) Orbis Seraphicus: *Historia de Tribus Ordin.*, 1888, ii. 293, 310.
[2] Poncet, C. J.: *Journey* in Pinkerton: *Voyages*, vol. 15, 1814, p. 105.

Chief among these was Bishop Pococke, whose *Description of the East*, first published in 1743, attained considerable celebrity. Several chapters were devoted to an account of Sinai and the progress of the Israelites. It contains a careful description of the monastic buildings with several plans. Bishop Pococke, like other travellers before and since, accepted the sites pointed out by the monks as the actual spots mentioned in the Biblical narrative, regardless of the impossibilities implied. He only questioned the spot where Dathan and Abiram were swallowed, remarking that when this happened they had left the desert of Sinai (i. 145).

Owing to the difficulties of dealing with the claims of the Bedawyn, the prelates of Sinai now found it preferable to take up their residence in one of the dependencies of the convent.

Nicephorus Mortales, surnamed Glaukos (1729–49), was from Crete, to which he returned and where he died. His body was conveyed to the convent for interment. The next prelate was Constantius (1749–59), who resided for the most part in Moldavia under Vaivode Michael, paying an occasional visit to Sinai. On one occasion he was accompanied by Khalil Sabag, who wrote an account of his visit. The next prelate Cyrillus II (1759–90) dwelt in Smyrna, Jerusalem and Moldavia. He was in contact with Carsten Niebuhr, who visited Sinai in 1762, where he was the first European to visit and describe the great ravines at Serabit. Cyrillus was in relation also with the traveller Volney, who visited the convent in 1783, where he found fifty monks.

It was owing to the efforts of Cyrillus II that the standing of the convent of Sinai as an independent centre was definitely established. A synod met in Constantinople in 1782, which declared in favour of its autonomy. The archbishop is elected by a council of the monks, who manage the affairs of the convent in Sinai and its branch establishment in Cairo. The archbishop is always selected from the priests of the monastery. He is consecrated as bishop by the patriarch of Jerusalem in consequence of the ancient connection, and he becomes one of the four independent archbishops of the Greek Church, the others being at Cyprus, Moscow and Ochrida.[1]

Cyrillus II was the last prelate who paid a visit to the convent for over a hundred years. The reason was that

[1] Robinson: i. p. 130.

large sums and gifts had to be presented to the Arabs by the new prelate on his installation. These were so considerable that the monks, in their impoverished state, were unable to raise them. Perhaps owing to this difficulty, there was an interregnum of four years, between the death of Cyrillus in 1790 and the establishment as prelate of Dorotheus of Byzantium (1794–96), after whose death there was again an interregnum of eight years.

CHAPTER XVIII

SINAI IN THE NINETEENTH CENTURY

THE close of the eighteenth century witnessed events in Egypt which directly affected the conditions of life in Sinai; they further reduced the man of the desert in his resources.

Since the conquest of Egypt by the Turks in 1517 the country was administered by a pasha who was appointed by the Sultan at Constantinople. But the order of the Sultan to Ali Bey to join in a war against Russia in 1769 met with a direct refusal; the Egyptian saw his chance of proclaiming his independence. The revolt of the pasha of Egypt gave Bonaparte an ostensible reason for occupying Alexandria in 1796. Bonaparte's imagination was fired by the thought of incorporating Egypt, the land of antiquity, in his world dominion. As part of this wider scheme he addressed a letter as *général en chef* to the monks of Sinai in 1798, in which he took them under his protection, "to the end," as he said, "that they should hand on to future races the tradition of his conquest, as he was filled with respect for Moses and the Jews, and because the monks were learned men living in the barbarity of the desert." He further decreed that henceforth the Arab Bedawyn had no claim whatever on the monks, that they should be left to devote themselves unmolested to the claims of their religion, that they should be exempt from paying tribute or tax on imports or exports on the produce of their property in Schio (*i.e.* Chios) and Cyprus, that they should freely enjoy their rights in Syria and in Cairo, and that their ruler should be independent of the patriarch.[1]

At the order of Bonaparte the gentlemen Coutelle and

[1] Renaudin, Dom: *Le monastère de Ste. Catherine* in *Révue de l'Orient Chrétien*, 1900, p. 319-21.

184

Rosières were sent on a tour of inspection to collect material
for the work which he planned. On this tour they came
to the convent of Sinai in 1800, where they found six monks
and twenty-two lay brothers in residence. The east wall of
the convent, built by Justinian, had collapsed. By order of
General Kléber at Cairo, the monk Hallil, with forty-two
masons and a hundred and fifty camels, were dispatched from
Cairo to do the necessary repair. The camels were furnished
by the Towarah.[1]

In the meantime Nelson, scouring the seas in search of
the French fleet, came upon it near the coast of Egypt, and
attacked and scattered it at the Battle of the Nile (Oct., 1798).
The Turks, aware that Bonaparte's descent on Egypt was
prompted by his desire for self-aggrandisement, felt called
upon to declare war on the French in Egypt (1799). Hereupon Bonaparte, with nearly the whole of his army, marched
along the desert road to Gaza and took Jaffa by assault, but
a few months later he was in full retreat. A Turkish army soon
afterwards reached Aboukir and joined forces with the
British fleet, but Bonaparte inflicted a crushing defeat on
them. He then left Egypt leaving his army in charge of
General Kléber. But a further expedition was launched by
the Turk, one detachment of troops was landed at Damietta,
another under Yussuf Pasha approached by the El Arish road.
They were defeated by the French, but General Kléber soon
afterwards was assassinated (June, 1808). The English now
effected a landing at Aboukir (March, 1801), and the French,
after some struggles, evacuated the country.

In Egypt itself confusion reigned. The Mameluks were
regaining their influence, when Mehemed Ali († 1849), the leader
of an Albanian corps, secured the adherence of the sheykhs
and claimed the Pashalik with the support of the French. An
expedition made by the British to oppose him in 1807 mis-
carried. In 1811 he caused a massacre of the Mameluks and
extended his influence by carrying war into Arabia and invading Syria. The interference of the English reduced, but
did not break, his power. In 1841 he secured the hereditary
sovereignty of Egypt.

The period of upheaval naturally re-acted on the desert
and rendered travelling unsafe. Seetzen visited the convent

[1] *Ord. Survey*, i. 200.

under Russian orders and found the road dangerous. There were twenty-five monks in the convent, who longed for the end of the Turkish government and the establishment of European influence in Cairo.[1] Seetzen was murdered in Syria on a later journey. Again the traveller Boutin was in Serabit in 1811, where he scrawled his name on a stone in the temple where Rüppell found it. Boutin also was murdered in Syria. Burckhardt travelled in the disguise of a Bedawyn and repeatedly visited Sinai, and the convent (1816, 1822). Both Rüppell and Burckhardt travelled in the interest of geography.

With the return of more settled conditions travellers became more numerous. Lord Prudhoe and Major Felix (1827) were among those who visited the ruins of Serabit. The account of their journey was lost, but Lord Prudhoe, after inspecting the temple ruins, was the first and, as far as I am aware, the only traveller to whom it occurred that this might be the sanctuary that was visited by the Israelites. The fact was recorded by Edward Robinson who came into Sinai in the interest of Biblical research in 1838 and 1852 (i. 79) and who was himself immensely impressed by the ruins at Serabit. Other travellers who made a prolonged stay were Laborde and Linant (1828), to whom we owe the first detailed and illustrated account of the convent church, its architecture, its great mosaics and its numerous side chapels ; Tischendorf, who secured the famous MS. for Petrograd, as mentioned above ; Bartlett, whose rapid visit in 1839 established interesting geological facts, more especially with regard to the lie of the land between Sinai and Syria ; and Lepsius, who came into Sinai in 1845 for the express purpose of copying the hieroglyph inscriptions at Maghara and Serabit, which he incorporated in his *Denkmäler* (1860).

Under the rule of Mehemed Ali safety was restored to the *hadj* route across Sinai by the rebuilding of the forts at Adjrud (near Suez), Nakhl and Akaba. The settlement of a garrison brought regularity of transport which reacted favourably on the Bedawyn who undertook it. Mehemed Ali, also, was favourably disposed towards the convent. His nephew, Abbas Pasha, who succeeded him in 1849, visited Sinai in 1853, and formed the plan of building himself a summer residence on Mount Horeb. A road was therefore planned leading up

[1] Seetzen : *Reisen*, 1807, vol. 3, on Sinai.

from Tur on the coast, which crossed the desert and then led through the relatively luxurious valley of Hebron, with its many streams and the tamarisk grove of Solaf. It was partly completed in 1854, when the Pasha was assassinated. His successor Said Pasha (1854–63), was in friendly relations with Ferdinand Lesseps, whom he zealously supported in the scheme for constructing a canal through the Isthmus of Suez. The enterprise was financed by French and Turkish subscriptions, and was at the outset worked by means of forced labour, later with the help of modern engineering appliances. The canal was completed under Ishmael Pasha (1863–79) in 1869, and the British Government became a large shareholder. Ishmael Pasha was an Oriental despot who depleted the treasury and robbed the people, but who modernised Egypt by building schools, laying down railways, and setting up telegraph communications. In return for a large annual tribute he was raised to the rank of Khedive, or viceroy, of Egypt by the Sultan in 1867. But the financial diffiulties, in which he became involved, were such that France and England brought pressure to bear on him and finally deposed him. He was succeeded by his son Tewfik Pasha (1879–92).

Among the visitors to the peninsula in 1845 was Major Macdonald, who came to inspect the turquoise that was left, and who settled near the mines at Maghara in 1855, where he remained ten years. His mining was done with the help of Bedawyn labour. He took considerable interest in the great inscriptions, and it was not he, but a French engineer, who took up the work after he left, who destroyed by blasting a large number of valuable rock inscriptions, including those of King Khufu and of the Pharaohs of the Sixth Dynasty. The general interest taken in the peninsula led to the sending out an expedition under General Wilson in 1868, who engaged in a survey of Sinai, *i.e.* the mountains of the south, under the auspices of the Palestine Exploration Fund. The work was published in 1871 and contains text, maps and a number of photographic views. Among those working on the Survey was the Rev. F. W. Holland, who had previously stayed in Sinai in 1861 and 1867 ; and the distinguished Arabic scholar, Prof. E. H. Palmer, who made the acquaintance of Sir Richard Burton on this occasion, and who was brought into prolonged contact with the Bedawyn. Prof. Palmer published in 1871 a special account that deals with the story of the Israelites in Sinai under the title *The Desert of Exodus*. Another visitor to the peninsula was the Egyptologist, Prof. Ebers, who published his work *Durch Gosen zum Sinai* in 1872. The interest in geography now caused travellers to journey along different routes and to explore different parts of the peninsula, but, in spite of the work accomplished then or undertaken since, the central part of the peninsula is still insufficiently known.

Fig. 22.—Sulyman abu Silm, a Bedawy.

From these writers we gain a further insight into the state of things at the convent, and the attitude of the Bedawyn.

The number of monks at the convent remained much the same. Seetzen found twenty-five monks there and a "guardian" who acted for the absentee bishop (i. 73) ; Edward Robinson found twenty monks in residence (i. 131) ; Lepsius in 1845 found twenty-five ; Ebers in 1871 found twenty-eight. In 1890 there were between twenty and thirty.

Of the property that is at present owned by the monks I fail to find a complete list. At different periods mention is made of priories in Alexandria, Jerusalem, Tripoli, Gaza, Constantinople, Crete and Cyprus, besides the house owned at Cairo.[1] Wolff, in 1839, mentioned property held by the monks at Constantinople, Cyprus, Belgrad, Bukarest, Jassy, Athens, India and Calcutta ; [2] Robinson mentioned houses at Bengal, Golconda, Crete and Cyprus (p. 549). According to Burckhardt the monks received their supplies from Gaza and Cairo.

After an interregnum of eight years Constantius II ruled as archbishop from 1804 to 1859, and was succeeded by Cyrillus III (1859–67). The next archbishop, Callistratus (1867–85), was the first prelate who returned to the convent in 1872, but his installation was attended by difficulties. His successor, Porphyrius, fell out with the patriarch of Alexandria, who caused him to be expelled from Cairo. He was in residence at the convent in the winter of 1905–6.

Modern accounts give a further insight into the temper of the men of the desert.

The pilgrims of the Middle Ages generally dreaded the Bedawyn who were apt to swoop down on them, clamouring for dues, as they passed from the territory of one tribe into that of another, but we hear of few excesses committed by them. Burckhardt, Prof. Palmer and Sir Richard Burton gave an account of the different tribes.

The Bedawyn of southern Sinai are collectively known as Towarah from Towa, Arabic for mountain, as distinct from the Tiyaha, or Bedawyn of the Plain and the tribes who hold the northern districts.

Among the Towarah Prof. Palmer included (1) the Sawaliheh, who are divided into three clans or families, of which each has its sheykh, so that there are three sheykhs to each tribe. In 1870 the sheykhs of the Sawaliheh were Fatir, Kadir Ibn Simhan and Abu Farh, of whom Fatir was *agyd* or commander-in-chief of all the military operations undertaken by the Towarah generally. Burton spoke of the Salihi (*i.e.* Sawaliheh or Benu Saleh) as the principal tribe of the Sinaitic Bedawyn.

The next tribe, included among the Towarah, were (2) the

---

[1] Gregoriades: pp. 88–117.
[2] Cited Weill : *Presqu'île*, pp. 250, footnote.

Auled Said, who include several families. The sheykhs in 1870 were Hasan Ibn 'Amir and Embarek ed Dheiri.[1]

The next tribe mentioned were (3) the Garrasheh, who are principally found in the neighbourhood of Wadi Feiran. Their chief sheykh, Ibn Nasir, was made responsible to the Egyptian government for the good conduct of the Towarah. He had died when the expedition returned to England. Husein Abu Ridhwan was the only remaining sheykh in 1870, Mansur Ibn Gormah also having recently died.

Another tribe were (4) the Aleyat (or Aliki), whose district was the neighbourhood of the (western) Wadi Nasb. Their sheykhs were Suleiman Ibn Emdakkhal, Juma Abu Shawish, and Amdan Abu Ukri. This tribe was described as not numerous by Prof. Palmer.

There were further, (5) the Emzeineh, (Muzaineh) the descendants of an illustrious tribe who are regarded by the Towarah as comparative strangers, though not excluded from the right of intermarriage. They roam over the eastern coast of the peninsula and are said to have come into Sinai from the Hedjaz in comparatively recent times. According to Sir Richard Burton five persons, ancestors of the Muzaineh, were forced by a blood feud to fly from their native country and landed at Sherm, where they were received by the Aleyat. With these they jointly own the palm trees at Dahab, and the rights of transporting the people landing at Dahab and Sherm. "Anyone who knows the Bedawyn," wrote Sir Richard, " can see that the Muzaineh are pure blood. Their brows are broad, their faces narrow, their features regular, and their eyes of moderate size, whereas the other Towarah clans are as palpably Egyptian. They are of an impure race, Egypto-Arabs, whereas their neighbour, the Hedjazi, is the pure Syrian or Mesopotamian."

Besides these tribes Prof. Palmer named (6) the Auled Shahin as the branch of the Towarah, who occupy the country immediately around Tur and the mountain which borders on the plain of El Kaa ; they are, properly speaking, a branch of the Aleyat.

There are also, (7) the Gebeliyeh, the so-called serfs of the convent, who are held to be the lineal descendants of the

---

[1] Palmer, Prof. in *Ord. Survey*, I, p. 456, ff. ; Burton : *Pilgrimage* (1855), ed. 1879, p. 100, ff. ; Burckhardt : *Notes on the Bedouin*, 1830.

four hundred Wallachian and Egyptian slaves whom the emperor settled in the peninsula. Their district comprises the Wadi esh Sheikh and the immediate neighbourhood of the convent. Their chief sheykhs in 1870 were Awwad Ibn Atiyeh, Eid Ibn Suad and Suleiman Ibn Ghanaim.

Of these tribes the Saidi and the Aleyat are the recognised *ghufara*, or protectors of the convent. The MS. account of 1710 calls them Waled Sahin, three tribes, the sons of Saleh, *i.e.* the Selim, the Saidi and the Haliq (Aleyat). These met at the annual festival at the tomb of Nebi Saleh.

The fluctuations of the tribes are insufficiently known. In Burckhardt's days Harun Ibn Amer, sheykh of the Saidi, was accounted one of the most powerful sheykhs of the Towarah (p. 594).

Of the Towarah generally, Sir R. Burton wrote that in the reign of Mehemed Ali no governor of Suez dared to flog or lay hands on a Turi, whatever offence he might have committed in the town of Suez. Later the wild man's sword was taken from him before he was allowed to enter the gates. In his estimation "the most good-humoured and sociable of men, they delight in a jest and may readily be managed by kindness and courtesy. Yet they are passionate, nice on the point of honour, revengeful and easily offended when their peculiar prejudices are misunderstood. I have always found them pleasant companions, and deserving of respect, for their hearts are good and their courage is beyond a doubt" (p. 102).

In distinction to the Towarah or men of the mountain, the Bedawyn further north are known as Tiyaha, or men of the plain, who go south as far as Nakhl. They have for their neighbours the Terrebin, a powerful tribe, whose territory extends from about forty miles south-east of Suez on the Sinai road as far as Gaza in the north. There are also the Heiwatt occupying the land between Akaba and Nakhl, who have a bad reputation for raiding, and their neighbours the Anazeh, whose pasture grounds extend from about Medina in Arabia to Palmyra in Syria, including the Arabah. Another wealthy tribe are the Howeitat who can raise as many as twelve hundred camels.

The difficulty of dealing with the Bedawyn, was shown by the events that attended the rising of Arabi in Egypt, in 1880.

When Tewfik became Khedive in 1879 dissatisfaction reigned. A military revolution broke out in Cairo, and Arabi Bey, a fellah officer, arose determined to diminish European influence. When rioting began at Alexandria the Khedive sought the protection of the British Fleet, and Sir Garnet Wolseley occupied the Suez Canal, whereupon Cairo surrendered. But the dread of Arabi's influence among the men of the desert led the British Government to request Prof. Palmer to bring his influence to bear on the Bedawyn of Et Tîh. His work in the Ordnance Survey had brought him into friendly relations with many of the sheykhs, and he was instructed to prevent them from joining the Egyptian rebels. With a *firmân* signed by Tewfik, Prof. Palmer left Jaffa as Abdallah Effendi, and crossed the peninsula to Suez, being conducted by Hamdan, the head man of the Tiyaha, and on his way met the great sheykh of the Heiwatt. His plan was to raise 10,000 of the Tiyaha and Terabin to fight Arabi. From Suez he therefore departed carrying the sum of £3000 in gold in order to buy camels, and arranged for a great meeting of the sheykhs. It was in vain that Sheykh Ode Ismaileh of the Aleyat, and Umdakhl, a minor sheykh, advised him not to go. He and his three companions were lured into an ambush in the Wadi Sudr, and were murdered, August, 1882.

Following upon the mission of Prof. Palmer to Sinai was the expedition to the Soudan for which General Gordon volunteered. He was killed in 1885, whereupon General Kitchener set out to reconquer the Sudan and occupied Khartoum. In 1892 Tewfik in Egypt was succeeded by Hussein Kamel. A misunderstanding with Turkey in connection with the Sinaitic frontier caused a passing difficulty in the year 1906-7. The Turco-Egyptian frontier was drawn from Rafa, now in Egypt, to the Gulf of Akaba, Akaba itself being included in the domain over which Turkey claimed supremacy. At this it stood at the outbreak of the Great War.

The population of the whole of the peninsula at the time was estimated as below 40,000 persons, including the settled inhabitants of El Arish, the Gebeliyeh (400-500), and the rest of the Bedawyn. From a military point of view these were looked upon as of small importance, except as possible secret

¹ Besant, W.: *Edward Henry Palmer*, 1883.

agents and scouts, and no effort was apparently made to organise them. Although Sinai was politically an Egyptian dependency, with the frontier line between Rafa and Akaba, the Suez Canal was chosen as the means of defending Egypt, and bridgeheads were constructed along it, chief of which was the one at Kantara. The peninsula was therefore open to the Turks, who advanced across it along three routes, *i.e.* along the coast, along the pilgrim road from Akaba by way of Nakhl, and by a route half-way between the pilgrim route and the Mediterranean. Nakhl became a Turkish military centre. The attacks made at different points along the canal were defeated. The Turk, from the first, engaged the help of the Bedawyn of the eastern desert, but he failed to raise much enthusiasm among them. Only the Terabin, the Ayayme, and some of the sub-tribes of the Howeitat supplied irregular lines, the Ruala and the Anazeh promised to defend Syria, other tribes failed altogether. When a raiding party of Turks advanced from Nakhl on Tur, they were joined by some Bedawyn from Midian and Sinai, who were tempted by the promise of loot. On the way, they requisitioned food at the convent, but they found Egyptian troops in occupation of Tur and were repulsed.

The advance along the shore of the Mediterranean, and expeditions from the bridgeheads and secured posts, engaged the Allied forces in 1916. Ayun Musa was fortified and connected with Suez by means of a light railway, and a railway was constructed along the Mediterranean. In the course of this progress the walls and water cisterns on which the enemy depended were naturally destroyed, and one does not wonder to find the Bedawyn acting in concert with the Turk in their defence. It was not till January, 1917, that Rafa was captured, and the Turk swept out of northern Sinai. Along the eastern frontier the Arabs were prepared to side with the Allies. As early as 1916 Prince Hussein of Mecca organised his forces to resist the Turk, but his progress was indifferent, when he was sought out by Capt. Lawrence, who urged him to advance and persuaded Auda Ibn Tayyi, the great sheykh of the Howeitat, to act in concert with him. The result was a camel charge on the fort of Akaba, which wiped out the Turkish battalion stationed there, and freed the Arab and the Allies from a centre of enemy plotting. By

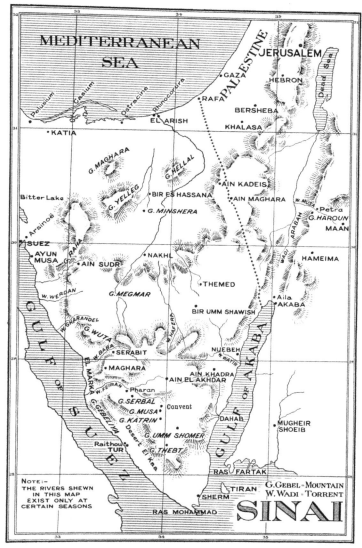

Fig. 23.—Map of the Peninsula.

their action the Arabs made a further step in realising themselves as a nation.[1]

In the light of these recent events, cne is set wondering
how they will affect the chances of well-being of the men of
the Sinai desert, and what future may be in store for the
convent.

[1] *Times History of the War*, parts 48, 128.

INDEX

195   O

PRINTED BY WILLIAM CLOWES AND SONS, LIMITED, LONDON AND BECCLES.

For EU product safety concerns, contact us at Calle de José Abascal, 56–1°,
28003 Madrid, Spain or eugpsr@cambridge.org.

www.ingramcontent.com/pod-product-compliance
Ingram Content Group UK Ltd.
Pitfield, Milton Keynes, MK11 3LW, UK
UKHW012347130625
459647UK00009B/612